# I saw a sunbird

RENUKA DAVID

© 2013 Renuka David

Published in Great Britain 2013 by Galle Face Publishing™

Renuka David has asserted her right under the Copyright, Designs and Patents Act 1988 to be identified as the author of this work.

This is a work of fiction. Names, characters, businesses, places, events and incidents are the products of the author's imagination or used in a fictitious manner. Any resemblance to actual persons, living or dead, or actual events is coincidental.

A few timelines and locations have been altered to fit in with the storyline.

A competent physician or qualified healthcare worker should be consulted before using treatments based on the information in this work.

ISBN 978-0-9575030-0-7

# DEDICATION

For my father.

# ACKNOWLEDGMENTS

Hill Slavid, for encouragement in my early period.
Shaun, for his creative advice and perseverance.
Maggie, for her experienced advice.
Anne, for editorial advice during workshops.
Jane, for her inspired cover design and generosity.
Natasha, for her kind words.
Ric, for wading through my early writing and still reading.
Another Anne, for feedback all the way from Australia.
Rohini, for letting me use her name.
And finally, not forgetting all those who gave constructive criticism in workshops and reviews. You know who you are.

I couldn't have achieved this without your help.

Below are reference works, novels and documentaries that provide details of Veddha culture and Sri Lankan history. Of particular help was the Seligmanns' anthropological tome as it phonetically documents songs and rituals in the Veddha tongue. The idea of a village *lost to all, except those who knew their way around winding tracks*, came from Dr Spittel's graceful writing about Ceylon and the Veddhas and Leonard Woolf's book about a Ceylonese village. Native songs and traditions that may no longer be sung or practised have been incorporated in the storyline to keep them alive, even in a small way. There's also a cookery book for those who want recipes.

*The Veddas* by C.G. and B.Z. Seligmann.
*Vanished Trails and Wild Ceylon* by Dr R.L. Spittel.
*Season of the Spirit Bear*, a wildlife documentary produced by Charith Pelpola for Animal Planet.
*Conversations with the Veddhas*, hosted by Dr Danièle Behn-Smith in the Medicine Woman series of documentaries first produced for the Aboriginal Peoples Television Network.
The Mahawamsa.
*Village in the Jungle* by Leonard Woolf.
*The Complete Asian Cookbook* by Charmaine Solomon.

Up into the cherry tree
Who should climb but little me?
I held the trunk with both my hands
And looked abroad in foreign lands.

*Robert Louis Stephenson: Foreign Lands*

# CONTENTS

| | |
|---|---|
| Make a wish | 1 |
| Once upon a time | 9 |
| Friends for life | 44 |
| Afraid of fear | 58 |
| Get ready | 69 |
| The fox and the cat | 90 |
| Christmas Day | 101 |
| First steps | 119 |
| Taking chances | 143 |
| Crossroads | 158 |
| Journey to Jaffna | 175 |
| Growing up | 186 |
| The worst happens | 202 |
| On Galle Face Green | 210 |
| Our Father | 221 |

## MAKE A WISH

I was allowed to pack two of my toys for our Christmas holiday to Sri Lanka, but wanted to take more so my cousins and friends could see what I played with in England. My shoeflower-red pyjamas were still too long for me and I had to pull them up while I ran about collecting dolls and teddy bears. After emptying my cupboard and shelves onto the bed, putting big toys at the back and small ones at the front, I looked at everything to choose what to carry on the plane. Most of all, I wanted to take the walkie-talkie doll I'd just got for my seventh birthday. She was too tall to lie down in the holdall and had to sit with her head and chest sticking up. Dad wouldn't let me take her like that. He wanted all zips closed and cases locked. I thought about pulling off her legs to make her fit in but Dad said he wouldn't fix her if I broke her again. I lifted her out with both hands and put her back on the bed, then ran around choosing smaller toys until Mum called me from the hallway.

"Rohini. Are you dressed?"

"Nearly."

She came thump, thump, thump, up the stairs. My heart started beating fast. I quickly shut the bedroom door and stuffed my Sindy and Russian dolls into the holdall, pushing them near the bottom to make space for more toys and games. Mum's footsteps were getting louder and a floorboard creaked. She must have been on the landing. I shoved in my Stylophone, a paint box and a ball of string for playing cat's cradle, then squeezed in a hot water bottle cover that looked like a dog, forcing it down so I could do up the zip before she came in.

I was too late.

The door opened wide and she stood there, hands on hips, giving me a funny look. I looked back at her, as if I hadn't done anything wrong.

"Is there something you want to tell me?" she asked.

"No . . ."

I stood in front of the holdall. It was no use. She took it and emptied it on the bed. Out tumbled everything I'd packed.

"Two toys," she said. "We need space for clothes and gifts we'll bring back."

"I can't separate them. They're a set."

"Two."

"You choose."

She picked up the Sindy and Russian dolls and left the poor puppy dog behind.

"You've broken his heart," I told her.

"It'll mend." She kissed the top of my head. "Off you go and wash."

"Post has arrived," Dad shouted from downstairs.

I jumped up and down. I'd been waiting days and days for a letter from my grandparents, kept waking early to see if they'd sent me their news. "Mum, do you think Appa and Amma will have written to me?"

"Sooner you get dressed, sooner you'll find out."

I ran to the bathroom and washed with the rose-scented bar of soap because she'd feel it afterwards to see if it was wet. She could also tell if I just threw water at the soap and didn't use it. As soon as I had my vest and *jungies* on, I tried to go downstairs. Mum pointed at the skirt and jumper she'd put on my bed. God gave me a mother to look after me, but he never meant her to make me get dressed when I was in a hurry to do something else. She watched as I went towards the door. Her mouth wasn't smiling and she pushed her eyebrows up. I gave in and put the skirt and jumper on. It wasn't going to be for long, anyway. The next day I was going to be in Sri Lanka, wearing summer dresses and not winter clothes.

I sang, "Jingle bells, jingle bells. Join in, Mum."

"Later, girl."

When I was older and had children of my own, I was going to let them do anything they liked even if they wanted to sing while getting dressed. I wriggled while Mum tried to plait my hair so she put it in two bunches instead. Her hair was long as well because we both liked to look Sri Lankan.

"You can go," she said. "That's all I can do while you're like this."

I rushed down to search the post on the hall table. Sometimes my grandparents sent an envelope with a letter and postcard of a sunbird inside, sometimes they sent a thin blue airmail form.

"Is there anything for you?" Dad asked from the sitting room.

"They're all for Mr and Mrs Palar."

"Keep looking. You never know."

I read names on the envelopes, letter by letter but all the post was for my parents. There was nothing for me. Appa and Amma had forgotten to write and I wanted to hear their news then, not wait until we saw each other in Colombo. I carried on searching anyway and was about to give up at the bottom of the pile when there it was: an airmail with my name on the front and theirs on the back. I hugged it to my heart and gave it to Dad while he sipped tea. He took a long drink then put his cup on the nest of tables.

"Sure you don't want to open it?" he asked.

"I might tear it."

I jumped onto his lap and leaned my head against his shoulder. He gave me the letter.

"Do you want to try and read it?"

"I can only read proper writing, not Appa's scribble."

He kissed the top of my head and laughed. I touched his long fingers as he ran them across the top of the letter. "Mum says you could be a concert pianist if you want." He thought about it but didn't say anything. "She said you became a lawyer, to send burglars to prison so they won't break into our house and steal my toys." He took a slow sip of tea, licked a drop off the corner of his mouth and began reading. His voice was quieter than when he read me bedtime stories.

*14 December 1972*

*Dear pretty Rohini,*

*Your grandmother and I are very happy to know we'll see you soon. We miss you all and look forward every year to your Christmas visit with us. This holiday is going to be special because the Temple tree is full of flowers and a Loten's sunbird has made a nest in the top branches. Remember, darling girl, our family has always stayed together while there is a sunbird in the garden.*

I crossed my fingers and made a wish for the bird to hang around so we could live again in Sri Lanka with my Appa and Amma. They sent me their love and said they were going to keep the letter short or they wouldn't have any news to tell me when we arrived.

*And don't worry about Saraswathie and the other servants. We're taking good care of them, although our new maid got homesick after a week and went back to Jaffna. So we've hired a houseboy from a family of Veddhas.*

"What're they, Dad?"

"They're the first people of Sri Lanka. They used to live in forests and rocks and hunt for food. There aren't many left. They're disappearing fast."

I hoped the houseboy wouldn't disappear before we arrived, so I could tell my friends I'd seen a Veddha.

"Did Appa and Amma go to the forest to find him?"

"Most Veddhas live in towns now. Only a few stay in the wild."

"I'd like to go to the jungle."

"Maybe we can take a trip there if we have time."

Mum came in and sat next to us, saying, "I've finished packing, Nathan." She asked him to read the letter again but she didn't really listen; she looked at the bamboo wallpaper then the stone-colour carpet. When he stopped reading, she looked at him and said, "I feel like I've forgotten to buy something."

He rolled his eyes. "Good grief, Uma. We've a suitcase full of shirts and shoes to take for this person or that one."

"Did you tell Tara we didn't get her fridge?"

"I'll enjoy telling her in person."

Poor Tara Aunty. She can't have known a fridge was too big to put on a plane or she wouldn't have asked us to bring one. I hoped Dad wasn't going to be rude when he told her off for being silly, or she wouldn't invite us to her parties.

He was still holding the letter. He liked to read it to himself when he was on his own. Mum had to cheer him up afterwards with a cup of orange pekoe tea and a joke.

I couldn't stop thinking about our holiday and was going to do all I could to make it the best ever. "I'm going upstairs," I told my parents. I knelt at the foot of my bed, shut my eyes and put my hands together, thinking carefully about what I was going to say. The Lord was ninety-four years old and got grumpy if he was asked to do too much.

"Hello, God. I'll pray for the poor people tonight, and I know I'm not supposed to ask for myself but I'd like a few favours from you. They could be your Christmas present to me. First, could you tell your angels to keep the sunbird safe in Appa's garden so our family can stay together? And if it's not too much trouble, can you ask Jesus to keep an eye on Amma in case her arthritis is bad again? And then if you're not ill with flu, please tell the airport not to lose our suitcases as my presents are in there."

I was also going to ask him to make Mum change her mind and let me pack more than two toys, but it wouldn't have worked because mothers can do what they want. I waited for him to tell me which of my favours he was going to say yes to. He didn't answer. He must have been in hospital having a knee operation. He was so old he should have retired, like Dad's boss, and let Jesus speak to children instead. I said the Lord's Prayer anyway, so he'd see I knew it by heart but instead of keeping my eyes shut, I peeped at the puppy dog Mum was making me leave behind. I was going to tell her she made him cry. I gave him a goodbye kiss and said I'd bring him a present from holiday.

Near the end of the plane journey to Colombo, I woke up to hear the pilot say, "We're in Sri Lankan airspace." I knew that meant we were flying over Sri Lanka but all I could see were clouds and you got those in England. When I saw the runway and palm trees that looked fuzzy in the heat, I jiggled in my seat. I'd already changed into summer clothes like the other passengers so we could begin our holiday as soon as we landed. Once the seatbelt sign went off, everybody jumped up, grabbed coats and bags from overhead lockers and pushed their way up the aisle. As I tried to squeeze past Mum, she put a hand on my shoulder. "Let your father go first." We said thank you and goodbye to the air stewardesses, who looked pretty in blue uniform and red lipstick then we marched off to pick up our luggage. I kept running ahead in the airport. Dad kept calling me back. My hand was hot and sticking to the handle of my holdall but it didn't matter. I loved seeing brown people everywhere and signs in squiggly writing.

I hopped around while we waited at the merry-go-round for our suitcases to turn up. When they did arrive, I went to climb on top of them for a ride, like at a funfair. Dad pulled me off and Mum tried not to laugh as she scolded me because a small boy was copying what I did.

Once I knew the airport hadn't lost my presents, I didn't want to stay any longer in Katunayake. I wanted to be on the way to Colombo, driving down country roads, watching car wheels kick up dust and people ride bicycles, carrying a friend on the handlebars. I wanted to drive down Perth Avenue to Appa's house, climb the Temple tree outside my bedroom and find the Loten's sunbird, if it was still there. And I couldn't wait to say hello to Saras, to wear the shoeflower necklace she made every year for me from the bushes in Appa's front garden.

Our porter followed us as we went through Customs to the meeting point. I searched the crowd left to right and back again but couldn't see my grandparents. Then in the middle, a lady with grey hair waved madly.

"Amma, Amma," I said, waving back.

Dad got to them first.

Appa held him tight. "It's good to see you again, son."

My grandmother was crying so I held her hand and said, "We're here now." She didn't speak while she dried her eyes with a white lace hanky she used for special occasions. I didn't think I should tell her she'd put on so much face powder that some had fallen onto her sari. Dad put an arm around her, not pressing hard, in case her arthritis was bad. We hugged each other for a few minutes until Appa moved away and said we should go. I'd hoped Saras might be at the airport but servants weren't allowed on family outings. I had to wait until we reached Appa's house to see my ayah.

After the porter put our suitcases in the boot, Mum tipped him thirty rupees. He looked at how much she gave him and said, "Thank you, thank you," while shaking his head from side to side. I'd done that at school once. My friends called me a nodding dog so I never did it again.

Appa said, "Uma, you gave him more than he gets in a month."

"It was worth it, to see the look on his face."

I tried to sit in the front seat of the car but had to go in the back between Mum and Amma, away from the door. I leaned forward to watch a man climb a palm tree, the handle of a long knife in his mouth. He cut off broken branches then let them crash to the ground.

"That tree must have been damaged in yesterday's storms," Amma said. "This monsoon comes and goes."

When I was older, I was going to climb a palm tree all the way to the top and when I was seventeen, I was going to do it with a knife in my mouth. I'd chop, chop, chop all the torn leaves and watch as they flew to the ground and landed on top of each other with a rustling noise. Then I was going to pick all the best coconuts and leave the rest to ripen.

Appa beeped a bullock cart in front of us but it didn't move to the side so he overtook it. I knelt on the seat to look behind at the driver. He stared ahead, like he hadn't seen or heard us, then he spat out red betel he'd been chewing.

The sun was shining on the car, making it stuffy. "Can you wind down the window, Mum?"

"We'll get grit in our eyes, sweetheart."

The cold air blower that Dad turned on didn't help much. At Appa's house, if I was hot and Saras wasn't busy, she'd sit me on her lap to cool me with a wooden fan.

"Amma, is Saras at home?"

"Yes, child."

We drove past a couple of villages then stopped at a crossroads. A beggar man with one hand tapped on my grandmother's window and frightened me. She pretended not to see him. "It's better to give to places that help them." I hoped someone would give him money to buy lunch.

All along the road were rows of huts with tin roofs, selling warm Fanta, Portello and king coconuts. Rich people never bought patties or Chinese rolls from them though because they'd have got an upset stomach.

"Are we there yet, Dad?"

"Nearly. This is Mount Lavinia."

Appa's house was a bit farther along Galle road, past the Hindu temple that had a totem pole of gods on the roof. I wriggled when we turned into Perth Avenue, which had houses one side and a field of palm trees on the other. When we went for walks, I stayed away from the field because a cobra lived there. "Mum, can you wind down the window? I want to smell the sea." I sat on her lap and stuck my tongue out to taste the salt in the air.

As we drove into Appa's house at the end of the road, I saw Saras waiting for us on the front veranda. She looked like she'd put on a new green sarong and blouse. I loved her as much as I did Mum and Dad and Appa and Amma but couldn't tell anyone. You weren't supposed to feel like that about servants, even if they were the same as family. Soon as the car stopped, I climbed over my mother and ran to hug Saras round the knees. I didn't want to let her go. Her long, black plait was shiny with coconut oil, the last thing I used to smell when she put me to bed. Stroking my head, she spoke softly in Tamil. I pushed my face into her sarong and cried my eyes out. When I finished, she wiped my cheeks dry with thumbs that were rough from doing servant's work, and put a necklace of red shoeflowers over my head. The petals around my neck were soft, like a silk sari.

"I really love this," I said.

"Come. I've written a poem for you."

She put an arm around me and we walked through the sitting and dining areas, along the back veranda and down the outside corridors. On the way, I waved to chickens in their coop and they clucked hello to me.

The kitchen was dark, even though the light was on. I leaned against Saras at the table while she pulled a sheet of folded paper from her blouse. I thought I knew everything about her but never knew she could read and write.

"When did you learn to write?"

"My father taught me. He was an English teacher in Jaffna."

"Is your poem like the ones in *A Child's Garden of Verses*?"

"Same," she said. "Same."

"Can you do sums as well?"

She smiled. "Yes, I can."

I took a petal from my necklace and stroked her cheek with it. "You'll spoil your eyes reading in the dark."

"I know it by heart, small one."

**All of the lives**

I sit on stone veranda steps
and wait to see my *kunju* girl,
hibiscus flowers at my feet,
to welcome my remaining joy.
The Lord seized those whom I loved most;
he chained them all to Heaven's gates.
No longer do I feel their touch,
nor hear familiar voices call.
Yet when she runs into my arms,
or turns her face to smile at me,
she wraps the shawl of gentle love
around my shoulders, brings them near.

I didn't know what she was talking about for some of the poem. I thought she was saying she loved me and missed me when I lived in England.
"It doesn't rhyme."
"Some poems don't."
"Have you written anything for children?"
She stroked my hair then pushed my chair back from the table.
"Go, kunju. Your Appa and Amma have been waiting all year to see you."

# ONCE UPON A TIME

Next morning, my bed was covered in sunshine from top to bottom. Saras must have opened the shutters above my head while I slept. My cotton bedspread was on the red cement floor, where I'd kicked it off in the night. I didn't mind that I only had two dolls sleeping with me. The sun was on my head and shoulders. England was far away and I was in Sri Lanka.

A rooster crowed twice. I stretched and yawned as I listened to its cock-a-doodle-doo. I was going to ask Dad if we could get a rooster in London so it could wake me up on schooldays, instead of the clanging of my alarm clock. I rolled over to look across the road at palmyrah trees. Appa had planted a few of them from seeds he brought from Jaffna. Amma told him they were the same as those that grew in Colombo but he said his were special because they came from his hometown. I was going to ask Dad if I could get a palmyrah tree to take to England.

The rooster crowed again.

I stood on the bed and put my arm through the metal bars in the window. I could nearly touch the sweet-smelling white flowers of the Temple tree. I stayed there for ages, looking around and over the garden wall, where the neighbour's dog was barking. Behind me, the grown-ups talked in the sitting area. They might have already eaten. Even if I'd missed breakfast, Saras would have left me something on the dining table, covered with a muslin cloth to keep flies away. I jumped onto the floor and opened my bedroom door.

Mum peeked over a newspaper, said, "You've slept well," and carried on reading. I nodded and sat next to my father on a rattan sofa. It was harder than our soft leather one at home, but it was Appa's, so I didn't mind. Dad was on the phone asking about train times. I listened to see if I could find out where he was going but didn't hear the name of a place.

On the wall to my right was a painting of Jesus' head. He was smiling and the sun shone behind his hair, making him look like an angel. The only other picture in the house was another one of the Son of God in Amma's room. Mum said Appa could afford to buy more, he was just eccentric. I thought that must mean he didn't like spending money. I looked around the room, even at hairy caterpillars that hid in corners, so when we returned to London I could close my eyes and be back in Colombo. On the other side of the room was a tall thing with a round, red and white mat at the top. I didn't remember seeing it before.

"What's that, Mum?"

She looked over the top of her paper. "Hmm? Oh, that's a *Sesath*, a sunshade. In the old days, they were white."

"Can you get them in England?"

"I don't think so. They're only made in Matale, by the same family who brought the Bodhi tree from India."

Dad put down the receiver. "There you are, Sleepyhead."

"Why were you asking about train times?"

"We're visiting Aunty Malathi in Kandy."

"Up the mountains?"

"After breakfast tomorrow."

"Yeahhh."

I clapped my hands. Everybody said going by rail to the hill country was the best, and Dad had remembered I asked to take the train that holiday, instead of driving up by car. I reached up and turned his face towards me.

"Can I have a rooster at home?"

"Are you nuts? Our neighbours would stop talking to us."

"Then can I have a palmyrah tree for our garden?"

"Whatever for?"

"To climb, like a coconut gatherer."

"You've already got your present for Christmas Day."

If a tree was a big gift, I'd have to wait for my next birthday. I didn't think I could hang on that long. When I went with Mum to buy plants for our garden, I'd ask her for one. She might have forgotten Dad had said no.

I wiggled my toes. Past the dining area, on the back veranda, Saras was grinding spices for the day's cooking. She was the only one Amma trusted to make good curry powder.

"Mum."

"Yes, dear?"

"Can we take Saras?"

"Home to England and keep her? No, sweetheart. She's happier living here."

I hadn't given up and was going to ask again later. Mum did the servant work in London and kept telling Dad we'd have to bring a maid from Sri Lanka to help her. If we took Saras and her sister with us, there'd be two people to help my mother.

My grandfather came in the room and saw me.

"At last, Lazybones has got up."

"Appa, we're going up the mountains by train."

"I know. Don't stay away long."

"Sorry," Mum told him. "It's my fault we're going so soon."

"I understand."

Every year we went to the hill country for my mother to see the Golden Temple of the Tooth. I didn't know why she had to keep going there. The monks never showed people the tooth, only the jar that it was in. Even then, you had to stand in a line for ages before they opened the door and brought it out.

"Dad, will we see Uncle Sohan in Kandy?"

"No."

"Nathan," Mum said, "will you at least try with him? You know he's like a brother to me."

Nobody spoke. I knew the day before my parents married, Uncle tried to kiss my father because they were best friends but Dad was too shy to kiss him back and got cross instead. They hadn't spoken to each other ever since. I hoped they didn't spoil our holiday by carrying on the fight like they had the year before. Whenever I asked grown-ups about it, nobody knew what was going on and they told me stories to keep me quiet. Even if I fell out with friends, I'd always make up so I could be friends with them forever.

Mum read the newspaper out loud. "The government's on its way out. Everyone's had enough of the Communists."

"This country's gone to the dogs," Dad said. He picked up a book on cricket from the side table and flicked through it.

Mum and Appa spoke about a new government and what it would mean for Tamils. I wasn't interested in what they were talking about so went to the back veranda to sit with Saras.

From the top of the steps, I watched chickens peck grain in the courtyard, their heads bobbing up and down. Appa liked to have fresh eggs each day, same as everybody else in Sri Lanka. If I was up early enough, I'd go with him to collect any that had been laid. Sometimes we'd have omelette fried in *gingelly* oil for breakfast or as a special treat, egg *hoppers*. I loved to break off the lacy, crispy top of the *hoppers* and dip it in egg yolk.

"You like the chickens, kunju?" Saras said.

I nodded.

She smiled. "We won't cook any."

The year before, she caught one to wring its neck and make into a curry. I cried when I heard it squawking so Appa told her to leave it then he drove to Pettah market to get one that was already dead.

The new houseboy swept the outside corridors with a scratchy broom, all the way from the back of the house, up the right side, to the kitchen and servants' quarters. My school-friends would be jealous when I told them I'd seen a Veddha. He had a pushed-out mouth, was as tall as Amma and looked grown-up. I wished my hair was long and curly like his.

"He's got lovely hair, Saras."

"All his people do. Ask him, he'll tell you more."

I knew I'd have to speak to him when he wasn't busy or I'd be scolded for disturbing servants while they worked. I watched his hair swing as he swept the next corridor. After he'd gone to the kitchen, I asked, "Did he burn himself?"

"What, kunju?"

"The black mark on his right hand."

"It's a birthmark. Did you see it's a teardrop, the shape of Sri Lanka? His father, chief of the Yala Veddhas, has it too."

If his dad was a chief, Herath must have been in a tribe like the Red Indians. I loved him already and when he wasn't working, I was going to play with him and have pow-wows in wigwams made from old saris.

Saras roasted coriander seeds over a small fire on the veranda, swishing them around until they were light brown, the way Tamils liked them. She took the *thachi* pan off the heat, a warm, spicy smell filling the air.

"Don't roast them dark," Dad shouted from the sitting area. "We don't want anyone thinking we're Sinhalese."

I ran to him. "I'll never learn good manners from you, if you talk about other people like that." Even though he laughed, Appa and Mum tried not to and looked away. I could feel them all watching me as I sat by Saras again.

She tipped the roasted coriander seeds into a stone bowl and smashed them into a powder. The smell made my mouth water as I thought about breakfast, better than the cornflakes and half-boiled egg I had in London.

Across the courtyard, in the kitchen, Amma talked to the cook she hired for special occasions and every day while we visited. My grandmother liked to make servants do the work but she stood over them while they baked, fried, or steamed food the way she wanted. Seer fish turned into *ambul thiyal*, drumsticks, my favourite vegetable, were cooked in *sodhi* until soft and best of all, they baked *wattalappam*, which my grandparents would have given me after every meal but Mum said, "No. Pudding only once a day."

As I wondered if I should eat as much as I wanted to for breakfast or keep space for lunch, Amma shouted at the cook, "I told you, not too much chilli. My son and his wife are English now." I hated it when she yelled at servants. They did their best to help. I stood up, ready to say something and guard the cook when Dad called me to the sitting area.

"Leave Amma alone, girl. She's busy."

I didn't want to but went inside and sat on the edge of the sofa, trying to listen to what was going on at the back of the house and what the grown-ups were talking about in the sitting area.

"Do you think the Tigers can make Eelam happen?" Mum asked my grandfather.

"Jaffna's always been Tamil. There's no need for independence."

I didn't know what independence was so tugged Dad's sleeve to see if it meant we could come back to live in Sri Lanka. He opened his mouth to answer when I heard loud voices at the back of the house. Appa rolled his eyes. Before anyone could stop me, I jumped up and rushed onto the back veranda, past Saras and up the outside corridors to the kitchen where my grandmother was shouting at the houseboy.

"Herath," she said. "You haven't swept the floors properly. You're worse than useless."

I stood between the two of them and put my arms out to separate them. "Amma, you shouldn't speak to him like he's dirt."

She put her hands on her hips. "Who do you think you are, Rohini? I'll rub chillies on your mouth if you use that tone with me again."

I didn't know what to do next.

Dad called my name from behind, came and put an arm around me. He patted my bottom. "Get washed and dressed, girl."

"Herath was doing his best."

"I'll deal with this."

I knew my grandmother only got angry because of arthritis pain but she should have learned from me. If I fell and hurt myself, I cried but never got cross. On my way to the bathroom, Saras stopped me and gave me a hug. I checked over my shoulder to make sure Dad was taking care of Herath.

After washing, I pretended I hadn't seen the pair of shorts and tee-shirt on my bed and tugged the almeira door until it opened. The clothes rail was too high for me to reach from the floor. I picked up a wooden stool by the bedside and carried it over. It was heavy, like all of Appa's furniture. I meant to put it down softly but dropped it with a thud. They must have heard that in the sitting room. My heart started thumping. I waited for someone to come running in. Nothing happened. Careful not to make any more noise, I listened again and climbed on the stool, one hand then the other then one foot at a time. I stood on tiptoe and stretched up to the rail. My body was half in, half out of the almeira when the bedroom door opened. I looked behind to see who was there and slipped. Mum ran in, grabbed me and dropped me onto the floor.

"What were you doing up there?" she said. "You could have fallen."

"I wanted to wear my party dress."

"I'll stay while you get dressed."

She watched while I put on the shorts and tee-shirt. My stomach rumbled so she helped me with my sandals, brushed my hair and plaited it. Then she held my hand as we walked to the dining area. I couldn't run to eat because Appa didn't like me rushing about indoors.

I'd have liked to sit at the top of the table but my grandfather sat there because it was his house and his table. The others had already said Grace so I didn't have to wait to start breakfast. Herath served *sodhi* and *stringhoppers*, his curly, black hair hanging loose around his shoulders. I said thank you as often as I could without looking straight at him, in case Amma got angry with me for being on his side. He didn't look at me either. Nobody did. My grandmother's eyes were on all of us.


For the fourth time that morning, Sohan's bedroom phone rang and for the fourth time he refused to take the call. Tara would make him suffer for not speaking to her but he wasn't going to change his plans. Why should he? He'd left his office before lunch to make an early start on his trip and was looking forward to peace and quiet in his hill country mansion. The phone rang again. Damn exchange couldn't cope when he had a call to make for an export client yet it was putting Tara through. He packed a shirt in his leather holdall and reached for another from the almeira. What if it wasn't her, but the office with a message about a late shipment? What if? What if? What if? He picked up the receiver and listened, without saying hello.

"Sohan? Tara here. Where have you been? Look, I'm ringing to say Nathan and his family landed today at Katunayake. Promise me you won't start a fight with him."

"Don't worry. The bigshot lawyer can have a pleasant holiday in Colombo. I'm going to spend a few days in Kandy."

"*Aiyo*, you know they take a trip there as soon as they arrive. I'd come to keep an eye on you, darling, but my father is ill with dengue fever. Tell me you'll behave if they turn up."

"You know me, Tara. Ever the gentleman. Give your father my love and I hope he recovers soon. I have to rush. Aunty Malathi's expecting me in a few hours."

Tara would make him pay for the quick end to the call but he didn't want any more delays in his journey.

In the softness of early evening light, he stood in the gardens of his Kandy *walauwa* and surveyed the ten acres of woods that came with the property. Hard to believe he could afford to rent this mansion, indeed, one that used to be the centre of a rubber plantation. It wouldn't be long before he could buy a place like this, sit on the veranda each night and watch stars in the sky, far from the town and its light pollution.

The head gardener would scold him later for leaving a trail of footprints on just-watered grass, but there was something satisfying about trampling a wet lawn. It was the same feeling he had on early morning treks in Yala jungle, when the air smelt of mist and dewdrops hung on blades of grass. Since Uncle Alagar passed away, Sohan had hardly been to the Veddha village, deep in a forest and lost to all, except those who knew their way around winding tracks and trees. His last visit there was when the north-east monsoonal winds had just started, so that must have been about a year ago. He often lay awake at night, imagined he was on a jungle path, watching each step because a Russell's viper might lurk nearby. In his mind, he walked through forest in all seasons, even drought, when dried leaves and twigs crackled under his feet, stirring up dust that scratched his nostrils and drifted into his lungs.

Yet as much as he missed the Veddhas, how could he return to see them? True, he'd paid rangers to protect Chief Aruma's village from illegal tree-loggers but he'd asked for a favour in return. Herath, the chief's son, was released from his training as a shaman to be hired as a servant in the Palar household. All Sohan expected was news of Nathan, to find out if his friend showed signs of wanting to end their feud. One word, a clue, something, anything, a torch to light the way out of enmity and back into friendship. Yet Herath, proud as the rest of his tribe, refused to exchange information for rupees. And then there was the chief's resistance. "Your Uncle Alagar told government ministers about our troubles," he said, stroking a grey beard that rested on his chest. "He never asked my son to spy."

"You know, I'm just asking for a bit of help."

Chief Aruma had spat out the betel he was chewing and sprayed the ground with red juice.

I looked forward all year to sitting in the Temple tree by the side of the house, pretending to be an angel in Heaven, flying through the sky with birds by my side. I knew every branch that was strong enough to stand on and those that were too thin, though I had to be careful because Amma didn't like it if holy flowers were knocked to the ground. One foot in the sitting area, one on the veranda, I said, "I'm going to the garden."

"Rohini," my grandfather said. "What are you going to do?"

"Climb the tree."

"It's too hot to sit outside and you want to run about and get even hotter?"

I nodded.

"All right. But take Herath. I don't want you falling."

I ran to the kitchen. Herath was at the table, talking to Saras. Even with the light switched on, I couldn't see his face very well so didn't know if he'd be cross with me for disturbing him. I touched his arm. "Can you come with me please, to climb the tree?" He didn't say anything. Saras told him it was all right. He could play with me and finish his work later.

We held hands as we walked down the side of the house, in the shade of trees and bushes. We were like cousins after I saved him from Amma's anger. I looked down at his bare feet.

"You'll cut your feet on stones."

"Wanniya-laeto don't need shoes."

"*Wattalappam*?"

He laughed. "We call ourselves Wanniya-laeto. You can say Veddha but I want you to say it properly before you go to England."

"I promise."

"Do you know what a Veddha is?"

"You live in rocks and forests."

"Gal Veddhas live like that, hunt deer and collect honey. Now we're mostly the Gam kind, *chena* crop farmers."

"Why?"

"Because our land has been stolen by the government and rich people."

When I was older and could look after myself, I was going to help him get his land back. All I thought about then was taking my sandals off to climb the tree. Herath made me put them back on, saying my feet were soft, not like his. I felt his thick, rough soles. One day, when nobody was looking

I was going to run around barefoot so I could be a Real Veddha too, and I was going to ask Mum if I could have my hair permed curly like his. I put a foot on the tree trunk and searched branches but couldn't see anything.

"What are you looking for?" Herath asked.

"The Loten's sunbird."

"It flew away a few days ago, *naga*."

I wished for another one to roost in the tree before the end of my holiday. Sometimes they appeared from nowhere.

I pulled myself up to the lowest thick branch then the next one while Herath stood underneath. I couldn't believe I was climbing the Temple tree at last. The garden was my kingdom. I was a hunter, going to the top of a hill. Appa's chickens clucking in the back yard were jungle fowl I'd eat for dinner. I climbed higher and higher, trying not to knock any of the white flowers. Each step up became more dangerous, branches were getting thinner. I stepped over one then had to grab another to stop myself falling, but it was full of flowers that broke off. Their petals floated down and around the tree trunk. I'd have to pick them up later and give them to Amma to keep by her bed. Sometimes she didn't mind that I'd knocked them off but after my scolding that morning, I was going to make sure another grown-up was in the room when I told her what I'd done.

Sitting on a high branch, I looked across the road at the field of palm trees. The sun shone on their leaves and made them sparkle. I put a hand over my eyes to spot the cobra that lived in the long grass but couldn't see anything moving. I hoped it had died and gone to Heaven. Jesus knows children are afraid of snakes, and wouldn't have wanted me to say sorry for wishing it dead.

Over the garden wall, the neighbour's servant boy came back from market, carrying a basket of fruit.

"What have you got?" I called out.

He looked at me but didn't answer. Herath had to tell him in Sinhalese what I'd said. The boy shouted something back then went into the house.

"Green plantains, mangoes and guavas," Herath told me.

I plucked a leaf from the tree, pretended I was picking a guava. I took small bites, made each mouthful of the sweet, pink flesh last. I'd just swallowed the last piece when Herath said, "Come. The sun is high."

"I'm not hot," I told him, my head aching a bit from the heat.

"Naga."

I climbed down, putting one foot lower, getting my balance, then moving down step by step. He caught me as I reached the highest branch I could jump off. I got a whiff of his armpits as he held me. He can't have used deodorant or talcum powder under there. Mum said villagers and poor people in Sri Lanka weren't ashamed of their own smell because it was natural. I loved Herath so his sweat didn't bother me much anyway.

"Be careful," I said as he reached up and picked a handful of leaves from the tree. "You'll get into trouble if you knock down the flowers."

Behind me, I heard a noise on the front veranda, like someone shuffling their feet. Had Amma come outside? No-one was there. Herath was safe for now. He threw leaves in the air, laughed and danced in circles around the tree, spinning round and round then he stopped as suddenly as he'd started.

"Veddhas dance if we're happy. You want to be one of us?"

"What do I have to do?"

"Sometimes throw leaves in the air, sometimes dance."

"And then what?"

"I'll teach you more another day."

He picked a few more leaves and put them in my hands. I threw them in the air, danced and laughed, only I spun round faster than he did.

"Naga, you'll make yourself ill."

Still laughing, I picked up leaves from the ground and threw them in the air. I was about to spin again when I saw Amma on the veranda, looking at the Temple flowers on the ground. She didn't say anything; she looked past me at Herath. He nodded at her. I didn't know what they were saying to each other and couldn't tell from her face if she was cross or not. After dancing with leaves, I was less afraid of her than I'd been at breakfast. Even if I got a scolding, I knew I'd have to tell her the truth.

"They fell while I was climbing. Sorry."

"These things happen, sweet girl. Spread them on my bed. It will keep me close to my faith." Then she looked at Herath and said, "Thank you for teaching her about Veddhas."

Sohan leaned against a wild breadfruit tree that was so tall and wide it towered over the landscape. It must have taken seed before the *walauwa* was built. A gust of air blew over him and drifted across the lawn, rustling the thatched veranda roof of the house. On each visit to Kandy, he meant to remind the landlord to secure the coconut branch covering before it was swept away in a hill country wind, but Tara or his import-export business always distracted him and he never spoke to the fellow about repairs.

If only he and Nathan hadn't kissed, a hug between two best friends that turned into something deeper. He should never have made the first move and put an arm across Nathan's shoulders. He should have guessed what would happen. After all, the clues were there: the constant touching of an arm or a hand as they talked, the peculiar smiles and compliments about hair, shoes and clothes. To his credit, he'd set aside the drunken lapse and moved on with his life so why did his bloody friend have to be so stubborn? If only Nathan could forget that night too, instead of glaring at him with 'I despise you' looks. Aunts and uncles said that becoming a father would ease the harshness in Nathan but it made him worse, wanting to protect his daughter. From what? The truth? Rohini had found out about the kiss, so there wasn't any point in stopping her from talking to Sohan at parties and outings. Surely even after their falling out, Nathan knew he cared for her as if she were his own child, and if the need arose, would risk his life to save hers?

That night, I didn't fall asleep until ages after I'd been sent to bed, because I couldn't stop thinking about dancing like a Veddha and what it would feel like to climb trees in bare feet. And we were going on a train journey to the hill country. My holiday was getting better and better.

In the morning, I packed my Russian dolls and a book in my holdall, so I'd have something to do if we visited people in Kandy who didn't have children. I took *Swallows and Amazons* because Dad read it when he was at school in Colombo and told me it was a great adventure story. I also remembered to ask Mum for a pair of socks though she looked at me in a funny way.

"Sweetheart, why do you want to wear socks all of a sudden?"

"Just because."

She knew I was up to something but she gave me a pair anyway.

We had to keep the windows shut on the taxi ride to the station, because roads were dusty and there was smoke from buses and tuk-tuks everywhere. With all the traffic, the driver dropped us off the only place he could, near where a man was being sick on the street. I thought this could only happen in poor countries then remembered how in London I hated spit on pavements and the smell of *choo* in car park lifts.

"Three first class tickets to Kandy," my father said at the ticket booth.

"Dad, first class is expensive."

"It's less here than a return to Oxford Street."

I became shy and wished I hadn't said something stupid.

The viewing carriage was at the front of the train, above the engine and had glass all around it. People were already in the front row so we had to sit behind.

"You'll still be able to see lots," Mum said. "You can read *Swallows and Amazons* until we get out of Colombo."

"Don't let me miss the jungle," I said, because when I was caught up in a story I forgot to do other things. After I finished a page, I asked, "Is it much farther?"

"Yes, darling, but look. Paddy fields."

I'd already seen some on the way from the airport so went back to my book. I was Captain Nancy of the Amazons and was going to capture all the boats in the sea to take my grandparents, Saras and Herath to England. I didn't look up again from the story until five pages later.

"I missed the jungle, Mum. You didn't stop me reading."

"I'll let you know before we get there."

I should have known she wouldn't forget about me.

The train climbed a mountain that was covered in grass and palm trees, except where there were villages. On a road between fields, a boy walked to school, carrying a satchel over his shoulder. He lived in Sri Lanka so if there was a cobra or viper hiding in the grass, he'd know to walk away and not look at it. I hoped the poor thing didn't have to walk four miles to lessons like Dad had to when he was young.

I bent my head to carry on with my story and had only read a page when Mum said we were getting close. Throwing my book into my holdall, I shot up in my seat, expecting to see a forest.

"I can't see anything."

"In a few minutes."

The train huffed and puffed and sounded like it wouldn't make it up the mountain. I silently prayed to God to let it get to the jungle. I shouldn't have asked him for a favour but I didn't think he'd mind doing it for one of his children. It was the only time in his life he didn't have broken bones or a fever because he answered my prayer.

First, there were only a few palm trees then we went through a tunnel of them, their leaves shining where there was sun in the forest. Giant ferns, a hundred times as big as the ones Mum had at home, grew all over the place. I'd never seen anything that beautiful. I jumped up and down and looked over the head of the man in front. He laughed then said I could share his seat. I asked Mum if I could move but climbed over before she could say yes or no. The train slowed right down. The man said we might have to get out and push. I wouldn't have minded helping if it meant I could walk in the jungle. My friends at school would be so jealous when I told them what I'd got up to on holiday.

"Over there," Dad said as he leaned forward to point over my shoulder. "The Sri Lankan Hanging Parrot."

"Ohmygosh."

I'd only seen parrots in films and zoos before. I didn't know how Dad spotted them. They were the same green as the trees, only their red beaks and blue tails were a different colour. The wind was blowing and made palm leaves swing about. I wanted to feel it on my face but the windows were shut and I wasn't allowed to open them in case I fell out and got lost. Though if that happened I could have lived with leopards and bears, like Mowgli in the *Jungle Book*. While Mum looked the other way, I reached up to undo the window latch. She pulled my hand down and held onto it, which was unfair. Children had to be allowed to do dangerous things or they'd never grow up.

When the train came out of the forest, I tried to remember what every tree, parrot and fern looked like so I'd only have to close my eyes to see them again. Dad pointed along the hills. "Nuwara Eliya is up there. They pluck two leaves and a bud to make tea." I wasn't listening. Appa had once given me a cup of tea made with warm milk and the taste made me feel sick.

The forest was disappearing fast. I looked all around, trying to spot more parrots, wanting the journey to go on forever but soon there were more office buildings and hotels than trees. I turned round to watch through the side windows and was still looking as we pulled into the station. After we stopped, I stayed on the train until Mum made me get off. A small girl was standing on the platform and asked me in Tamil what it was like seeing the jungle from the viewing carriage. She'd wanted to sit there as well but her family didn't have enough money for the ticket. I didn't know what to say. My mother held my hand and told the girl it was nice and the same as being in other carriages. I felt bad that I'd had a great time when there were poor people around.

"You're quiet," Dad said to me. "What's wrong?"

"One day, can we bring Saras up here in first class?"

"It's not for servants."

"The bible says we're all the same."

"We are, but not in that way."

I didn't know why he had to be horrible. Even God would have let Saras ride in the viewing carriage.

The hill country was windier than Colombo. Only my feet were warm because I wore socks and I was proud of myself for remembering to put them on. I hoped my aunt wasn't going to be late because I really wanted to get to her house. Mum put an arm around me when she saw me shiver and said she'd get my cardigan from the suitcase if Aunty didn't come soon. I wanted to stay in my summer dress, said I was hot but she wasn't listening.

People got on and off buses at the bus halt outside the station. The air smelt of petrol and made me feel a bit sick. Children around me were in torn dresses and shirts. I didn't have enough pocket money to share among them so they could buy sweets, and it wouldn't have been fair to give some and not others. A beggar with a bleeding hand sat on a wooden box near the bus stop. He saw me looking at him and started to walk towards us until a policeman shooed him away. It wasn't a nice thing to do, but I was glad we weren't going to be bothered.

Dad put his hands in his pockets and stared in front of him. "Wonder where Aunty Malathi's got to. She's bound to be late if she's been at the hospital today."

"She's a wonderful doctor," Mum said. "Would have made a great mother. Shame she never got married."

"You know she prefers women."

"Nathan. Rohini's here."

"I like girls more too," I told him.

"Let's hope you grow out of it."

"I won't. Boys fight and pull my hair. Aunty doesn't have a husband because she's too busy to do a man's job and be a wife."

I couldn't wait to see her again. She treated me like a grown-up when we were alone, asking me what I wanted to do and telling me gossip. I was looking up and down the road for her when a car drove fast around the corner and a lady inside shouted. It was my aunt, telling her driver she'd seen us and to stop so she could get out. I'd forgotten how noisy she was. She kissed Mum and Dad on both cheeks then all I could see was her yellow sari coming for me.

"Come, child. Give me a hug. I have missed you."

She squashed my face into her body. I couldn't breathe and was afraid to move in case her front pleats came undone and the whole sari fell down. I counted all the way to five before she let go. When she tried to grab me for another hug, I hurried into the back seat of the car.

The driver looked over his shoulder at me and said, "Hello." He had a bit of red betel-dribble on the corner of his mouth. I'd never seen him before so pretended he hadn't spoken to me. "Small one doesn't remember me," he said and laughed.

Aunty patted my hand. "She's only young."

I moved closer to her in the back seat.

Dad got in the front so he could sit by the handbrake and steering wheel and act like he was in charge. We drove along bendy mountain roads, while poor people walked by the side. They must have got tired going up the hill. We couldn't give them a lift though, they might have been robbers or beggars. Cars drove around potholes, trying not to hit each other or anybody walking on the road. It was more dangerous than Dad's driving in

London.

"If this country wasn't run by crooks," my mother said, "stealing aid, they could have mended roads and built schools and hospitals."

"Don't go on, Uma," Dad told her. "I left here to get away from this kind of talk."

I looked past Aunty, at the valley. It was a long way to the bottom. Just then, the driver swerved so he wouldn't hit a goat and we nearly went down the mountainside. I grabbed my aunt's hand and screamed. She told the driver, "*Aiyo*, go slow, will you. You're frightening her." She put an arm around me. "We'll be there soon." I pressed close to her and sat back in my seat, trying not to look out of the window.

"I've forgotten how exciting the hill country can be," Dad said. "I'd like to get behind the wheel while we're here."

"You wouldn't brake in time," I told him.

Everybody laughed.

We drove along until we reached Kandy Lake, where Aunty told the driver to let us out because, "Small one likes to watch the storks." I didn't want to stop. I wanted to get to her house but didn't like to say anything when she was trying to do something nice for me. Mum and Dad held hands and walked ahead to the lake while I came behind with my aunt. She was staring at a car parked by a jewellery shop across the road. A tall man in a straw hat and sunglasses got out and leaned against the bonnet. He touched his left thigh before he put his hand in his pocket.

"It's Uncle Sohan," I whispered to my aunt.

"Honestly. I told him we were coming here and to stay clear." She waved at him to go away then put a finger to her lips. "Don't say a word to your parents."

"I promise." I wasn't supposed to lie to Mum and Dad but Aunty was like a mother so they wouldn't have minded.

Mum told me to stand behind the *walakulu* wall, arrow-shaped stones as tall as my chest, to watch *Kokku* birds dive for fish in the lake. I climbed up the wall for a better look and tried to sit on the top. Dad put his hands on my waist and made me come down even though I wasn't doing anything very dangerous. The birds stood on one foot and dived into the water. Sometimes they pulled out a fish, sometimes they missed and had to go hungry. One flapped its wings to dry them and sprayed us with water. Dad said, "Bloody hell," and wiped his hands on his trousers.

"Did I tell you the story of the lake?" Aunty asked me. "The last Sinhalese king, Sri Wickrama Rajasinghe, made it out of paddy fields he stole from local villagers. The tyrant and his family were exiled to India where he died fifteen years later."

He shouldn't have stolen from the poor, though if they'd put him in a Sri Lankan prison he could have been in his beloved country, instead of dying of a broken heart in India.

I couldn't help it. I looked at the shop where Uncle had been standing. His car was gone and so was he. I tugged Aunty's sari and pointed to where he'd parked. She nodded at me then spoke to my parents.

"Nathan and Uma, I've organised a get-together for you to meet the old crowd."

"Great," Dad said. "So long as it's not all the old crowd."

"Come. Let's head home."

We waited at the car for the driver who'd gone off for a cup of tea and chat with his friends. When he popped his head out of a cafe and saw us, he came running. I looked for Uncle and was ready to warn my aunt if he showed up. I didn't see him and thought he might be hiding in a shop. As we drove away, I knelt on the seat to see if he was following us but there was a bus in the way. Aunty said, "Don't worry. Everything's fine."

I was glad I didn't have to think about him anymore and looked down the valley at the green river; it was too far away to see if the long dark things in it were logs or crocodiles. The bus followed us until a bit farther up the road when we pulled into my aunt's front garden, which was full of pretty white flowers.

"I forgot what those are called," I told her.

"Boo-gain-villia."

I was going to call them boogan. After shoeflowers and Temple flowers, I liked them the best.

The front doors with elephant and deer carvings had been left open for us. Nobody locked houses in Sri Lanka during the day because servants were always there to get rid of thieves. I ran through the hallway to my favourite room, a garden in the middle of the house with guava and frangipani trees and plants everywhere so it didn't need air freshener to smell nice. I closed my eyes and breathed in the flower scents. Heaven must have been like that, with God telling angels to grow their best plants in his house.

Dad helped the driver take our luggage from the boot and carry it upstairs, where a maid waited to show us our rooms. I stepped onto the first stair and saw something move at the back of the house in the dark. A small boy was watching us. He didn't have any shoes on; he must have been a servant's son. He smiled, showing his teeth and I waved to him, thinking we could run about later. I wasn't supposed to play with poor people in case I caught head lice from them but Aunty would have looked after me if I got ill.

My father tipped the driver and maid with lots of rupee notes. They shook his hand for ages and smiled at me on the way out. The room my parents were going to sleep in was lovely. In the middle was a huge bed with a mosquito net, like a bed for princesses and there was a desk and tall bookcases against the walls.

Mum picked up a notebook. "I see Aunty Malathi hasn't given up her writing. I don't know how she finds the time, what with the hospital and her charity work."

"Does she write books for children?"

"No sweetheart, Aunty writes medical text books."

They sounded like they were for doctors and nurses, with long words I wouldn't understand. We had a quick wash to freshen up then Dad wanted to go down.

"I want to unpack first so I can relax," Mum said.

"I'll see you downstairs," he told her.

She folded her arms. She wasn't going to let him get away with it while she did all the work. I looked at both of them to see who was going to win the row. Dad wasn't good at fights with her. He always gave in and said, "Yes, dear." He stood in the doorway like he didn't know what to do then he came back in the room, lifted a case onto the bed and opened it.

"What goes where?" he asked, holding a shirt in each hand.

"Nathan, you sit, while I put the clothes away."

He lay down on the bed. "Yes, dear."

When I had a husband, I was going to make him work as hard as I did. He wouldn't get away with anything. I helped Mum unpack our cases and hoped Dad was watching me so he could learn how to be nice.

Soon as Mum opened the chest of drawers and almeira to put the clothes away, I got the strong scent of mothballs. I asked her if we could buy some to take back to London so I could have the smell of Sri Lanka every day. She said she'd think about it, which meant no or she'd think about if for days then we'd both forget about it, and I still wouldn't get mothballs.

Mum put the empty cases by the wall. "Nathan, I've finished."

He put an arm around her waist and we went downstairs to join Aunty in the indoor garden. I'd have liked to eat guavas from the tree but there weren't honey bees nearby to make fruit so only flowers grew there. The reddy-brown floor tiles were clean and tidy as they always were, because each morning the servants plucked weeds and swept fallen petals. If Temple flowers floated down on me, I saved them to give to Amma, to sprinkle on her bed. She told me God made them all with five petals because he loved everybody and everything the same. He must have made them when he was young because he was too ill from heart attacks to do anything anymore.

Mum and Aunty sat on the sofa, talking about relations who were getting divorced and which ones had clever children. Dad and I listened to them from the pond. We didn't join in the gossiping because we liked to be better than ladies who talked about friends when they weren't there. He watched the fish swimming and didn't notice me taking off my sandals.

At last, I got to do what I'd been looking forward to since we left Colombo and why I was wearing socks. Like a skater on an ice rink, I put my arms out for balance then slid across the tiles, whizzing past lilies and tiny rose trees. Mum said, "What do you think you're doing?" I turned to look at her, tripped over a weeping fig plant and fell towards the pond. I'd have drowned if Dad hadn't caught me. We both got frightened. He said if I tried it again he'd let me fall in. Aunty looked away, trying not to laugh and Mum told me off. It was just my luck she saw me before I'd done much skating, but even if she was cross with me, her mouth smiled so I knew I wouldn't be punished. Dad saved me from her anyway and talked about something else.

"The pond looks different, Aunty."

"I had it rebuilt so I could put a heater underneath. It's Japanese, best in the world."

"You waste your money, Aunty Malathi."

"What else do I have to spend it on?"

He didn't answer her. He showed me two clownfish and angelfish that chased each other in and out of seaweed and coral. I was so busy looking at them, I didn't notice a green lizard on a wall until it jumped on the floor by my feet. It looked up at me with its big eyes, as if it was going to pounce on me. I ran to Mum.

"You'll have to get used to these again," Dad said. "Come and get close to it."

I wasn't going to listen to him and moved nearer my mother until I was almost on her lap. I held her dress with both hands and looked at the lizard, wondering what it was going to do. My father picked it up and started walking towards me.

"Let her be, Nathan," Aunty said. "Besides, I want to talk to you about the get-together. Do I invite Sohan or not?"

Dad looked cross. He stood holding the lizard then walked away to put it near the wall it had jumped from. We all went quiet and waited for him to come back. I held onto Mum while she talked to Aunty with her eyes. I didn't understand what they were saying to each other.

"Nathan?" Aunty said.

My father stood with his back to us, hands in pockets, watching the lizard climb up the outside wall then disappear over the top. Only Uncle Sohan could upset him like this. I moved closer to Mum until I pressed against her legs.

"This is your house, Aunty," he said. "If he turns up, I'll say hello to him. That's all."

"We'll leave it for your next visit."

Dad sat with us and everybody went quiet again. I was thinking of something grown-up to say when the small boy I saw earlier, walked in with a bowl of *murukku* and put it on the coffee table. He'd put on a pair of flip-flops to serve us shorteats. I took a handful of cashew nuts and sultanas, leaving the crunchy pieces behind. Mum didn't allow me to pick my favourite bits, uncles and aunties didn't mind.

"This is Ganesh," Aunty told us. "My new maid's son. The father ran off and left them penniless so they live with me now. He only speaks Tamil."

Ganesh smiled at me in a shy way. I'd forgotten some of my Tamil but remembered play words. I was glad his mother kept him when his dad went away, and hadn't given him to monks to look after because she didn't have enough money to bring him up.

"Aunty, can he play with me?"

"After he's finished the sweeping."

I didn't have long to wait to find out if he'd have to clean the whole house or only the kitchen. I'd just eaten my *murukku* when he came rushing back in. Aunty asked him a question and he nodded. "I'm not so sure he's finished," she said, "but *ponghal*."

Bamboo and palmyrah trees grew down the sides of the back garden; yellow firecracker flowers were everywhere and in a rockery grew my favourite plant, the Sri Lankan Red Ginger, a tall red tongue in the middle of leaves. Mum said it was just called Red Ginger, it didn't have the name of a country in front, and anyway, it came from Malaysia. I didn't listen to her. It was growing there so it must have been Sri Lankan. At the end of the garden was what Aunty called the wild wood, where she let everything grow the way it wanted to because, "That's how God made nature."

I taught Ganesh how to say tree, grass, run and chase in English. I'd forgotten what grass was in Tamil and asked him to teach me. He giggled and didn't understand what I was saying so we played chase around croton and rose bushes. He ran faster than me and took his flip-flops off to go even faster. As he looked behind to see how far away I was, he tripped by a rockery in the middle of the lawn. He didn't cry when he fell; he was still laughing. I checked his knees and hands. He hadn't hurt himself, he only had green marks on his skin. Then he ran off without saying goodbye when his mum called him to help her make lunch.

I sat with the grown-ups, not interested in their chatting. After Aunty had gone into the kitchen to see how the cooking was going, I told my parents Ganesh should be allowed to play.

Dad said, "He has to earn his keep."

"Small boys shouldn't be servants."

"I'm not discussing it anymore."

When I was a grown-up, I was going to listen to my children, especially if they were trying to help someone else.

"What's wrong?" Aunty asked when she came back.

"I'm not allowed to say," I told her, looking away from my father.

She patted my hand and said that after lunch she'd take us to Kandy Temple, so my mother could see Buddha's tooth.

Dad looked straight at Mum. "Why do you want to go there, Uma, when you know it upsets you?"

"It keeps me close to them."

"Rohini, girl," Aunty said. "Fetch me a hanky from my room."

I went out of the room but waited in the corridor to hear what they were saying. Mum cried a bit before saying, "My whole family gone. All of them."

Poor Mum. There were riots in Colombo while she was on a school trip to Kandy Temple and her home burned down. Her family were so scared they ran away, forgot where they lived and never came back, leaving her all alone. I fetched a white lace hanky for Aunty and stood outside the door again, listening to my mother.

"I don't know what I would have done without Sohan. He walked me to school every day, wouldn't let anyone play jokes on me, made sure I did my homework and passed exams, even though I didn't want a career. I only wanted to be a wife and mother. Nathan, please can't you try with him for my sake?"

"I'm sorry. He's not the same person you remember."


Sohan hung around the Golden Temple of the Tooth, hoping to catch a glimpse of Uma. Not that he could do anything by watching but he had to know she was all right. He also wanted her to know that if she needed him, he was where he always had been, by her side. And he wanted Uncle Alagar to know his daughter was being taken care of. Above all, he had to tell her it was okay to grieve. It wasn't her fault she was alive and her family were gone. If she was in tears, he'd have to take a back seat as he had since she married, and let Nathan do the comforting. He wasn't sure he could stand back anymore, which is why he'd gone to the lake that morning. And God knows how Aunty Malathi and the small one recognised him in his disguise of a straw hat and sunglasses. I suppose, he thought, not many people in Kandy drive a sports car. He was only surprised Nathan hadn't spotted him too. Perhaps his friend had given up fighting and hadn't been on the lookout. Standing up straight, he squared his shoulders. Is that why Tara rang before he came to the hill country? To say the quarrel with Nathan was over so for God's sake, for all our sakes, don't start it up again. Christ Almighty, what should he do? Stay or leave? Uncle Alagar would have put an arm around him, saying, "Let your heart guide you." Fat lot of good the heart was. Sohan had to know what was going through Nathan's mind and if his friend was ready for reconciliation. He scanned the crowds. Perhaps they'd already turned up and he'd missed seeing them. That looked like Uma from behind. No, couldn't be her, that woman was with a bald man. What if they'd come and gone and he was too late to see how she was? He should never have lost sight of them at Kandy Lake, and if that damn bus hadn't got in the way, he could have followed them to Aunty's house. He didn't know what he would have done if they'd spotted him. He could hardly have pretended to be driving through the neighbourhood.

Flower sellers showed him cardboard trays of purple lotus flowers, the petals of which were sprinkled with water to stop them wilting in the heat. He paused to look for the briefest of moments, felt obliged to take off his sandals and make offerings to Buddha, yet he said, "*Eppa,*" and shooed the sellers away. When a man in a torn sarong approached with bowls of rice for the shrine, he hesitated before waving him away too.

Still unsure what to do and without knowing why, he turned to the right. His head throbbed when he glimpsed Uma and the others arrive, separated from him by two lines of worshippers. He tried to see if her face was tear-stained and took a sharp breath when he saw she wore sunglasses: an accessory she claimed was for tourists and Sri Lankans who wanted to ape Westerners. Nathan's arm was around her waist, guiding her to the shoe hut where they left their sandals before strolling through the temple gates. Aunty Malathi and Rohini followed close behind. As if the small one knew where to look, she turned in his direction and lifted a hand to wave.

Aunty shook her head at him and mouthed, "Not now."

He mouthed back, "Uma?"

"Fine," Aunty mouthed. "Fine."

Sohan nodded his head, waved to the small one and walked away. The sun was bearing down on him and he touched his left thigh. Lately, as much as he'd got used to being on the outside, one rejection after another made his scar feel like it was burning through his jeans.

In the Golden Temple of the Tooth, I asked my aunt, "Why have they kept the pictures from last year on the walls and ceilings?"

"They're hundreds of years old."

"At school, we paint new murals every term or it gets boring."

"These are religious. They mean a lot to Buddhists."

I still thought it would have been nice to see something different.

There was a strong smell of incense all over the place and small rooms were foggy with smoke. There was nothing fun to do. I couldn't even sing to the music because it was just men banging drums or blowing a trumpet. Statues of Buddha were everywhere.

"I've never seen a statue of God in church, Aunty. I don't think Christians love him much."

"It's for other reasons."

I didn't know why grown-ups always had to argue with children.

Mum and Dad bought purple and white flowers to put on the shrine upstairs. They'd have to queue for ages until a monk came out of a room, carrying the jar with the tooth in it. I stayed downstairs to have a chat with Aunty and held her hand. I didn't know how upset Mum was going to be, even with Dad looking after her. I was glad he hadn't seen Uncle Sohan because he might have had a row in a holy place.

"You should ask your parents to bring you to Kandy for the Esala Perahera next year," Aunty said. "The whole town is alive, for ten nights of parades to celebrate Buddha. Whip-crackers start it off, followed by fire-eaters, dancers and drummers. Then there are the elephants. It's magic."

I'd already seen photos of the Perahera. People with burning torches walk on the roads, next to elephants whose bodies and trunks are covered in red, blue and orange cloth, all lit up by fairy lights. The monks want to show the tooth to everyone on the streets, so they take it out of the temple and give it to the oldest elephant to carry on his back. The younger ones aren't allowed to have it because they'd only get over-excited and break it. I couldn't wait to see the festival for myself.

When Mum came back with Dad, her eyes were red and she was quiet. She smiled at me so must have been feeling better after crying. I let go of my aunt's hand and held hers instead. I didn't know what to say so asked my father, "Can we see the Perahera?"

"It's in July and August. We'd have to miss our Christmas trip if we came for the festival." He thought about it some more. "We should bring you to see it one year."

The next day, Mum and Dad had a lie-in while I ate breakfast with Aunty. She'd asked me the night before what I wanted. I told her egg *hoppers* and that's what I got. When we had special food like that, servants made extra so they could have some too. My aunt didn't like a fuss being made about them having nice meals, so I didn't ask her what Ganesh and his mum were going to eat. I broke off a crispy piece from the top of a hopper and was careful when I dipped it in the egg but still got yolk on my palm. Only grown-ups could eat without getting their hands dirty.

"Aunty, do Veddhas live in Kandy?"

"That's a strange question. Why the sudden interest?"

"Amma's new houseboy, Herath, is a Veddha. I really love him. You have to promise not to tell Mum and Dad though. They'll think he's trying to marry me when he doesn't have a good job."

"Your great-grandmother was a Veddha."

I put down the piece of hopper I was about to eat. "Which one?"

"On your Amma's side and Herath is related to her. Do you know what *waruge* he comes from?"

"*Wattalappam?*"

She laughed. "*Waruge*. He's *Morana waruge*. The top clan."

Wow. Herath and I were King and Queen of the Veddhas.

"That's all I know about him," she said. "I'm ashamed to say I don't know much about his race. They collect honey and hunt, want to be left in peace to follow their lifestyle and we wipe them out by taking away their lands. It all comes down to greed and corruption."

I broke off a piece of hopper, dipped it in coconut sambal that had been made without chillies for me, and ate it.

"Let me see," she said, sipping coffee with black pepper on top. "How do you think they stop food spoiling in the heat?"

"Is that corruption?"

"No, sweetheart. Corruption is stealing."

"I forgot what you asked me."

"How do you think Veddhas stop food going off?"

"They use fridges?"

"There isn't electricity in the jungle, at least not where they live. They cut into a hollow tree, put honey in it, fill it with flesh then stop it with clay."

"Why are they allowed to keep food in trees but Mum makes me wash guavas before I eat them?"

"I'll let your mother explain that to you."

I finished breakfast and wiped up every bit of egg yolk with my fingers, which I then licked. Mum didn't let me do that at home, sometimes Aunty didn't mind. When I asked to be excused from the table, she told me to wait a minute.

"I've a surprise for you. I've got tickets to see a Kandy ballet."

"Can Ganesh come?"

"I only have four tickets."

"I have two rupees left of my pocket money. Is that enough for a ticket?"

She took a long drink of her coffee before putting the cup down. "You really want him to come?"

I nodded hard.

"All right. Tell him to put his best clothes on and be ready after lunch."

I rushed to the kitchen to tell his mother he could come with us. Even on hot days like that one, stone floors at the back of the house never warmed up but she stood in bare feet at the worktop, thumping roti dough. I wondered if she was a Veddha too, with thick soles like Herath or if she didn't want to complain about a cold floor in case she was scolded or sacked. I used all the Tamil words I remembered, waved my hands about and did a little dance. She still didn't understand me. Then I saw Aunty behind me, laughing before she explained what I couldn't. Ganesh's mum stroked my cheek. I felt so good about helping her son, I didn't mind that my aunt thought I was funny.

In the afternoon, I changed into my going out clothes: a new red cotton dress with white dots. Ganesh was waiting in the hallway in his grey school shirt and shorts, white socks and sandals. I was sorry he didn't have anything else to wear but knew not to say anything to the grown-ups. On the way to the ballet, I let him hold my hand because he wouldn't pinch me like boys in my class would have done.

At the theatre, I asked Aunty, "When are ballerinas in tutus and pointed shoes coming on?"

"In Kandyan dance, women wear red blouses and white skirts. Men are dressed in white skirts and their chests are covered with silver breast plates or jewellery."

Even if it wasn't proper ballet, I was looking forward to the dancing, until my aunt spoilt it for me by saying people sang during the show. Sri Lankans sang through their noses and sounded like they had a cold.

"Is the music nice?" I asked, hoping I could listen to that instead.

"They dance to drums, often a Geta Beraya, a long instrument with cow skin over one end and monkey skin over the other, which make different sounds when hit."

"Why can't they use cow skin at both ends instead of a poor monkey?"

"They use monkeys that are already dead."

"Where do they find the dead ones?"

"Now and again, drums used are Yak Beras, from the Veddha word for spirits. You could say all our dances started with the Veddhas, the true race of our country."

When I returned to Colombo, I was going to tell Herath I'd learned about his people and their music. He'd be so proud of me.

I asked Aunty to tell Ganesh the story of the dances and drums in Tamil. She said a few sentences, not as much as she had to me. I wanted to ask her to treat him the same as me, but knew I could only stand up for him if something bad happened. He didn't say anything. He just listened. It must have been the first time he'd been taken to a show.

The lights went out in the theatre and I waited for the dancing to begin. Nobody came onto the stage. I fidgeted and wondered if Ganesh and I would be allowed to run up and down the aisle, so long as we promised not to bump into anyone. Then Aunty said, "Here they come."

Drummers showed up first. They bowed to us before banging away on drums with their hands. I felt pain each time they hit the end I thought was monkey skin. Then the singing started and dancers came on from the side. They looked as good as my aunt told me they would. Women danced in front, with men behind, jingling bells on their hands and legs and wearing silver hats that looked heavy. I don't know how their heads stayed on with all their neck wiggling. I was so caught up in watching them I forgot about the poor dead monkeys and that I didn't like nose singing. Ganesh couldn't stop looking at the stage either. He was dancing in his seat, hanging on tight to the arms of the chair. We both clapped loudest of all at the end of the first dance. I waited for the next one, hoped something exciting would happen but it was the same as the first. Men and women stood in different places, the drum banging changed a little and the nose singing sounded the same. In the third dance, Ganesh and I fell asleep. We woke up when Aunty gently shook us by the shoulders. The curtains had closed and the lights were on. "At least you saw some of it," she told us. Ganesh rubbed his eyes and said sorry to her. I wasn't sure if she was going to scold him for wasting her money on the ticket.

"Never mind," she said and smiled at him.

Party day arrived. Soon, other children would come for the get-together and we could play games, get up to mischief or watch grown-ups get drunk. I ran in and out of rooms, upstairs, downstairs, up and down corridors. I couldn't even sit still to watch fish swim in the pond. Aunty Malathi didn't mind me racing round her house, until she began to arrange flowers. "Careful, girl," she said. "Don't break my cut-glass vases." I ran close to her, meaning to be careful but didn't look where I was going. I tripped over a Chinese rug she put down for special occasions and fell against her, knocking a vase on the table. She had to grab it to stop it tipping over. "Enough, Rohini. You can run in the garden when the guests arrive."

Then I had nothing to do. Ganesh was helping his mother in the kitchen and had to finish before he could play with me. Mum and Dad had gone up to take an afternoon nap and I wasn't allowed to disturb them unless I'd done something dangerous and broken my neck. I couldn't even go for a walk on my own while they slept, which was unfair. I belonged to the Tufty club and knew how to cross roads without getting run over. Aunty told me if I wanted to be useful, I could count the plates on the table to make sure we had enough for all the guests.

"There's fifty-two," I said.

"Good. Just enough."

"Is it fifty-two with or without children?"

"With. Fifteen young ones, including you."

"And Ganesh?"

She picked up a bunch of roses and measured the stems against vases. "Sixteen with him, but he'll have work to do." I played with the skirt of her dress, wanting to ask if he could join the rest of the children. When she started cutting rose stems, I let out a long sigh. In a kind voice, she said, "That's the way it is, small one. Now if you want to help, you can answer the phone and tell those women I'm not around."

I dragged a chair to the phone to wait for calls, which were always from ladies who wanted to find out who was coming so they could choose what to wear. "Honestly," Aunty said. "Does it matter if they're seen in the same sari twice in one month?" I didn't see what the fuss was about either. I liked wearing my favourite party dress all the time.

Aunty put the roses in vases, bent them this way and that and stuck leaves in between. After her fifth vase, the phone stopped ringing. I passed her flowers to arrange when another call came. The man didn't tell me his name but he had a nice voice and wanted to know if I liked school and living in England. I chatted with him about the party and asked if he had any children. He laughed. "None that I know of." I wasn't sure what he meant, I only wanted to know if he had any or not. When Aunty wanted me to find out who was calling, he waited before telling me his name.

I said, "It's Uncle Sohan."

She took the phone from me, scolded him in Tamil, then spoke to him in English. "Come another time. Not today." Mum said he always did what he wanted. I thought he'd obey Aunty because most people did, and it would have been selfish if he turned up to start a quarrel with my father during a party.

I'd had enough of holding flowers so helped Ganesh put bowls of roasted chilli cashew nuts and *murukku* around the house. Patties and *cutlets* would be served hot later. At home, Mum made the best meat *cutlets* with tomato ketchup but Aunty wouldn't let her cook use it because, "It's not a Sri Lankan flavour." She made my favourite chocolate butter cake though, and cut it into squares to serve, letting Ganesh and me have a piece each before guests arrived. I took a bite. Sweet butter icing melted in my mouth and then came the chocolate taste of the cake. I ate small mouthfuls, wanting to make it last. After finishing the last crumb, I licked my fingers clean and wiped them on my dress when I thought Aunty wasn't looking. "Wash your hands or use a serviette," she said. "Then get changed."

She put the vases in the sitting room and corridors. She'd picked some of the flowers from her garden, the rest were delivered from town because she didn't have enough. There weren't any of the white ones from the front of her house though.

"Can you also use boogan flowers?" I asked her.

"You like those?"

I nodded. She picked a big bunch and soon the house was full of boogan, jasmine, roses and other flowers I didn't know the name of. I closed my eyes and breathed in the perfume, which was much nicer than the air freshener Mum sprayed around our house in England.

After changing into my party dress, I put the last bowl of cashew nuts on a coffee table and was allowed to take Ganesh to play in the courtyard. He didn't know how to skip and copied me until he got the hang of it. I didn't think anybody had played with him before. We were going to have so much fun when other children arrived in the afternoon. I couldn't wait to make new friends.

"Aunty, when are the guests going to turn up?"

"They'll start arriving at four o'clock."

"What time is it now?"

"Three-thirty."

Just then a car pulled up outside.

"That can only be the Fonsekas," she said to a maid she'd hired for the day. "That woman arrives earlier with each party."

She told Ganesh to wait in the kitchen with his mother. I was so used to seeing servants go into their quarters while rich people had fun that I forgot about him. The maid opened the door to a man with a moustache. He said sorry for arriving early, his wife wanted to come then. I put my head out of the door and peeped past him. There was a boy and a girl in the car. I ran back into the house and bumped into my aunt.

"Can they come in?" I asked. "We'll be good."

"Now he's heard you," she whispered, "they'll have to."

The maid put the Fonsekas in the sitting room and gave them passion fruit juice and *cutlets* to keep them quiet. She didn't serve cake because they weren't allowed to have a good time until the party started at four o'clock.

"I have to go upstairs and get ready," Aunty told the Fonsekas.

"You've just changed," I said.

"Thank you, darling, but I have to put on lipstick and perfume."

The children, Victor and Leela, wanted to know what it was like living in England and if I was allowed chewing gum every day. While we chatted, their father sat quietly, smoking and drinking. The ash on the end of his cigarette got longer until it curled and looked like it was going to drop onto the floor. I grabbed an ashtray from the coffee table and gave it to him before he got into trouble with my aunt. His wife walked round the room, picked up a brass head of Buddha, screwed her nose up at it then put it down again. She should have left other people's things alone. She showed a wooden elephant to her husband.

"How much do you think this is worth?"

"I haven't the slightest idea."

"I've seen these in the market, for fifty cents."

"Put it down. We're here as guests."

I took Victor and Leela into the garden to show them the fountain with a mermaid sitting on the edge.

Victor told his sister, "Try the water, you'll like it."

Leela dipped her hand in the fountain.

"You can't drink it," I said before she swallowed some. "You'll get ill."

Victor laughed. "I nearly got away with it."

"I'm going to tell Mum on you," Leela said.

She shouldn't have said that. She should have fought her own battles without running to her mother.

Aunty Malathi came down as soon as more people arrived and took everybody to the back garden to have a chat and a drink, leaving a maid to answer the front door. Whenever someone knocked, I also went to see who had come. I took children to the garden while the maid looked after grown-ups. A servant boy my aunt had borrowed from neighbours tried to come in through the front. He was told to go to the back entrance and stay in the kitchen unless he was serving food to guests.

Soon the lawn was full of men in batik shirts and ladies in saris, one the colour of Sri Lankan Red Ginger. Not all the families had children. I still had more playmates than I knew what to do with. We ran around, chasing each other, laughing and shouting. Grown-ups told us to play quietly then gave up when we carried on making noise. An uncle said, "At least stay at the other end of the garden."

When Ganesh brought us a tray of shorteats, I was too busy to take much notice of him; he went back to the kitchen as quietly as he'd come. I had all the girls playing Veddhas. We picked up leaves from the ground, threw them in the air and danced in circles. The boys liked throwing leaves at the girls but didn't want to dance, even when they saw how much fun we were having. They just wanted to play cricket with pretend bats and a ball. I wished Herath had taught me songs so I could show the others more about his people. The girls and I played at being honey-gatherers. We weren't allowed to climb trees in our party clothes so had to collect from rocks on the ground. We put our hands in beehives to pull out the honeycomb and were so good at it that we didn't get stung. Then we hunted pigs and deer with twigs for spears. Victor chased us with a spear until his father said he'd thrash him if he tried it again. We'd had enough of the boys by then and told them they were Gam Veddhas, *chena* farmers, while we were Gal Veddhas, hunters living in rocks.

Houseboys kept bringing bottles of arrack and ginger beer for the men and bowls of fruit punch for the women. They put the drinks in a corner of the garden, away from the children. Aunty Malathi was the only lady who drank arrack with the uncles and told rude jokes about men and women playing together.

Mum and Dad came down from their nap, holding hands and smiling at each other. A sleep in the afternoon always made them happy. One of the uncles at the other end of the garden shouted to Dad to grab a drink and join the men. Mum served herself a cup of punch then went to gossip with the ladies. Soon as I saw her do this, I stopped playing and ran to her. I wasn't allowed to drink alcohol and get drunk but could have a taste. She gave me a piece of apple from her cup of punch then carried on talking. The ladies asked her to tell them about smocks and bell-bottomed trousers that were the latest fashion in England and what colours people were wearing for winter. I sucked the punch out of the fruit and listened to their chatting.

Aunty Daisy was the only one not talking about clothes. She was a bit fat so pleats at the front of her sari spread out in a fan. She boasted about her sons, how much cleverer and better looking they were than everybody else. "My youngest is top of his class at Royal," she said.

"You can't beat St Thomas for education," another lady said, winking.

Aunty Daisy's face puffed up. "Let me tell you, my first son went to Royal a man and came out a boy."

"Exactly. Mine went to St Thomas a boy and came out a man."

Everybody laughed except Aunty Daisy whose cheeks went bright red. She was so angry I thought her blouse hooks were going to explode. Mum put an arm around her shoulder and said she was glad Royal was still a good college.

I pulled my mother's glass down to take another piece of apple.

She said, "That's all, girl."

The ladies gossiped about how husbands never wanted to go to church and only wanted to watch cricket or go to the club for a drink. I ate my piece of apple and went to Dad at the other end of the garden.

"Can I have a sip of arrack?"

"I suppose it won't hurt. It's watered down with ginger beer."

He put the glass to my mouth then looked away as he carried on chatting. I didn't think he'd notice me tipping the glass to take a gulp instead of a sip, but he did, and took it away, saying, "Cheeky monkey."

I laughed. "I nearly got away with it."

Aunty Malathi took a puff of a cigarette. She only ever smoked at parties because she didn't want to get a cough from it. I watched as one smoke circle came out of her mouth then lots of them, one after the other. "After small one has gone," she said, "I'll tell you a funny story I heard." I stood there, as if I were allowed to hear rude things. I only knew bloody as a swear word and had to learn more if I was going to grow up quickly.

Dad patted my bottom. "Play with your friends, girl."

I walked away slowly, pretended my shoe buckle had come undone and I needed to do it up. They were all looking at me, waiting for me to go away. When I got to the children I heard my father and the others laugh loudly. It must have been a funny joke.

"Come on, Rohini," Victor shouted. "We're playing hide and seek. I'm going to the bathroom to count to a hundred."

Everybody screamed and giggled as they ran to hide. I stood alone, upset at being left out of Aunty Malathi's story. Dad called me over, pointing to a bush by him. "Hide in here." I got down low among crotons and tried not to move in the long grass that tickled my legs. There were bamboo trees nearby I could have hidden behind but I wouldn't have been able to hear the men's talk from there. I stood up to trample the grass and had just got out of sight again when Uncle Sohan turned up. He went straight to my father and held out his hand.

"Nathan, how are you doing?"

Dad put his hand in his pocket.

Aunty Malathi rushed over to stand between them. "Don't start trouble, Sohan. I told you to keep away."

"I'm sure my friend won't mind me being here, Aunty." He slapped my father on the shoulders. "What do you say, Nathan? Do I bother you?"

Dad turned away. All I could see from behind the bush was his back. I should have gone to him but didn't want to show myself and be the first to be found. Mum came over and put her arm through his. She asked Uncle please not to create a scene. He didn't pay any attention to her and was only interested in quarrelling with my father.

"Shame you had to go overseas to get a job, Nathan. Rest of our crowd are doing well here."

Dad straightened his back. I couldn't help myself. I got up from my hiding place and stood by his side, holding his hand then I gave Uncle a bad look to warn him off. Two other uncles came over to join in. I carried on holding my father's hand so he'd know I was there to help him. If there was a big fight, like in cowboy films, I was going to bite Uncle's leg.

"Enough Sohan," Aunty Malathi said.

She followed the uncles as they took him away. She must have told him to get out of her house because he didn't show up again. Even after he left, I wanted to stay and look after Dad. When Victor called me to play, I wasn't sure what to do.

Mum said, "Run along, girl. Everything is fine."

Ganesh leaned out of the kitchen window and waved to me. He'd been watching us play but hadn't been allowed to join in. I should have taken care of him instead of only wanting to make new friends.

"Can Ganesh play with us, Aunty Malathi?"

"I suppose so. He's finished his duties for now."

He ran out of the kitchen, nearly tripping over his flip-flops. While the rest of the children were in party clothes, he wore an old shirt that pulled. Victor told Leela to explain games to him in Tamil. She wasn't nice and only said a couple of words. Ganesh still smiled at her. I held his hand, chose him if we played in pairs and stood next to him in other games. We were in the middle of Statues when Aunty called him to serve shorteats. He was trying to stand still on one leg and didn't go straight away. Even though my aunt called him again, he stayed where he was. She walked quickly to where he was and smacked him.

"That wasn't fair," I told her.

"Play with the others, Rohini," she said before marching Ganesh away.

I complained to my father. "She shouldn't have hit him."

"It wasn't a hard smack and he has to learn."

"He's small."

"Enough, girl," he said gently.

"Can I say one more thing?"

"If you must."

"When I grow up, I'm not going to be horrible to servants and I'm going to listen to my children."

"Okay, but that's the end of it."

I kept quiet. Although Sri Lankans were good people, I hated the way they behaved towards servants. I wished I could do something to make it all right for children from poor families. God wasn't much use. I'd prayed to him the night before, asking him to be kind to child servants and he'd done nothing. I looked at where Ganesh had been wrongly punished. One day, I promised myself, I'd come back to rescue him, Saras, Herath and all the others.

Sohan revved the engine, put the car into gear, and roared away from Aunty Malathi's house. He'd gone there to enjoy himself not provoke an incident yet he'd been thrown out of the party like a pariah dog. The crescent-shaped scar on his thigh seared through his trousers. He'd hurt himself in childhood, climbing a tree to catch a Loten's sunbird for Nathan's family; an injury that only bothered him after his friend moved to England.

He slammed the brakes outside the nineteenth hole at his golf club and strode into the bar, which was furnished with Dutch colonial furniture and not even a batik print on the walls. None of the usual suspects was around and he didn't want to drink alone, yet other than returning home there was nowhere else to go. Everybody was at Aunty Malathi's party and nothing and no-one waited for him at home. Who was Nathan Palar to turn away from his handshake and have him barred from the party? Who the bloody hell was Nathan Palar to ignore him?

He clicked his fingers at the new barman, a chap as black as the ace of spades. "Give me an arrack, Harry." He emptied his glass in one gulp. "Give me another." Without drawing breath, he swallowed a second drink. His head was starting to feel woozy. If he had one more, he'd be in trouble driving home. He'd taken Nathan to the cricket club the night before his friend's wedding. Both had drunk whisky on the rocks. Who'd have thought a quick shot would have had so much effect?

"Harry, my glass is empty."

"Sir, you always ask me to remind you after the second."

"When I want your opinion, I'll ask for it."

He'd ordered a single measure for Nathan and added several ice cubes, telling his friend it was a double. Having promised Uma he wouldn't deliver her groom with a hangover, he vowed to be true to his word. He twirled his third drink around. Mountain roads were treacherous in the dark. He lifted the glass to his mouth then put it down again and clicked his fingers at the barman.

"Remind me of your name again."

"Harry, sir."

"Not that foreign thing. Your Sri Lankan one."

"Sir, Harry is my name."

"Well, whatever your name is, get rid of this bloody drink."

"Let me take your keys, sir. I'll get one of the boys to drive you."

"And make them walk three miles back here? Don't be ridiculous."

Outside, night air stung his face, good old Kandy night air, with a chill that sobered up the worst of drunks. So steadying was it, he could walk a straight stagger to his car. He started the engine, put his foot down, and raced home along unlit roads, although he ought to have learned his lesson after the last accident, when the front wheels of his car ended up over the edge of a hill. Tara, typical woman, had flung her arms around his neck and screamed. Luckily, they'd been spotted by a passing motorist who organised two rescue trucks to get them back on the road. Days later, Tara was still blackguarding him over the incident until he told her to shut up: she'd made her point and he wouldn't drive again while drunk. He never said anything about driving while tipsy. Besides, it wasn't his fault. Those conceited idiots at Aunty Malathi's had made him unwelcome and put him in a bad temper. Anyway, didn't he know every inch of the mountain's twists and turns? No doubt about it, he could control the car as well as if he'd given the nineteenth hole a miss.

He sped along, not seeing a cyclist in the middle of the road until he was feet away because the bloody fool didn't have any lights on. There wasn't enough time to toot the chap to move to one side. The cyclist fell into a ditch, his sarong coming undone in the process. Sohan swerved, slammed the brakes on, then reversed to where the bike lay on the road. The fellow was most likely a Plantation Tamil from a nearby tea estate. He grabbed hold of the man's arm and pulled him up.

"Are you hurt?" he asked in Tamil.

"No, sir."

"Is your bicycle damaged?"

"All is fine."

Sohan checked the bike. The front wheel was buckled beyond repair and he could feel the roughness of rust on the frame. Even though it belonged on a scrap heap, he tossed it into the boot of his car.

"Get in. Where do you live?"

"Sabara Tea Estate, sir. Over there."

"Yes, yes. I know where it is. Get in. Get in."

At the plantation, the fellow guided him past dwellings by the factory to a row of line rooms farther away, kept for the lower castes.

Sohan took a bunch of rupee notes from his wallet. "What are you? Barber? Washer?"

"Yes, sir. Washer."

Sohan pulled out another wad of rupee notes. "This will pay for a doctor, if you need one. There's also enough for a new bicycle."

"Thank you, sir. A thousand times."

"And get some lights for the next one."

He drove off, smiling. The bugger had thanked him as if he'd saved his life, not run him off the road.

The near miss had added an hour to his journey and sobered him even more. Taking it easy on the accelerator, he cruised home and called for his houseboy from the front veranda. The young chap came running.

"Was it a good party, *mahathya*?"

Sohan had forgotten all about Nathan. "Get me a cold beer. And why is this still on my chair?"

He threw the crumpled newspaper onto the floor, unable to remember what it was he wanted to read, something to do with leopards, but he was damned if he could recall what. Nathan, Nathan, Nathan. All he could think about, as if nothing and nobody else existed. His friend had changed over the past year, a few grey hairs around the temples, crow's feet around the eyes and a thinning patch at the back of the head. Perhaps it was early promotion to partner at his law firm that had caused the aging, not their fight. He picked up the newspaper and put it on a side table with the article about leopards face down.

Crickets shrilled over the rush of a nearby waterfall that snaked its way down hills and tributaries, then flowed through the Mahaweli River into the ocean at Trinco. If only he could also escape into the wild sea, let it engulf his body and leave it lifeless, drifting in peace for eternity. Yet he knew he was destined to face the following day and the one after that; he wouldn't give up on himself because Uncle Alagar hadn't.

Stars dotted the clear midnight sky: balls of burning gases, Uncle had taught him. They sat for hours in the garden trying to spot constellations. Ursa Minor was the first he'd learnt. According to Uncle, legend had it that Tamils used its North Star to escape to Jaffna during foreign rule. If you can find Polaris, the old man added, you can always find your way home. Nobody else had heard of that legend, however Uncle repeated the story to

Sohan as often as he needed to hear it.

The houseboy crept onto the veranda and left a carafe of water on the side table. Sohan downed two glasses so that when the dawn chorus started, he could watch the forest without a hangover and marvel at rays of sunlight filtered by palm leaves, or laugh at a troop of grey langurs jumping from branch to branch, hanging around the veranda, hoping to steal scraps of his breakfast.

An owl hooted in the distance.

"*Mahathya*," the boy asked, "do you want anything more tonight?"

Sohan waved him away with his hand. "You can go to bed."

As he watched the boy retreat, he reflected on the maid he'd been offered, a thirteen-year-old girl from one of the islands off Jaffna. She'd have been better at housework than this kid, but it wouldn't have done for a single man to have a girl in his home, especially in a town like Kandy, full of country bumpkins. He'd rather have been in Colombo, walking along Galle Face Green after Sunday lunch, as he had when he was young. Yet since he'd started to do well for himself, scrounging relations pushed him to the point where he couldn't stay there for long. "*Aiyo*, Sohan, can you buy us a small car to run around in? Sohan, we can't afford to pay for this one's school fees. Look at the holes in our shoes, son. Your father would want you to help us." True, one or two had been good friends and he spent his business profits on them, though hangers-on who wanted to trade on his success could take a flying jump.

He went indoors, locked and bolted the door behind him. Out of the corner of his eye, he gazed at the frayed edges on sofa cushions that had come with the house. On her first visit, Tara had commented on the worn-out furniture yet was soon distracted by the antique sideboard with lion claw legs that, unknown to her, he'd won in poker rather than bought.

"At last," she said, "you appreciate the finer things in life."

After he'd negotiated the deal in India that would turn him into a rupee millionaire, once that business was up and running, he'd be able to fill his homes with antique furniture without having to win it in games. And he promised himself that when he had all the money he needed, he was going to buy the Kandy *walauwa*, a home in every town in Sri Lanka and the whole damn lot of those people at Aunty Malathi's party.

# FRIENDS FOR LIFE

When we had to leave Kandy, I asked Mum, "Who's going to look after Ganesh now that I'm going back to Colombo?"

"Don't worry. Aunty takes care of him like he was her son."

I loved my aunt but knew she'd make him work in the kitchen with his mum because he was poor. I didn't speak much on the train journey back through the mountains, even when Dad pointed out a Hanging Parrot. I wished Ganesh could have been in the viewing carriage with us, watching the jungle. Although I wanted to stay in Sri Lanka to look after him, I didn't know how to make that happen if there were Troubles at the end of our holiday and Dad wanted to go back to England. God couldn't help because he'd broken his leg and was walking on crutches. All I could do was ask Jesus to bless Ganesh and keep him safe. To make my prayers come true, I was also going to promise again to be good.


Back at Appa's house, I was helping Mum put dirty clothes in a bag for the dhobi man when I heard Herath in the back yard, calling the chickens for their food. I took the shirt I was holding and listened to him from the doorway.

"You're not much use to me from there," Mum said. "Go to him if you want, but don't disturb his work."

I couldn't wait to tell him about Kandy and dropped the shirt on the floor then ran down the back veranda steps. The sun was behind a cloud so I didn't have to cover my eyes to look up at him.

"I learned about Veddhas. You put meat in trees and your devils are called yakas. And you were the first dancers in Sri Lanka."

I was so proud when he patted my head and said, "Yaku are spirits of dead Veddhas. One yaka. Two yaku."

"Are they angels?"

"They're our long-gone family and heroes. We ask the spirit of the greatest hunter, Kande Wanniya, for help when we track deer."

"You pray to him?"

"We perform the Kiri Koraha ceremony."

"Show me how?"

He finished scattering the chicken feed. "Saraswathie is cooking lunch. Let me see first if she needs my help."

I followed him to the kitchen so he wouldn't forget about me. The chilli smell of *tempered* onions being fried made me want to sneeze but I didn't. Amma was in the middle of the kitchen, telling Saras and a cook she'd hired for the day, what to do. "This curry powder is too dark. Have you checked the oven? You'll have to add more coconut milk to the snake beans. Rohini, don't come near the fire." I waited by the door while Herath asked if he could play with me. "Go with her," my grandmother said. "Mending the fence can wait."

He told me to stand in the back courtyard while he fetched something from his room. I hurried down the steps and stood to attention in front of the chicken coop, arms by my side, ready to do Kiri Koraha. It sounded more important than winning a gold medal on sports day. Herath came outside, carrying a long metal arrow, which he gave me to hold while he went into the kitchen. I couldn't believe I had a real arrow in my hand. My school friends would be jealous when I told them about it. I held the sharp tip above my head in case I accidentally killed myself with it. Herath came back with a clay chatty and put it on the ground.

"What's in there?"

"Coconut milk for the yaku."

He collected three twigs from the ground, tied them together at the top and spread the legs.

"What are you doing?" I asked.

"Making a stand."

He put the chatty on it then laid the arrow across the top. "The milk is the Kiri Koraha. This arrow is the *aude*. I am still learning to be a shaman, so yaku may not appear."

I looked around the courtyard, along the outside corridors and in the sky. "I can't see any angels."

"I haven't started yet, naga." He checked the chatty wasn't wobbling on the stand. "All right. Now I do it."

He bent over forwards, put his arms out in front, then stood straight again and took a step forward until he was dancing around the chatty. I wasn't sure if I was supposed to join in so stayed out of the way but near him in case he called me to dance too. He started to sing a song that didn't have a tune and his voice went funny deep. The chickens didn't take any notice of him and went into their hen house. I couldn't stop watching him. The way he was throwing his head around, I thought he was going mad. He'd danced round the chatty once, when my parents and Appa came onto the back veranda to see what the noise was about. Then my grandmother came out of the kitchen and stood in the side corridor.

Appa put his hands in his pockets. "Kiri Koraha."

Everybody was looking into the courtyard, watching Herath and me. I was still just standing there, not taking part in the ceremony and thought I should put on a show as well. I didn't know the words to Herath's song or how to do his dance so put my hand over my mouth to make Red Indian noises. Whooping, "Waah, waah, waah," I skipped around the yard, making sure I didn't bump into the arrow. I looked at the grown-ups to see if they'd noticed I was also taking part in the ceremony and that Herath and I were making a good job of it. Appa watched me skip and I caught him trying not to laugh at me, which was unfair. I was doing my best. Dad put a finger to his lips and called me over to stand between him and Mum.

Herath enjoyed himself so much that he shook his body and head. He looked like he'd forgotten about the rest of us. After a few minutes, Appa went down the veranda steps and held him until he calmed down.

I looked in the trees to see if Herath's magic had worked, if angels and yaku had come down to Earth from Heaven, but couldn't see anything. Then I saw a shadow move by the outside kitchen wall. It was only Saras coming onto the corridor. The sun shone on her, making her golden. She looked lovely and holy, like the picture of Jesus in the sitting area. I forgot about everybody else and stared at her beautiful face and smile and then, I couldn't believe it, I saw her wings and a halo. I should have known it all along. My beloved ayah was one of God's angels.


After lunch, I was playing Kiri Koraha with dolls in my bedroom when Uncle Theo rang. I stood in the doorway and listened to the call.

"Does Uncle have children?" I asked my father after he put the phone down.

"A daughter, about your age."

I clapped my hands and jumped up and down.

"Come here, girl," Mum said.

She wasn't smiling so can't have wanted a cuddle. Appa and Amma watched me climb onto her lap.

"Uncle Theo is divorcing Aunty Jyoti," my mother said. "You're not to speak to him about it."

"I promise. Why are they getting divorced?"

"Aunty Jyoti has a boyfriend," Dad said.

Mum scolded him with her eyes. She always stopped him when he told me grown-up things. I felt sorry for my new friend. My parents would never divorce because Mum didn't want boyfriends as well as a husband. Anyway, Dad would have had a row with her if she kissed another man on the mouth, like in films. He might even have made her stand in a corner.

I brought *Swallows and Amazons* from my bedroom, hoping that if I sat quietly, the grown-ups would forget about me and start gossiping about Uncle. Pretending to read, I turned a page in my book.

Amma said, "Theo stayed with that woman too long. She was running around with other men straight after their honeymoon."

"Beautiful women can be like that," Appa told her. "That's why I - "

Wow. Grown-ups had never said anything like this while I was around. I had to say something and show I was a big girl.

"I'm going to tell Uncle I hope he gets an ugly wife next time."

"Rohini, you're not to speak to Theo about his divorce. Your grandmother's right, sweetheart. Listen to Amma, girl."

They were all ganging up on me when I was trying to help. Even if I wasn't allowed to speak to Uncle about his wife, I wanted to cheer him up and went to look for Saras in the servants' quarters. It was so dark in her room I couldn't see clearly then I saw her having a nap on the stone floor. I bent down and pulled out coconut hairs that poked through her thin mattress so they wouldn't prick her skin. I wished my grandparents would buy beds for her and Herath but Amma said servants were used to sleeping like that. I went back to the sitting area and every now and then, as the grown-ups chatted, I left the room to check if Saras had woken up. Mum nearly caught me once.

"Where are you going?"

"Nowhere."

"Don't disturb Saras. She's got a headache."

"I won't."

She went to her bedroom to get a hanky. I crept onto the back veranda and down the side corridors, looking behind to make sure nobody was following me. Saras' room was empty. I found her at the kitchen table, rubbing her eyes. She still seemed tired.

"You slept a lot," I said. "Are you ill?"

"I needed to sleep, kunju. I was preparing food late last night."

"Can you bend down? I want to whisper something to you."

Amma came onto the back veranda and saw me across the house. I turned my back to her so she wouldn't guess what I was saying.

"Rohini, please leave Saraswathie alone," she said.

"I'm just coming now."

Hoping she wouldn't catch hold of me, I ran past her, back to the sitting room.

"Mum, can I wear my new green dress with the big pockets to visit Uncle Theo."

"If you like."

I picked up my book again and read until Dad said we were leaving for Uncle's place. I ran to the kitchen. "I'm just saying goodbye to Saras," I said and came back with my hand in my dress pocket, holding what Saras had just given me. As I got into the car, Mum gave me a funny look but didn't say anything. I acted like I hadn't noticed her watching me.

Before we went to Uncle's house, we drove round Colombo, looking at places we used to visit when we lived there. First we stopped at Galle Face Green, where people flew kites, some diamond-shaped, some long like cobras. Dad said he used to have kite fights there when he was a schoolboy. "We rubbed ground glass on the strings to cut down another kite when it was flying." That wasn't a nice thing to do but boys are like that.

On the other side of the grass, waves crashed into the sea shore in a wind that also made ladies' saris blow about. One old lady looked like she was going to take off any minute. My father said it was perfect flying weather and if we hadn't been going to visit Uncle, he'd have got out of the car and taught me how to fly kites.

"Can we come here one day anyway so you can show me?"

"Sure." He put his hands his hands on the steering wheel and stared through the windscreen. "You know, Uma, this takes me back."

Mum covered his hands with one of hers. "I know."

We drove to Elephant House next, which had the best ice cream in the whole world. Dad stopped the car outside, left the engine running and said we could come there another time too. I was glad we weren't going to stay any longer. It was hot and my hand was getting sticky. Dad took a long look at the building then changed gear and pulled away, nearly hitting a tuk-tuk that overtook us.

"Careful, Nathan," Mum said.

"Relax. I saw the fellow coming."

They started talking about the traffic in Sri Lanka and the fools on the road. It was my lucky day. They'd forgotten about me and nobody had found out what Saras and I had got up to. I bent my head down for the rest of the drive so my parents couldn't see in their mirrors what I was doing. I kept looking up to make sure they weren't watching me. When I finished, my hands were sticky and I licked them clean. It was only when we stopped outside Uncle's house I remembered that I'd gone and spoilt my surprise for him. I climbed out of the car and cried. Mum wiped my tears away with her thumb and asked what was wrong. I didn't know how to tell her I'd been bad.

"What is it sweetheart?" she said again.
"I asked Saras to make milk toffee for Uncle to cheer him up."
"That was nice of you."
"I ate some in the car."
"You can give him the rest."
"I finished it."
"Oh. Do you feel sick?"

I nodded. I didn't really feel ill but thought I should say yes. I was so upset, I didn't even feel like laughing when Dad played a joke on Uncle and banged the door knocker hard.

"What's all this noise?" a man shouted from inside. He came stomping out then saw us, laughed and hugged my father.

Mum said, "Rohini's not feeling well."
"Poor thing. Come in. Come in. Kana, let her lie down on your bed."

A girl as tall as I was took me upstairs to her room. She sat next to me on the bed, held my hand and kissed me on the forehead, saying, "I'll take care of you."

I felt blessed to have her near me. She made me go quiet inside, like nothing would trouble me again. I didn't want her to know I'd been play-acting so carried on pretending to be ill for a few more minutes. After drinking the glass of water a servant brought me, my mouth felt clean and the sugar taste went. I could have eaten more milk toffee if I'd had any. Kana held my sticky hand in her warm one and we stayed on the bed, not looking at each other. A few minutes later, she brought a wet facecloth and wiped our hands. When I'd had enough of lying down, I sat up, saying I felt better. I'd been told not to mention the divorce to Uncle Theo but nobody had said anything about his daughter and anyway, it must have been all right, because we were children.

"Your mum left you and your dad."
"She loves me, even if she doesn't live with us."
"Do you miss her?"
"She didn't look after me much. When I wish she was here, I meditate or pray to Buddha."
"Is he any better than God?"
"He's different."

I thought I might try talking to him. The Lord might even like it if I asked someone else for favours instead of bothering him. I knelt by the foot of the bed. "Hello, Buddha. It's Rohini speaking here. I'm Kana's friend. Can you please tell Aunty Malathi to take good care of Ganesh without making him work a lot. He's only small."

"You can't ask him about any one person. He helps all living things."

"Look after everyone, Buddha. Most of all, Ganesh." I waited for him to talk to me but couldn't hear anything. "He doesn't listen either."

"It's not about listening. It's about meditating to find peace."

"Huh?"

"Like this, and put your hands on your lap."

I copied the way my new friend sat, cross-legged, hands one on top of each other and palms up, thumbs touching at the tips.

"Close your eyes," she said, "and relax your body, from toes to head."

I shut my eyes tight and waited for her peace to happen. I didn't feel any different and Buddha still didn't speak to me. "It's not working."

She jumped off the bed. "You have to practise at home."

I'd have liked to learn more about Buddhism but didn't ask her to teach me then in case she thought I was a nuisance.

She pulled out two brand new dolls from her toy box, which we played families with, then we made dinner on a cooker that had lights, then we played with her new dolls again.

"Rohini," Mum shouted from downstairs. "Say goodbye. We're going now."

I ran down. "Can Kana come over tomorrow?"

"If that's all right with Uncle Theo, then yes."

"Of course," he said. "It'll do her good."

On the drive back to my grandfather's house, I told my parents I was now talking to Buddha as well as God.

"How will you get to temple to have these chats?" Dad asked.

"I'm going to speak to him at home."

"You're her mother, Uma. Explain why we're Christians."

Mum looked out of the window. "Never mind that. I want to know why Saras gave her so much milk toffee it made her ill."

It wasn't my ayah's fault; she was only trying to help me and I'd gone and got her into trouble.

The sky was getting dark. It wasn't a pretty orange or purple, the sun just fell below houses and buildings. I hoped Saras was sleeping because in the morning Mum would have forgotten she was angry.

Back at Appa's house, Dad parked in the front port and patted the steering wheel. He loved the Mercedes and would have taken it to London if my grandfather had let him. Mum rushed out of the car and went straight to the kitchen where Saras was cooking dinner. I followed her, wanting to stand up for my ayah, also afraid to in case I was told off for being rude and talking back. I wasn't sure how much trouble I was in and stood by the door.

Mum said, "Saraswathie, why did you give Rohini milk toffee to take to her uncle? She ate it all and was nearly sick."

Saras laughed. "I only gave two pieces and kept the rest here. I knew small one would eat it."

Mum stood like she was for a couple of seconds then apologised for being wrong and unkind. It was my turn to be told off. I waited to see if I was to be scolded for eating the milk toffee or for asking Saras to make it. Luckily, my mother had forgotten about me. I wondered what to do next when Amma called me from the sitting room. Before Mum remembered I was there, I ran to my grandmother.

"Your father tells me you're taking up Buddhism," she said.

"God never does what I want."

"There are better reasons for choosing a religion but you're young. Go bring me the statue of Buddha from my dressing table."

I hurried to her bedroom and opened the dressing table drawer, which smelt of cough linctus and pills. I took out the statue and carried it in both hands, even though it was so small I could have put it in my pocket.

"Here, Amma."

"I want you to have it, child. Look after it. I was given it when I was about your age."

I gave her a kiss and showed it to Dad.

"I can talk to him properly now."

He pulled a face. "That's what I'm afraid of."

I put Buddha in my pocket and kept him there for the rest of the evening. Every now and then, I took him out and talked to him in my bedroom with the door shut. I told him about Ganesh, how he was only a small boy and Aunty Malathi shouldn't smack him. I said to take good care of Kana and to make her mum come back and love her. And please look after all living things as well. At night-time, I pushed him under my pillow before kneeling at the foot of my bed.

"Are you going to pray to God or Buddha?" Mum asked.

"I'm speaking to the good one."

"Do you want to pray out loud?"

"He likes to have peace and quiet."

She smiled and let me finish without asking any more questions. After tucking me in, she went to join the others while I lay in bed, falling asleep. Through the open door, I heard Dad ask whom I'd prayed to.

"I have no idea, Nathan," Mum told him.

They started talking about religion. I tried to listen but felt my eyelids close. The last thing I heard before I dropped off was Amma saying, "The child will find the right path for her."

---

The next morning, holding Buddha in my pocket, I sat on the front veranda steps and waited for Uncle Theo to drop off Kana. Behind me, Appa drank a cup of tea while playing chess with Dad. The sun shone through the carport, a warm sea wind floated across me, just touching my hair. I lifted my nose to breathe in the salt. I loved being in my summer dress, feeling sunrays on my legs, arms and face. I gave Buddha a rub and made a wish we'd never leave Sri Lanka again. It was my seventh wish that morning. I hoped he wasn't counting how many things I'd asked for.

"Dad, when is Kana coming?"

"Soon."

"When is Uncle picking her up?"

"Hmm? They'll have dinner with us then leave straight after."

"To get back before curfew?"

"Yes."

I wasn't sure why there was a curfew every night. I thought it might have been to stop people playing cricket in the dark and fighting if they lost. If Uncle stayed out after nine o'clock and got arrested, his police friends would have got him out of jail but he didn't like taking chances.

Mum joined us on the veranda, a newspaper under her arm. "Prabhakaran and his Tamil Tigers are dangerous," she said to nobody. "Thank goodness they aren't as organised as the IRA."

"They soon will be," Appa told her.

Dad looked up a move in his chess book. "I wish you'd move to England."

Appa moved a pawn forward. "I won't be driven out of my country by thugs."

I rubbed Buddha again. If he couldn't let me live in Sri Lanka, could he send my grandparents, Saras and Herath to live with us in England? And Uncle Theo and Kana and not to forget Ganesh, his mum, Aunty Malathi and everybody else I loved and had forgotten. I was saying thank you to him when an ant crawled up my arm. I flicked it off then stamped on it in case it came back angry. I thought it must have been okay for Buddhists to kill if it was to stop an insect biting them.

Uncle Theo drove through the gates and into the drive, his tyres scrunching on the earth. Kana was leaning out of the front car window, waving to us. I waved back and hugged her when she got out.

Uncle gave her a goodbye kiss. "See you later, alligator."

"In a while, crocodile."

I asked Mum if we could go to the beach. She lifted her head from the paper. "Let me read for a bit, then I'll walk you there." She wouldn't be long. When Dad and Appa played chess, they didn't talk much to her about what she'd been reading.

I took Kana to my room and pulled Buddha out of my dress pocket. "Amma gave him to me. I carry him around so he can be everywhere, same as God."

"He has to be on a table. Like this. Then you pray in front of him or meditate."

I didn't want to pray or meditate then. I'd been speaking to Buddha from waking up to waiting for Kana, which was a long time to be religious. Even Sunday school didn't go on that long. I kissed my statue and said I'd chat to him later.

I put my hands over my mouth. "I forgot. I want Saras to bless you."

"Is she a nun?"

"She's an angel. Quick. I'm not supposed to disturb servants while they're working."

We ran to the back of the house and past Herath who whistled as he swept the dining area.

I put a finger to my lips. "Amma's sleeping."

"Your grandmother's awake. I took her a glass of warm water."

I looked behind at Amma's closed bedroom door. "Is she going to come out?" I whispered.

"She'll lie down for a few more minutes."

"Is Saras busy?"

"What are you up to, naga?"

"I want Saras to bless Kana."

"She's in the kitchen."

I grabbed Kana's hand and we ran to the back of the house.

"Saras. Saras," I called softly.

"Here, kunju. What's wrong?"

"I want you to meet my new friend."

"Let me finish cleaning my teeth first."

She used her fingers to brush with burnt paddy husk then rinsed her mouth to get rid of the black. Afterwards, she stroked Kana's hair. "*Nalla pillhi*," she said. "Sweet child." I sighed. Now that Kana had been blessed, she had God and his angels as well as Buddha to keep her safe. And as Herath was my cousin, his yaku spirits were already watching over us. We were lucky to have all of them.

"Do you want milk toffee?" Saras asked. We held out our hands, hoping she'd fill them from the jar she took down off a high shelf. "One piece each," she said. Less than we wanted, it was still a treat we took to the dining area. I sat in Appa's chair at the top of the table and swung my legs. We took small bites of the crumbly toffee, trying to make it last. Mum walked in from the front veranda and wanted to know what we were eating.

"Saras gave us milk toffee," I said.

"How much have you girls had?"

"One piece each."

She smiled. "When you finish, we'll go to the beach. Kana, I'll give you a pair of Rohini's flip-flops and shorts to wear."

She let us run ahead by the grass pavement until we got to the railway line, where we had to hold hands and wait for her to check both ways for trains, then tell us it was safe to cross. There wasn't a switch to turn off the electricity so we had to walk on the wooden parts of the track, which were cracked and dry because nobody had polished them. The beach was on the other side of the railway line.

"Mum, when we get to the sea, can I put my foot in? I won't jump into the water."

"Absolutely not. You know the currents are strong."

Dad had held onto me the year before and let me dip my foot in but I didn't think I should tell her.

Kana and I ran about, picking out shells from seaweed and driftwood to make necklaces and bracelets. We had to be careful not to get bitten by tiny crabs in the sand. She found more than I did because I danced about without really looking for shells. She shared hers with me anyway. One had all the colours of the rainbow when the sun shone on it, so I gave it back to her because it was special.

She said, "You have it. It's a present."

I asked Mum to keep it safe so I wouldn't lose it.

Near me was a long, thin piece of wood that looked like an arrow. I wanted to take it back to England to do Kiri Koraha there but Mum made me throw it away. "It's dirty," she said then she sat on the sand, which was just as dirty.

When Kana and I weren't playing together, my friend stayed close to my mother and cuddled her. I wasn't jealous like I'd have been with other playmates. I picked up a few shells and gave her the prettiest ones. I was going to look for more but the sun was so high it covered the sea with a silver blanket. I put a hand to my head because I was getting a headache.

Mum stood up and brushed the sand off her dress. "Come, girls. If I'd known it was going to be a scorcher, I wouldn't have brought you here."

"Can we stay a little longer?" I asked. "I'm not hot at all."

"Please, Aunty Uma?"

"Another time. You're both wilting."

At the railway line, she stopped to look left and right but didn't cross over. She looked down the track at a man who was coming towards us. The way he walked on the sand, one hand in his trouser pocket, made me think I'd seen him before. Maybe he lived down Perth Avenue. When he reached us, Mum looked around before saying his name, just to make sure my father wasn't nearby.

"It's good to see you, Sohan."

"How are you, Uma?"

"Can't complain. And you?"

"Can't complain. Business is doing well. So are Tara and I."

"I'd ask you in for a drink - "

"I understand."

"How did you know we'd be here?"

"I didn't. Just came down on the off chance. And for old times' sake. I miss walking with Uncle Alagar to Galle Face Green."

"Dad said you stopped him going mad in his family of women. Sohan, can't you apologise to Nathan? Put it behind you."

"It's not easy. I wish it were."

My head was getting hotter and started to pain me. I closed my eyes and leaned against my mother.

Uncle said, "Small one is fading fast."

"I'd better get them back."

"It was good seeing you again, Uma. I'll see you around."

He put his hands in his pockets and walked back down the railway line. Mum said it might be better if we didn't tell Dad we'd seen Uncle. I didn't like keeping bad secrets from my father but liked fights even less, and she knew about it so it wasn't like I'd be telling a lie.

Back at the house, Appa's politician friend was on the veranda, saying riots were expected in town. He stopped talking when he saw us. Dad said, "Girls, clean up then play in the back garden." He looked worried.

Mum put a plastic bag on my bed for the shells and Kana and I emptied our pockets into it. The three of us washed the sand off our feet in the bathroom then my mother went to join the grown-ups, asking Herath on the way to get cold drinks for Kana and me. We quietly drank the glasses of iced water he left on the dining table and only felt like speaking after our heads cooled off from the sun.

"What did they mean about riots, Kana?"

"*Thathi* said the trouble between the Sinhalese and Tamils is getting worse."

"That's why we moved to England."

"My mum wanted us to live in Australia but *Thathi* stayed here."

"Your dad's Sinhalese. Why do you need to leave?"

She started to cry. I didn't know what to do and took her to my mother. "She just started crying. I didn't say anything to upset her."

Mum held her and stroked her hair until she was quiet. She kissed the top of her head and asked if she was all right. Kana nodded then wiped her eyes and blew her nose loudly on my mother's hanky.

Mum said, "Look after her, Rohini."

In my bedroom, I asked Kana why she was so upset.

"Jyoti wanted to go to Australia because her boyfriend moved there."

I'd never heard my friend call her mother by her name before and wanted to know why she was doing it then. I wasn't sure if that would make her cry again, so said, "Shall I call your mum, Jyoti, too?"

"I think you should."

We played Snap and I let her win to cheer her up, like Dad and Mum did with me if I was upset. She smiled a little bit. I didn't know what else to do for her until I saw my statue by the bed.

"We can start a secret club so we can be Buddhists."

"I'm already one and it shouldn't be a secret."

Herath walked up the side garden, past my window, carrying a basket for fruit and vegetables he was going to buy from Pettah market.

"Then we can use it to be Veddhas."

"I'd like that. Then your dad will have to let you stay in Sri Lanka."

"Huh?"

"Veddhas only live here. They don't leave like Tamils and Sinhalese."

Sohan watched Uma take the girls up Perth Avenue and into Roshan Uncle's garden. He counted her paces from the front gate, up veranda steps and to the sitting and dining areas. He and Nathan had often walked the same path, returning from a school cricket match, discussing wickets they'd taken and runs they'd scored. Whichever team they played for, if they'd won or lost, Nathan's parents would congratulate both boys on having played their best.

He crossed the railway track and climbed a boulder at the shoreline. Taking a lungful of air, he held his breath until he thought he was going to pass out then he exhaled slowly and let his breathing settle. Ocean waves smashed into the shore, drenching his jeans, making the denim heavy and stick to his legs. Children ran along the beach, pointing at the man on the rock while their parents hurried them past. A young girl asked if he was going to dive into the water and was dragged away by her mother. Standing as tall as he could, he faced the sea and horizon. He was cricket captain of the school team; they'd just won a match and he flaunted the school flag at evening celebrations, ready to belt out the words and tune of the school song, *Nil Desperandum*, with Nathan by his side. So absorbed was he in memories, he half-expected his friend to come running down the road and join him on the beach. As seagulls circled above, calling to each other, his heart beat faster and he hoped and prayed, watched to see if Nathan would race out of Roshan Uncle's house and come to him. He stood there so long his neck hurt from straining to look behind, yet he stayed where he was, getting soaked by sea spray until what seemed like a lifetime later, the seagulls' calls turned to screeching. When he finally conceded his friend wasn't going to appear, he edged his way down, inch by inch, from the boulder. The days of cricket trophies were long gone.

On the sand, a young boy sat on his father's shoulders, holding onto his dad's ears. Sohan could feel the man's bristles scratch the child's bare legs, as his own father's had one afternoon when, farther north along the coastline, he too was carried on shoulders on Galle Face Green. In all honesty, he couldn't be sure what the weather had been like that day, but he thought of it as a cloudless blue sky, with enough wind to lift kites and make them soar. That was long before his parents' divorce. And since then, somewhere along the way his life had taken a wrong turning, all favours done had been forgotten, relationships twisted until they snapped and he was left at the end of Perth Avenue, watching the world.

# AFRAID OF FEAR

Later that evening, Kana and I were in the Temple tree when Uncle Theo came for dinner. He drove fast into the front garden and stopped just in front of Appa's Mercedes. He was going to get a blackguarding for nearly having an accident. Also, my grandfather was on the front veranda and didn't like being disturbed while the sky changed colour.

"Do that again," Appa said crossly, "and I'll ban you from driving in here. You boys never grow up."

Uncle laughed. "Has my daughter been behaving herself?"

Kana jumped down from the tree and ran to hug him. "As much as you, *Thathi*."

She ran back to join me on a branch and we sat there, swinging our legs, watching the sky turn pink. I was going to ask Dad to paint my bedroom in London that colour. Uncle Theo tried to chat to Appa and was told to be quiet. I wondered how long it would be before the grown-ups remembered Kana and I were up the tree and made us climb down because it was getting dark. After the sun disappeared, a curry smell came out of the kitchen to the front of the house. Although I wanted to stay where I was, I'd been on a branch for so long I couldn't feel my bottom and was glad when Amma called, "Come and eat. I won't warm it again." Kana and I tried to climb down by ourselves but had to ask Uncle Theo for help because we couldn't see where to put our feet.

At dinner, Appa opened a couple of bottles of wine we'd brought him from England and served everyone except Kana and me, even though we asked nicely for a glass each. After we'd finished eating and Mum and Dad were a little drunk, I said, "Can Kana stay with us for the rest of the holiday?"

"What do you say, Theo?" Dad said.

"If it's all right with your parents, Nathan, I can leave her here during the day and pick her up after work."

Kana and I clapped our hands. "Yeahhh."

Appa coughed loudly. "Children, you haven't asked me yet."

"Please?"

"You'll have to promise to be good."

"We will."

"And quiet."

"That too."

"Now you've promised to do the impossible, I suppose the answer has to be yes."

Soon as Uncle Theo finished his wine, he said Kana and he should get going. It was half an hour to curfew. "Besides, I don't like driving at night anymore."

"In the good old days," Dad said, "I remember when we didn't have to worry what time we got home."

"Apart from when you had your parents' curfew, Nathan," Appa said.

"Apart from when I said I was staying at Sohan's house."

"And he said he was staying here. You think we didn't know?"

Dad smiled.

Suddenly there was a loud bang outside and we all went quiet. The men told everybody to stay in the dining area then they closed the front doors. Amma called Saras and Herath into the house. "Stay inside with us. I don't want you two at the back where anything could happen. And bring a paraffin lamp in case the electricity goes out." The men looked out of the front window but it was too dark to see anything.

"Better lock the house," Appa said.

Mum ran to his bedroom to get the keys while Saras and Herath ran to check that all the windows and shutters were closed. When Dad heard loud voices on the road, he went outside with Appa, Uncle Theo and Herath.

Mum was afraid. "Be careful," she told them.

"Keep the door shut," my father said.

She closed it then watched out of the front window. Kana and I held hands tightly and stayed at the dining table with Amma and Saras. I didn't know what was happening. The bang had sounded like a gun in cowboy films. It might have been Uncle Sohan come to shoot my father. If he started a fight, I could attack him but I couldn't stop bullets. I got scared and jumped down from my chair, wanting to be with my mother.

"Come on, Kana."

We ran to Mum only for her to push us away.

"Girls, sit with Saras at the back of the house. I want you away from the front."

I wanted to stay with her, even if it was more dangerous. Saras took us back to the dining area and lifted us onto our chairs. She put an arm across Amma's shoulders to stop her shaking and spoke softly to her in Tamil. The grown-ups were too busy to look after Kana and me so we hugged each other. I jumped if I heard a creak in the house or if shadows, made by the flame in the paraffin lamp, moved on the walls. Saras said everything was going to be all right. I didn't believe her because she didn't look like an angel in the dark. She looked as frightened as the rest of us. The men talked on the road for ages. I could only hear their voices, not what they were saying.

Mum said, "They're coming back." She quickly unlocked the door. "What was it, Nathan?"

"A car backfiring."

He still looked worried.

Appa took the house keys from the door. "I shouldn't have panicked but it reminded me of the riots in fifty-eight."

Uncle Theo went straight over to Kana. "I should have known it was only a car backfiring. Your dad's getting sillier as he gets older."

She didn't laugh.


In the morning, Uncle dropped Kana off while we were having breakfast. I was eating my favourite mashed purple yam with sugar.

"Do you want some?" I asked my friend.

"I've already eaten."

I fed her a couple of spoonfuls anyway. I was still eating when Herath and Saras started to clear the dining table.

"Rohini hasn't finished," Amma told them.

"Storm coming," Saras said and pointed at the sky through the back veranda doors. I turned to see what was happening outside then the room got darker. I swallowed my last mouthful and gave Saras my bowl. She picked up the stringhopper plate with her free hand and used her elbow to switch on the lights. I jumped with each thunderclap. I looked behind and saw a flash of lightning. Rain came pouring down outside. It splashed on the back veranda and a couple of drops bounced off the floor onto my legs. Dad told us to count between the lightning and thunder and the storm would soon be gone.

I held Kana's hand. "We don't want to."

Saras shut the front doors then helped Herath clear the table. They were about to take plates and serving dishes to the kitchen when Amma told them, "Stay here. You'll get soaked on the outside corridors."

"Lot of work to do," Saras said.

"It can wait."

I was starting to miss England, where the only Troubles were cold winters. It wasn't fair we had to live there, and my grandparents and Kana had to live where there were riots.

"There's always trouble in Sri Lanka," I told my mother.

"It was just a car backfiring last night, darling, and thunderstorms happen in London as well."

Herath said something to her in Sinhalese, which I didn't understand and she nodded her head. He told Kana and me to come with him to the sitting area. We ran and sat either side of him on the sofa. I felt a bit funny being next to a servant on good furniture until Amma smiled at us. Rain poured so loudly onto the front garden that Herath had to raise his voice for us to hear him.

"My mother used to sing to me when there was thunder."

"Is it a Veddha song?" I asked.

"Yes, naga."

He opened his mouth and started to sing. Close-up, his lips looked even bigger than I'd noticed before. Amma told me later that most Veddhas had mouths like that.

*Aemminan aemminan* [1]
*Sat muduru kandiyeta piten*
*Silman Silpawanali widinnegi neweyit neweyi*
*Balapawu denno nam bala paw denno*
*Ayiyinan ayiyinan disi muduru nagala*
*Balapa gena ena raga narakayi*
*Maya aga bawiri karanneyi*
*Rajawalo galgamata nuwannu denna nam*

I didn't understand what he was singing and it wasn't a pretty tune. "What does it mean?"

"Rohini, he hasn't finished," Kana said as he opened his mouth to sing some more.

"Let me see," he said. "It means, darling, darling. There you see the wind and rain are coming down from outside the Seven Seas. See the two. See brother, thunder and lightning, coming from the direction of the sea. Things are getting bad. My body is losing strength. Let us two go to the Rajawalo cave." [2]

"Where's Rajawalo cave?" I asked.

"Near my village, Nilgala."

"Where's that?"

"Near Yala."

Kana sat up. "I know where Yala is, Rohini."

Herath said if we had time that holiday, he'd take us to see his family.

"What if we don't have time?" I asked.

"Then next year."

I didn't want to wait until then but none of my prayers were working and I didn't know how else to change things.

When the storm passed and the sun came out again, I looked through the dripping leaves and white flowers of the Temple tree, to see if a Loten's sunbird had taken shelter in the branches. I couldn't see anything moving or sitting there.

"It's never coming back, Amma."

"They turn up every now and then, girl, like they always have."

She said we should all go out to cheer us up, and what about a craft shop to buy presents for friends in England? Dad and Appa grunted but she told them they were coming too. Mum thought it was a great idea and went to her room to get ready.

Kana and I watched as she put on eye shadow and mascara and asked if we could have some too. She said no but let us put a bit of rouge on our cheeks, though not enough for it to show much. Kana gave her a hug. "My mum never let me try make-up." I prayed to Buddha in my head to make my friend's mother start loving her and to please do it soon.

"Are you ready?" Dad shouted from outside. "We're waiting for you."

"Be right there," Mum shouted back.

Amma said in a loud voice from the front veranda, "You must be joking, Nathan, if you think I'm going to make my joints stiff by sitting in the car before I have to. I'll wait until Uma's ready."

My mother quickly put on red lipstick. "We'd better go. It won't take much for him to stay behind and give the shopping a miss."

I asked her to bend down so I could whisper in her ear. "Can Kana sit next to you?"

"Of course she can."

As Mum climbed into the back seat of the car, she called my friend, "Come, girl." Kana rushed in and snuggled up close to her for loving. I got a bit jealous, even though I said she could sit there, and squeezed closer to Mum. When we were all inside and had clunked the doors shut, Amma took my hand and put it on her lap. She smelt of Eau de Cologne and face powder she wore to church. I got worried and didn't know how to escape.

"Darling girl," she said.

Kana and Mum were cuddling and hadn't noticed what was happening to me. Dad was driving so he couldn't help. I was going to have to save myself. "Amma, Jesus doesn't want you to tell me a bible story while the car's moving. It'll make me sick."

"*Aiyo*, child, can't I hold your hand without it being about religion?"

"Highly unlikely," Appa said.

"I'm ignoring you, Roshan. I see my granddaughter only once a year."

She stroked my cheek and I leaned against her arm, glad she wasn't going to tell me God and Jesus stories.

"That's the third police car we've passed," Appa said as we drove along Galle road.

"Think we should go back?" Dad asked.

"Drive on. It's probably a rehearsal."

Dad bombed along, swerving round tuk-tuks and beeping cyclists who got in his way. Mum told him off for not stopping at crossings when there were people waiting to go over the road.

"You've forgotten, Uma. This is how everybody drives round here."

"Exactly. Enough maniacs on the road without another one."

He pretended he hadn't heard her and carried on driving dangerously until we got to the shop, where he slammed the brakes on. "There you go, ladies and young ladies. Service with a smile."

"I'll give you service with a smile if you try that trick again," Mum said.

Dad told us he was going to hang around the car with Appa while we shopped, but we'd only been inside a few minutes when they came in too.

"Did you come to help choose presents?" I asked.

My father shook his head and wiped his forehead with a hanky. "It's too hot outside. What are you two girls going to buy?"

"We haven't got any money."

"Choose something as a treat."

Kana and I stared at each other. We couldn't believe our luck. We rushed around the room that was full of painted masks and statues of villagers and Buddha. There were even elephants as tall as my waist. I sat on one but couldn't stay long on it, because Dad lifted me off. "They're ornaments," he said.

Kana held my hand after that and pulled me if she thought I was going to sit on an elephant, but she let me lie back on a leather pouffe. Up on the ceiling, fan blades were grey with dust and paint was peeling. A lot of places in Sri Lanka were dirty like that, because nobody sold Jif cleaning cream there and decorators were always on strike with the miners for more pay.

The floor was crowded with things to buy and I had to step carefully so as not to trample anything. Kana already had shell bracelets at home like those we saw in a basket. We chose one each anyway, so we could have the same.

As we waited for Mum to finish her shopping, I looked around at Batik prints that were mostly of elephants in the Perahera and flowers. I couldn't make out what a picture on the opposite wall was supposed to be then I covered my mouth with my hands. Oh my goodness. "Kana," I said softly, afraid the shopkeeper might hear, "look at that picture of ladies showing their bosoms. I don't think children are allowed in here."

She looked up to where I'd been staring. "They're not rude, they're Sigiriya frescoes. We learned about them at school."

"But they're showing their bosoms."

Dad heard what we said and came up to us. "We may be able to fit in a visit to Sigiriya this holiday so you can see the frescoes for yourself. And yes, if we go, Kana can come too."

I grabbed her hand and we jumped up and down, even after Appa said, "Stop it girls. You're starting an earthquake." Then he held our hands and jumped with us until Amma gave him a look.

Mum had a basket full of wooden serving dishes, table linen and coconut shell spoons. Dad spotted hopper pans so she got some of those as well. "I'll have to teach you how to cook," she said, "or you'll have me making *hoppers* all day long."

"I'm a lawyer. I'm best at supervising."

"For that wisecrack, Supervisor, you can pay for this lot and I'll keep my money to spend on myself."

He laughed and went to the counter, asking Kana and me to give him our bracelets so he could pay for everything with traveller's cheques. Kana watched him take his wallet out of his trouser pocket.

"Why does your dad have to show his passport?"

"So the man knows he hasn't stolen the cheques."

I was proud to be able to explain something to her after I didn't know anything about the frescoes. We hung around Dad while he took the shopping from the man. He fished in the bags and took the price tags off our bracelets. "I suppose you two want to wear these now." We held our hands out and took our new jewellery from him.

Amma was waiting on a chair by the door, cooling herself with a fan that had flowers cut into the wood. She promised I could have it when I was old enough not to break it. I didn't know when that would be but didn't think it would be soon.

Mum said now we were out and about, she'd like to go to a sari shop. Dad wanted to have a cold drink instead with Appa at Elephant House, saying they'd be back in half an hour. My mother lifted her eyebrows.

"And if we need longer?"

"Then take longer. But you won't need it."

She called him back after he walked off with Appa and gave him her shopping to put in the car. Before he ran off again she said, "Girls, do you want to have something to drink too?" Kana and I shook our heads. We wanted to go shopping with the ladies.

As soon as we went in the sari shop, I got the smell of incense that was like sandalwood furniture polish we had at home. Mum had a good look at saris hanging in the middle of the floor. She touched each one and pulled a face if it was thin cotton. She should have had better manners and pretended to like clothes that belonged to someone else. Kana and I played peek-a-boo between the hanging rails until Amma told us to stop because we were making the saris dirty. We giggled and hung round Mum while she picked material for sarongs. She asked the shop owner to show her what he had at the back. He went to and from his storeroom fetching silk saris that he put on the counter.

"Choose, choose. Best material in Colombo."

She took a green one and a dark pink one, wasn't sure if she should take a blue or purple one, so wanted to know which sari Amma liked best.

"They both suit your colouring. But I thought you didn't wear blue."

"It's not for me." Then she told the man, "I'll take all four. I can't get this choice in London. Oh, and can you make sure the blouse material is also in there?"

Amma said, "This will surprise my husband and son. We've only been here a short while." She never wore a watch so everything was a short while or a long one. Mum looked at her wristwatch. "Half an hour on the dot. Nathan knows me better than I realised."

On the way back to the car, we met Dad and Appa. They were chatting and laughing and must have been telling rude jokes to each other or gossiping about ladies. Around the corner, two policemen were getting out of a police van by Appa's Mercedes. One of them grinned when he saw my grandfather. "I thought this was yours, Mr Palar. If you ever want to sell it - "

"Joseph Mendis. My God. How are you?"

I looked at Amma's face, expecting her to be cross. And she was. Oh, she was going to punish him at home for taking the name of the Lord in vain. On our last holiday, she scolded him for a whole day. Appa carried on talking as if he hadn't done anything wrong.

"I heard your family had moved to Bentota, Joseph."

The policeman put his arm inside the van and pulled out a rifle. I'd never seen a gun so close before and was scared of it. Kana didn't seem to mind so I acted like I didn't either. She told me later she wasn't afraid because Uncle Theo had a couple of rifles at home, which his grandfather had used to hunt tigers in India.

"I've come back to Colombo because we can't find enough sharp-shooters, Mr Palar," the policeman said.

"Sad days, indeed, Joseph. Let's hope you never have to use your skills."

As we drove off, I waved goodbye to the policeman through the back windscreen but he wasn't looking. He was putting his rifle back in the van. Dad must have been scared of the gun too because he drove carefully on the way back and stopped to let people cross Galle Road.

When we got near Appa's house, I asked if Kana and I could have a bottle of Portello from the man at the corner of the road. Dad parked nearby but kept the engine running. The drink man's stall was rustier than hot dog stands in London and the pictures painted on it were worn out. A beggar man sitting on the pavement stood up and started coming towards me. I bought two bottles of Portello with straws then hurried to the car before he caught up.

Back at the house, Kana and I ran inside to the sitting area to drink our fruity, purple Portello. We weren't often allowed fizzy drinks so we made it last by drinking it slowly. Appa sat in an armchair, stretched his legs and put his hands behind his head. Amma sat up straight on a chair next to him then put her hands on the armrests.

"Can you come into the bedroom for a minute?" she asked him. "I want to talk to you."

"Later. I've had a hard day's shopping and want to relax."

He wasn't going to get away with it. When my grandmother wanted to give someone a blackguarding, she never forgot about it.

Mum put out everything she'd bought on the dining table and called Saras to come see it all. Saras came from the kitchen, looking tired and like she had other things to do. I was going to make sure she didn't have to stay long because then she'd have been late doing her work, and might have got into trouble with Amma. Mum gave her the blue silk sari and a piece of material for a sarong and blouse. Saras ran her hand up and down the silk and said something in Tamil I didn't hear.

"What did she say?" I asked Kana.

"It's the most beautiful sari she's ever seen."

Mum closed her hand around Saras'. "You are like family to us," she said. They stayed like that for a few seconds until my mother pulled her hand away and took something out of a brown paper bag. "Can you give this sarong material to Herath? He'll sell it and send the money to his family but it's up to him." Saras touched my mother's cheek and looked at the gifts on the table. She didn't pay close attention to them as Mum wanted her to, she just acted like she was interested.

Amma was in her armchair still looking cross with Appa. I wondered if he might get away with it because we were all in the room but he was out of luck, poor thing. My grandmother pushed herself up and stood over him. "Have it your way, Roshan Palar. I'll do this in front of everyone if I have to." She wagged a finger at him. "How can you expect the children to respect the Lord if you don't set the example?"

"Amma," I said. "Dad swears about God, too. Mum tells him off but he doesn't listen either."

I looked at my father and waited for him to tell the truth. He couldn't see me because he'd covered his face with a newspaper. It rustled and folded in half when I bent it down. He was laughing.

Amma took one look at him and threw her hands up. "Child, at least you have the sense to know what's right and wrong. Saraswathie, help me to my chair. My husband and son are driving me up the wall."

Even though Mum was still showing Saras her shopping, she let her go help Amma. Kana and I carried on drinking our Portello. After we finished, we put our empty bottles on the dining table for Herath to take to the drinks man and get money back, which my grandfather always let him keep. Kana whispered to me about the secret club we were supposed to have started. I covered my mouth with my hand. I'd forgotten about that.

"Now what are they up to?" Appa asked as we hurried through the dining and sitting areas to my room.

"No doubt, something you and your son taught them," Amma said.

Dad joined in. "I hope you glued down the furniture, Uma."

"And nailed it."

I closed the door. We threw off our sandals and sat on the bed to talk about our club, but it didn't feel like a secret with the sun shining on us. I started to take the pink cotton coverlet off the bed. It was so big I got caught up in it and Kana had to rescue me. We sat cross-legged on the bed and put the coverlet over us, like a tent, so we could talk in private. It didn't matter that we were hot and stuffy and breathing was hard.

"What shall we decide about first, Rohini?"

"I don't know."

"Who are we going to have in our club?"

We spoke about children we knew and which ones we didn't like. Kana told me about a boy at school who was rude to her because her parents were getting a divorce.

"I hate him," I said.

"A Buddhist shouldn't hate anybody."

"Then I just don't want him in our club."

"And I don't. Do we have to invite boys?"

"We need them to do the heavy work."

I didn't know what heavy work there was to be done but wanted to be ready, just in case. I told her about Victor Fonseka at Aunty Malathi's party in Kandy. I'd have to find out later if he was just visiting there and lived in Colombo, which meant he could play with us. The only other boy I knew was Ganesh and Aunty wouldn't have allowed him to join because he was poor, which was unfair. Kana was going to think about who else there was. Everybody was leaving, or had already gone to live overseas because of the Troubles, so it wouldn't be easy to get the right sort of boy.

Mum called, "Girls. Lunch is ready."

"Just coming," I shouted.

My mother's voice got louder. "Now, please."

The door creaked open. Kana and I looked at each other under the coverlet.

"Nathan, take a look at this," Mum said from the doorway.

He lifted the coverlet off us. "My Go - I mean good grief. What are you two doing under there?"

"We were talking," I told him.

"What about?"

"It's a secret."

He had a serious look on his face. "That's what worries me." As he turned to leave, he tried not to smile.

We jumped off the bed and headed for the dining table. Mum put her hands on her hips. "Where do you two think you're going?" I waited to be told what Kana and I had done wrong. "Give me a hand to make the bed, girls. It isn't fair to ask Saras to do it twice in one day."

At lunch, I let Kana sit next to Mum so she could have a cuddle and I sat with Dad. After the food had been put on the table and the grown-ups were serving themselves, I asked if Victor could come to play.

"They live in Kandy," my father told me. "And we won't be going back to the hill country this holiday."

Appa shook his head. "Victor and his family are in Colombo. Mahen was transferred here because they need more judges to deal with the extra cases."

Dad looked worried. "Things are really hotting up here."

"Don't upset yourself. If it gets really bad, we'll take the servants and move to the country or India for a while."

My father looked more relaxed but I didn't think I should ask again about playing.

## GET READY

After nightfall, Sohan lounged on his bed in a five-star Delhi hotel, listening to the melodious tones of a muezzin calling Muslims to Isha prayer. He wished he could submerge himself in faith like a devotee and not just hope there was a God.

In his hands were his get-rich-quicker plans. He'd been through them the day before, the one before that and each day since hatching the idea. He knew how many leopard skins he needed, how many *lakhs* he could afford as bribes; every revenue and cost was as familiar to him as boyhood scars on Nathan's arms and knees. Fists clenched, he rolled onto his side and closed his eyes. His past was sliding away faster than he could run after it. Only business forecasts were within his grasp those days, and to achieve his latest plan he'd spent months fostering contacts in India: businessmen who knew the price of government ministers. He ought to have been ashamed of striking a deal that way. In fact, he could picture Uma's father wagging a finger at him and saying, "Be careful what mistakes you make. You can't always put them right." If Uncle Alagar had been around to advise him, Sohan knew he wouldn't have embarked on such a risky scheme, but, and his eyes moistened, the old man wasn't around.

His sleep that night was disturbed by nightmares of walking through Colombo streets, only becoming aware he was naked when Uma floated over him, pointing at his body. Aunty Malathi said that kind of dream meant he was unprepared for something important. What did she know? He couldn't have been more ready to poach and export leopard skins, and had already planned a meeting the following day with government officials.

On the way to breakfast he paused to admire antique maps of India by the stairwell. One in particular, a celestial map in parchment, grabbed his attention. He let his gaze hover over stars on a tea-coloured sky. That constellation was Cygnus, this one Ursa Minor, and wasn't that Draco? Some things, and some teachers, you never forget.

A clock in the foyer chimed sixteen notes then struck nine, the same Westminster chimes as in the clock outside his headmaster's study. How often he'd sat there, waiting for the cane or a scolding. You name it, he'd done it all. Flicking ink at a teacher's back, cutting classes to play cricket or see a girl. Not always the ringleader but often at the centre of trouble. After his third detention, Uncle Alagar turned up at his house, escorted him to the school gates and threatened a severe thrashing if he played up again. Although the old man would never have resorted to that punishment, Sohan stayed out of trouble and came second in class at the end of the year.

Strolling past the clock in the foyer, he asked the hotel receptionist where the celestial map had come from and to let the manager know he wanted to buy it.

"It is here since we opened," he was told and, "Sorry, sir, it isn't for sale."

"Everything has a price. I come to Delhi often and will buy it on my next visit."

The restaurant was empty apart from a group of Americans wearing red and orange shirts, talking in voices louder than their clothes. Soon the whole of India got to know first-hand that the city of Agra wasn't as big as the state of Texas and by the way, "In the US, there are motels larger and grander than the Taj Mahal." Naturally, these people were at the table under the chandelier, an ugly thing, which for reasons known only to the hotel owners was the centrepiece in the room and worst of all, dangled from loose fittings. The builder had no doubt used the son of a neighbour's cousin to fix it to the ceiling. The foreigners couldn't have noticed how unstable it was and he wasn't going to warn them. He glanced at their plates of pancakes covered in syrup and wanted to say, for God's sake at least try the local food. Instead, he nodded good morning then sat at a window table with his back to them.

Outside, bullock carts trundled along in sunshine, carrying food and people to markets. Trucks, buses and cars darted in and out of lanes, driving to their own rules and God help pedestrians and cyclists. Horns tooted endlessly in a language of their own. Short beeps warned others, usually tuk-tuks, to get out of the way and a long beep said, what the bloody hell did you think you were doing?

The menu on his table lay unopened. He hadn't come down because he was hungry, he wanted to use the hour before his meeting to prepare: he'd never met these officials before and only knew their reputations. One had made his fortune when Bali Nagar was turned from farming land to development opportunities. A clever move by that chap, in at the start, sucking up to government ministers so he'd be the first to know which plots were being sold, the lowest price he could pay. Sohan wondered how many poor Bali Nagar farmers had been played out of their land so others could profit.

Stood behind the tourists was a young waiter pulling at the collar of his jacket, which he wore over a sarong. Look at him, a local dressed like a Westerner to keep tourists happy. He must have been used to wearing a string *banyan* with his sarong, if anything at all. Sohan clicked his fingers at the fellow who hesitated between keeping watch over the Americans and seeing to the Asian. Sohan clicked his fingers again. The waiter hurried over, throwing an occasional look over his shoulder at the tourists.

"Sir, you are ready to order?"

"Bring me *khichri* and freshly squeezed orange juice."

The boy looked at him with glazed eyes, not understanding a word. Must have been a relative or friend of the hotel owners if he'd been hired without knowing much English. Didn't those fools understand the value of educating staff before throwing them at guests? He repeated his order in Hindi and shook his head as the waiter scurried away. He had enough going on in his life without having to deal with other people's failings.

Eager as he was to get his scheme off the ground, he wasn't sure that day would be the great beginning he hoped for. In Colombo or Delhi or even the great US of A, you could sit through meetings from dawn to sunset and win promises of contracts that never materialised. Businessmen said yes to everything then refused to answer phone calls or letters. Perhaps you hadn't paid enough of an incentive or the other side had only agreed to meet to find out what your company was up to. Whatever the motive, he couldn't take the risk that morning was a false start, which is why he'd booked the Royal room at the hotel. If you wanted to close an illegal deal or negotiate a law that couldn't get passed, that was the place to meet. Everybody who was anybody had used it at one time or another.

The waiter served breakfast, putting the plate down on the table as if his life depended on not spilling anything. Sohan pushed rice and lentils around with a fork until he thought he should eat something. At home, he'd have eaten with his fingers. In a five-star hotel, you never knew who was watching and the last thing he wanted was for wealthy tourists to think of him as a peasant. Tara often laughed at his double standards. "If it's good enough for you at home, darling, it should be good enough for others. After all, this is our country and culture."

As he lifted the fork to take his first mouthful, a boy about nine years old came down the stairs to reception, on his back a laundry basket as long as he was tall. It seemed like the child would buckle under the weight. Normally Sohan wouldn't have given him a second thought. Lately he noticed barefoot children on pavements, hands outstretched for a few rupees while the hungrier settled for a few cents. Or he'd see kids running in torn clothes on beaches, their toys the driftwood chewed by rabid dogs. All since Rohini had come back to Sri Lanka.

He longed to have things the way it used to be: he and Nathan chasing the same girls, usually Shiranthi, getting drunk at parties then returning to Nathan's home, their alarm call in the morning being a scolding from Arul Aunty. She'd bang the door to their bedrooms, storm in, shake the cotton coverlets they'd crawled under and yell in their ears. "Look at the state you're in. Who'd want to marry good-for-nothings like you two? My precious son and his best friend. I'm ashamed to say I know either of you." She may have had a tongue that sliced you in pieces but she was the only aunt who looked out for him and treated him like a son when his parents divorced. He was sure all it needed was a trigger, something to let Nathan explode, get rid of his anger then they could be buddies again. A quick glance at his watch told him he ought to finish eating and head for the meeting room. He clicked his fingers at the waiter and pointed at his empty glass. First he'd see to business in India and when he was back in Sri Lanka, he'd find an end to the deadlock with his friend.

He'd have to negotiate hard in that morning's meeting yet the trip to Delhi would be worth it if he could pull it off. He was delving into no-man's land with the transaction, the only shortcut to getting richer he could think of. He'd need co-operation from these people; they were supposed to be the right kind of officials, banana skin types who could put him in touch with an Indian government minister. Sri Lanka would have been easier to operate from. He knew who and how much, yet it was too small a country to run the risk of exporting leopard skins; whereas in India it was easy to blend into thousands of businesses that sent exotic fruit, tea and cheaply-made clothes to every corner of the world. All he needed was someone to turn a blind eye to his own exports.

He made his way across the reception area to the great Royal Room, pausing outside the double wooden doors before pushing them open. So this was it. Wood panelling and furniture from the colonial days. Must be over a hundred years old like the hotel he thought, same as the chairs that were carved out of mahogany, upholstered in olive green leather. The matching oval table with marquetry inlay had dents and scratches but polished to a gleam, looked all the better for them. Leaning back in a chair, he clasped his hands behind his head. He'd done well with his planning.

"Son, you'll go far," Uncle Alagar used to say, "with the effort you put into organisation. Remember though, other people have their own ideas and ambitions."

A waiter came in with a jug of iced water and four glasses. "Sir, the gentlemen have rung to say they will be late."

Sohan had expected this delay. Hard to say if it was urgent business that kept his associates or the usual lack of respect for time. "Put the ceiling fan on slow, will you?" he asked. In his mind, he sifted through his figures again then waded through a week-old copy of the English Times that lay on a sideboard. No harm in seeing what the mood was over there. Miners' strike. Three-day week. Nothing of any use. What's this? USA passing The Endangered Species Act. Could be good. Selling leopard skins would be more risky but more profitable.

The waiter returned, shaking his head. "Sorry, sir, the gentlemen have cancelled the meeting. They want you to ring again when it is quieter."

Sohan shot up in his chair, slammed the paper on the table. Nobody liked upsetting America, the big hope of Asia. Those government buggers must have read the news too and panicked that overseas aid would stop if they were caught helping him. Not that they gave a damn about poverty in their own country, it was losing the chance to fill their back pockets that scared them. He didn't have a choice, he'd have to postpone the rest of that week's meetings. Without that lot on his side, he didn't have a hope in hell of smuggling.


One afternoon, Mum and Dad were going to drive my grandmother to visit her sister outside Colombo. My great-aunt didn't have any children for me to play with so I asked if I could stay behind.

"I'll look after small one," Appa said. "That way, she won't disturb Saras and Herath while they're busy."

Amma gave him a look. "Busy, my foot. Anything to get out of seeing relations."

He pretended not to hear her and said nothing.

After the others had gone, I sat on the front veranda talking to my dolls while my grandfather looked up chess moves in a book. I hoped he wasn't going to try and teach me chess. It was as slow as cricket and sometimes took longer.

Herath came down the side garden, dressed in only a nappy and with an axe over his shoulder.

"Why is he wearing that, Appa?"

"What? Oh, that's his loin cloth."

"Why isn't he wearing a sarong?"

"Sometimes he likes to wear the clothes of his ancestors."

Herath walked in front of the veranda to the carport and, oh my gosh, I couldn't believe it. He'd forgotten to put on underpants and was showing his bottom. I shook my grandfather's arm and made him lift his head from his book.

"Look, Appa. I can see his *kundy*."

"That's how to wear a loin cloth."

Veddhas must have been really poor if they couldn't afford underwear, though if my grandfather didn't mind seeing Herath's bottom, it can't have been rude to dress like that so I tried not to mind either. I also tried not to look but couldn't help myself. I'd never seen a grown-up's backside before. Herath turned round and took his axe off his shoulder.

"What's he going to do?"

"He's going to cut that shoeflower bush."

"No, Appa. He mustn't chop it down."

"Calm down, child. He's only trimming where it grows into the carport."

I watched Herath while he worked, to make sure my grandfather wasn't telling lies to keep me quiet. I loved the shoeflower bushes as much as the Temple tree, dreamed all year in England about seeing them again and of Saras making me a shoeflower necklace. A sunray fell on Herath's axe, making it sparkle.

"His axe is shiny."

"He polishes it every night. There's a small chip at the top of the blade, where he tried to cut an ebony tree." Appa folded the corner of the page he was reading and put his book down. "I can see I'll have to read this later. What else can I help you with?"

"He's acting like he hasn't seen us."

"When he's dressed like that, he likes to pretend he isn't in Colombo. His head and heart are in the jungle with his people, hunting Sambhur deer with his bow and arrows, using the axe to cut up animal flesh or clear a path in the forest."

I waved to Herath. He didn't look at me. I waved with both hands. He carried on with his work and still didn't look at me.

"Let him be, child," my grandfather said. "He misses his village and way of life."

The servant boy next door came back from the market carrying fruit and vegetables in a basket, long *murunga* sticking out over the top. When he saw Herath, he ran inside his house then came out again, still holding the basket. A fat lady in a green sari followed him out. She stood on her veranda, hands on hips, and took a good look at Herath's bottom.

"Appa, she's staring."

"Let her. Herath isn't doing anything wrong. These Colombo snobs should be proud of his background, not ashamed."

I wasn't sure why you had to be proud of being poor and almost in your birthday suit. I stroked the soft hairs that covered my grandfather's arm. "Why does he live with you, if he likes to be in a village?"

"Among other reasons, it's money, child. The government let loggers chop down the forest on Veddha land, even though it's supposed to be protected. He sends what he can to help his family live the way they always have."

"Dad says you're rich. I think you can pay Herath and let him live in the jungle."

"Then who will help your grandmother with her chores?"

I didn't know. If we got another servant, they'd want to live with their family too, instead of in Colombo. I was going to say prayers that night for everyone who couldn't be with people they loved.

We were still chatting on the front veranda when the others came back in the late afternoon with Kana. We'd all been invited to Tara Aunty's place in the evening and Uncle Theo was going to join us after he finished work. Aunty's parties were the best and she always had something special for children. Last time, she hired a clown and I couldn't wait to find out what the surprise was that evening.

"Sohan had better not cut short his India trip to turn up tonight," Dad said.

Everybody looked away from each other and didn't say anything. We listened to dogs barking and seagulls making a racket above us. A crow hopped by the carport, trying to find worms. Saras brought *vadai* and fish *cutlets* onto the veranda with poppadum, which wasn't a shorteat but she knew I liked it. Mum served Kana and me half a *vadai* and one cutlet each with pieces of poppadum, so we could keep space for party food. Appa ate as much as he wanted to. He and Amma weren't coming in the evening because Tara Aunty had borrowed money from them once and never paid it back.

"It was a long while ago," my grandfather said before taking a mouthful of *vadai*, a few crumbs falling onto his side plate. "Let it go, Arul."

"Not until she apologises or repays the loan."

"Come on, Arul. I haven't seen my son for a year. We should spend as long as we can with Nathan and his family."

". . . All right. For Nathan's sake."

Dad looked surprised she was coming.

Mum got up, saying, "Rohini and Kana, we need to get ready."

In my parents' room, as my mother wrapped her silk sari around her petticoat I asked her, "Why are we going out tonight when there's a curfew?"

"It's been lifted for the day," she said, pleating the sari at the front, then tucking it into her petticoat, "because there's a state function going on." I didn't know what a state function was but was glad there was one so we could be out late. Mum threw a long piece of sari material over her shoulder and looked at herself sideways in the mirror. "That's about the right length," she said. Then she stuck a safety pin under the front pleats to stop them falling down.

Kana was also getting ready. She put her dress on, turned her back to me. "Can you zip me up?"

"You look pretty."

She smiled at me but didn't say thank you for helping her. I didn't need her to either, because we were best friends.

Mum sat at the dressing table. "Can one of you hand me hairpins while I put my hair up?"

I played with my Buddha statue and pretended I hadn't heard her.

Kana ran to her. "I'll do it, Aunty Uma."

Mum pulled her hair tight at the back, then wrapped it round a black hairpiece to make a French plait. I'd tried putting it up for her like that once but it fell down again. When I was older, she was going to show me how to do it properly. She stuck in hairpins and Kana helped push in loose bits of hair.

Soon as Mum was ready, she got up and looked at me. I was still running round in my vest and *jungies*, playing with Buddha while she and Kana were dressed. I looked back at her, ready to be scolded.

"Rohini," she said, "if you don't hurry up, you'll have to come as you are."

"Okay," I told her, laughing. "I'll go like this."

She caught me and put my dress over my head. I kept my arms by my side so she couldn't get it over my body. When she said, "I'll leave you behind if you don't behave," I gave in and put my arms through the sleeves so she could zip me up. She brushed Kana's and my hair then told us to sit with the others while she put on make-up and perfume. Kana wanted to stay a bit longer with her though.

"I'd like to watch you, Aunty Uma."

"I'll wait with Dad."

I tried to sneak into the garden. Amma saw me at the front door and called me back. "Come in. You'll dirty your party dress."

"I'll be careful while I'm climbing the tree."

She fixed me with her Evil Eye. I ran back in, sat next to my father and tried not to look at her in case she put a spell on me. It didn't matter that I'd been caught anyway, because Mum didn't take long getting ready so I wouldn't have got far up the tree. My mother looked lovely and smelt of roses when she came out of her room. Dad wolf-whistled at her.

Saras waved goodbye to us from the front veranda. She never went anywhere nice; I wanted to take her with us but she wouldn't have been allowed to come because servants aren't allowed to enjoy themselves at rich people's parties, so I decided to bring something back for her.

Tara Aunty's front garden was beautiful, with pretty lights on the path and white, red and pink flowers everywhere. I didn't think anyone would mind if I picked a few for Saras.

"They stay in the garden," Dad said.

"I was only looking."

A maid opened the door and took us into a long corridor. Down one side was a water garden with purple flowers that Kana told me were called Nil Mahanel. "We offer them in temples to show discipline, purity and truth." I didn't know what purity was and thought it might be something to do with finding peace. I wanted to take purple flowers home for Saras and was sure Buddha would understand if I picked a few later when nobody was looking.

"Join the others," Dad said, "and leave those alone."

I let out a long sigh. I'd have to do something else nice for my ayah.

Appa patted a grand piano that was by the back doors. "This is new. And it's a Steinway."

"Must have bought it with our money," Amma said quietly.

My grandfather coughed loudly and looked around him. He'd been lucky. Even though the room was full of guests, they were all gossiping loudly and hadn't heard my grandmother being rude. He stroked the piano wood. "Why don't you play a tune, Nathan? Show this lot what our family's made of."

"Next time. I'm not in the mood this holiday."

"You know, Sohan was proud of your school recitals. He played merry hell with me when I missed one because of a Board meeting."

Dad didn't smile at how nice Uncle Sohan had been. He wanted to stay cross with him.

There were so many people in the room I had to peep round the grown-ups' legs to find children to play with. All I could see were saris and long trousers. An aunty saw me searching and told me the children were in the garden.

Lemon oil burning by the back door to keep mosquitoes away stung my nose when I got close to it. Crickets made a threeeee threeeee threeeee sound in the garden and there were lanterns and electric lights everywhere.

"It's like daytime," I said.

"It was like this for Uncle Sohan's birthday," Kana said.

"I didn't see him inside."

"He's in India. Tara Aunty just spoke to him on the phone."

"He might have pretended to be there, when he's really in Colombo."

Kana shook her head. "He's not coming."

Tara Aunty came outside, wiggling her bottom because the uncles were looking at her. "Time for the surprise, children."

"What do you think it is, Kana?"

"Don't know but look over there."

An uncle walked onto the lawn, carrying a tall round packet, which he put on the ground. "Over by the croton bush, everyone. I don't want you too close."

Kana clapped her hands. "It's a toy firework."

If it was a toy, I didn't understand why we had to stay away. I didn't know what it was going to do but all the children jumped up and down so I did too. After the uncle lit the firework, I waited for something exciting to happen. At first, there was nothing then it spat out a few lights then it became a giant sparkler and then it exploded and threw out lots of things. It wasn't as pretty as Catherine wheels in London on Guy Fawkes Night.

"It's broken," I said.

"Those are toys coming out," Kana told me.

We all screamed and shouted and tried to find toys but had to stay where we were until the uncle said it was safe, then we ran around collecting what we could. When one of the boys pushed girls out of the way, Tara Aunty told him to behave and not to be selfish. "Share what you find," she said to us, "and make sure all the small ones get a gift each."

Kana picked up a pink hair slide and gave it to a girl who didn't have anything. I gave Kana a whistle I found and kept a magnifying glass. Even though I didn't like gifts like that in Christmas crackers, it was magic then. Something shone in the bushes and I hurried there before the boys found it. It was only the eyes of a lizard and it ran into the bushes as soon as I got near. When we all had something, Tara Aunty called us into the sitting room to eat. The girls had to keep our toys in our dress pockets to stop the boys snatching them.

Maids served trays of club sandwiches, crispy Chinese rolls and other shorteats. On the table was a butter cake that tasted just like the ones Mum baked. She made one for me to take to school on the last day of term and share with my class, but the teachers ate it and didn't give any to the children. She said if they were going to be like that, she wasn't going to make any more cakes for school.

When Uncle Theo turned up, he spotted Kana straight away. He had to stop on the way to her and kiss aunties on both cheeks. She squeezed her way through guests to give him a big hug. I only saw her looking that happy when he was around or after she'd found her peace. Uncle went to talk to grown-ups and left Kana and me playing near the piano, looking at each other with my magnifying glass. A tall boy and girl came over to where we were.

"I dare you to play Chopsticks on the piano," the boy said to the girl.

"I can't, Vivi. We're only allowed to play proper music on it."

"Cluck, cluck, cluck, cluck. Chicken."

God ran out of sugar and spice when he made boys, which is why he used frogs and snails. He had enough nice things though, when he made Herath and Ganesh. And Appa and Uncle Theo, and he must have put some sugar in Dad and Uncle Sohan too because they hadn't always fought.

The girl stood up and was about to do the dare when an uncle lifted the piano lid and shouted, "Hey Vivi, let's hear some music." She ran back to her friends, glad she hadn't had to play Chopsticks.

Vivi said, "I'll start with *Let's Twist Again*."

He must have practised a lot because he knew the tune without having to read sheet music. Kana grabbed my hand and we started dancing. Other children joined in then so did the grown-ups. Uncle Theo did the Twist and went down all the way to the ground. We all copied him to see which of us could get the lowest. Kana and I got to the floor and twisted our way up again.

"Now for some *Baila*," Vivi said.

Everybody started cheering as he played, *Hai Hooi Babi Aachi*, a song I'd been waiting to hear ever since we'd come back to Sri Lanka. It was never played on the radio in London but when I heard it on the record player there at family parties, I remembered how much I missed living with my grandparents and Saras.

Whatever Vivi played, everybody danced and we all danced, *Baila* style, apart from Uncle Theo who only wanted to do the Twist. Most of the guests had a good time in the middle of the room while Dad, Amma and a few old uncles and aunts watched.

"Shake a leg, Nathan," Uncle Theo said. "If your old man can get up, so can you."

"Not so old," Appa said and danced faster.

"Keeping my mother company," Dad shouted.

Tara Aunty was drunk and wobbled over to my father then sat on his lap. "In that case, Nathan, I'll keep you company." Dad pushed her off. Mum was at the other side of the room when an aunty whispered in her ear. My mother shoved her way through the crowd towards Tara Aunty. I stood by Appa who was throwing his arms and legs everywhere. I had to be careful not to get knocked over by his dancing. Mum was going to give Aunty a huge scolding for sitting on Dad's lap and pretending to be his girlfriend. While I watched to see what she was going to do, I also had to keep an eye on my grandfather and dodge his legs when he kicked them out. Dad saw Mum coming, put an arm around her and took her into the back garden to talk behind tall palm plants. The party noise was so loud, I couldn't hear what they were saying. They stayed outside for two whole songs. When they came back, he stayed by her side. Although she was angry, her mouth wasn't so I knew she wasn't going to start a fight and make everybody look at us. She wasn't going to forgive Aunty soon though, like she didn't forgive my teachers for eating all the cake she made.

The party finished early because the next day Appa had arranged a picnic for friends and relations. He tripped over his feet on the way out of Tara Aunty's house and Dad had to hold his elbow to help him walk. He'd drunk so much he was going to have a big headache in the morning. As the guests left, servants gave all the children *cutlets*, Chinese rolls and a piece of cake wrapped in a paper napkin. I took mine and held it with both hands all the way back to our house. I also sneaked a purple flower from the water garden while Dad was taking care of Appa. Uncle Theo saw me take it and winked at me.


My grandfather had hired a coach and driver to take us to a beach where we could swim and play on the sand. It was a *Poya* day, when nobody worked, so all the grown-ups came too. Amma was on the front veranda with my parents, waiting for Appa while he took tablets for his hangover. I said good morning to him when he came out of his bedroom, but he waved me away.

While the grown-ups chatted, I took my chance and crept into Saras' room to leave the flower and napkin parcel of food I'd brought from the party. She was having a nap and I wasn't sure about putting the shorteats and piece of cake on her pillow because it would attract ants, but didn't know where else to leave it. My kiss goodbye woke her up and she gave me a sleepy smile. I loved her more than ever and wanted to take care of her like I did with Kana. I pushed the food into her hands and joined the others on the veranda before anyone caught me in the servants' quarters. When my grandmother saw me, she said, "Rohini, my husband has given Saraswathie and Herath the day off today, which should make you happy." I knew though that Saras had woken early to make and fry patties for the picnic. Even on a day off, she had to work.

Dad drove us to the pick-up point, St Vincent's college, and parked outside. Appa knew the college principal so we were allowed to wait in the playground for the coach. I searched for Kana and Victor in the huge crowd that had already arrived but couldn't find them.

"Looks like most are here," Amma said as we got out of the car. "And a few are hung over from last night. Serve them right."

"No need to talk so loudly," Appa told her.

He didn't look well at all. If he was ill on the coach, he'd spoil the day out for everyone. When Uncle Theo turned up with Kana, Appa told him he was in charge of counting the grown-ups to make sure nobody got lost.

"And don't shout," he said.

Mum said she'd count the children. She started to walk round the playground, collecting kids when Tara Aunty came up to her.

"Uma, I want to apologise for last night. You know how it is. I'd had too much to drink and all."

Mum didn't say anything then lifted her hand. Oh my goodness. She was going to hit Aunty. I'd never seen her smack anyone and wasn't sure she should do it in front of me.

"You had no right," she told my aunt.

"*Aiyo,* Uma. I don't want to fall out with you."

Mum's eyes and her mouth were still angry. Aunty touched her arm.

"Please. I really am sorry."

". . . All right. This time."

"Thank you. It means a lot to me."

I was glad they'd made friends again or we might not have been invited to Aunty's next party.

"Kids," my mother shouted across the playground, "stand in one group over there, so I can see how many of you there are."

Kana and I walked to the wall she was pointing to. Victor still hadn't arrived. A girl who lived next door to him told me the Fonsekas were still getting ready when her family had left their house.

Mum started to count children but everybody kept moving around. She was getting annoyed with us. "Stand still till I finish, will you? I'll have to start again now." I tried to help her by clapping my hands to get attention. Nobody took any notice of me. She counted again. "Twenty-four," she said then went back to the grown-ups.

Kana talked to a boy she knew from school, until his mother called him to stand with her. He wasn't allowed to be Kana's friend because her parents were getting a divorce. When his mum called him again he didn't do as he was told and carried on talking to us. "*Thathi* lets me play with her," he said. He held one of Kana's hands and I held the other while we looked at his mother. We were doing something brave but I didn't know if we'd be punished for it. His mum started to walk towards us when a man put a hand on her shoulder and pulled her back. "Are you mad? Taking it out on children. Leave them alone." She gave us a dirty look. The boy whispered he wasn't afraid of his mother. He always got her in trouble with his dad if she was unfair to him. We stood still, not sure what to do next, only letting go of hands when his mum turned away to gossip with other ladies.

I'd been in the playground for a long while and the Fonsekas still hadn't come. Leaving Kana with the boy to look after her, I went to ask Dad what was happening.

"They'll be here," he said. "Mahen needs something to take his mind off that wife of his."

Mum pointed at me. "Behave, Nathan."

I rushed to tell Kana what my father had said. I didn't know what he meant but it sounded bad. Someone called my name from behind.

"How's my favourite girl?" Uncle Sohan asked.

"I'm Dad's girl."

I wasn't sure if I should run away or bite him. My father hurried over and stood between Uncle and me then, in a voice so soft I could hardly hear him, he said, "Stay away from my family, Sohan." They stared at each other until Uncle shrugged his shoulders and walked towards the ladies, as if he didn't care that my father wasn't friends with him anymore. Tara Aunty grabbed his shirt sleeve as he passed her and marched him to a street corner. She must have given him a good talking-to because he came back looking cross.

Kana whispered she had a secret to tell me and took me away from the others. "I don't like Uncle Sohan."

"Did he kiss your dad too?"

"He was one of my mum's boyfriends."

"Have we stopped calling her Jyoti?"

"No. I just forgot not to call her Mum."

"Is she still his girlfriend?"

"He only goes out with Tara Aunty now."

Even so, I didn't know why he was allowed to come to parties and picnics if he'd also gone out with married women. When I told Amma this, she said some people you've known since they were children are family and a part of your life. You can't get rid of them if you've shared a good past.

Uncle Theo spotted Kana looking a bit upset and came over to give her a hug. He said we'd better wait with the other kids or Aunty Uma might forget to count us when the coach arrived, then we'd never leave because everyone would be looking for two missing children. Kana cheered up a little. We were returning to the others when at last the Fonsekas turned up. Victor and his sister came running. They'd had to park round the corner because there wasn't any space nearby.

"I thought you weren't coming," I told him.

"We nearly didn't. My parents were having a row because Mum changed her sari four times before she decided to wear trousers. Then she had to put on lipstick and rouge for the picnic."

All the children started cheering and shouting when the coach pulled up in front of the college gates and we rushed to climb in. The ladies told us to stay where we were: they wanted to put the food in before anyone got on. I'd never seen so many *lampries* in my life. Mum watched as the driver put the food on the coach then she let us on after everything was loaded. Children were allowed to sit at the back if we promised to be quiet. We said we would but ran on, shouting. Kana and I got seats next to each other. I was by the aisle so I could see what was going on down the coach and she sat near the window because she wanted to wave to people on the road.

Mum counted the children as we got on. "Twenty-six."

"We'll have to bring back the same number," Dad said. "But they don't have to be the same kids."

Amma pinched his ear.

"Ouch," he said. "That hurt."

"It was meant to."

As she walked past him to a seat, I quickly looked away in case she asked me to sit next to her.

To stop the children fighting, the ladies got on next and sat near the back, except Tara Aunty. She grabbed Uncle Sohan's shirt as he climbed in and made him sit in the front row with her. Uncle Theo was the last one on and walked up and down the aisle, counting grown-ups.

"Forty-three. We've lost one and we haven't even set off."

Dad said, "Did you count yourself, Theo?"

"Forty-four."

Everybody laughed.

The driver shut the coach door and we all waved goodbye to Colombo. Uncle Sohan stood up and called to the driver.

"I say, put the radio on, will you? I want to hear the cricket score."

"When we're out of the city, sir. I need to concentrate on the traffic."

Uncle tripped and fell into his seat as we went over a pothole. Tara Aunty gave him a bottle of beer and told him to drink it and shut up.

We drove through town, past dirty shops with tin roofs, and people on bicycles in the middle of the road, some carrying small children on their laps. Mum said most Sri Lankan families were too poor to travel any other way. When we got to the countryside where there were green paddy fields and no traffic lights, the driver switched on the radio at a music station. Uncle Sohan was busy drinking and didn't notice there wasn't any cricket news. I couldn't understand what the Sri Lankan bands were singing about when the songs were in Tamil or Sinhalese, then one in English came on.

*Pink and blue,*
*I love you,*
*Red and green,*
*You're my Sri Lankan queen.*

Older children who had moved overseas and come back for Christmas giggled when they heard the words. It was one of Kana's favourites so she sang along and I joined in too. Mum always told me my singing made her happy and one day I'd be able to sing in tune.

Two boys across the aisle started fighting because they'd been told to take it in turns to sit by the window, but one wouldn't move when he was supposed to so his mum shouted at him to share the seat with his brother.

"I'll give you what for, if I have to come over there."

He still didn't shift so she got up from her seat and asked if he wanted a smack.

Laughing, he said, "Yes please," so he got one on the leg.

He didn't cry because it wasn't a hard hit but he had to move.

All the children went quiet for a few minutes afterwards until another of Kana's favourite songs came on the radio. She started singing and the rest of us joined in, one by one.

Uncle Sohan got up to talk to the driver. "Make a quick stop, will you? I need to relieve myself."

Tara Aunty scolded him. "Can't you wait, man? We're nearly at the beach."

"I have to go now," he said, running out when the coach driver opened the doors.

Uncle Theo took a picture of him doing his business in the long grass. The children leaned into the aisle to look out of the windscreen as well but couldn't see anything. Uncle Sohan was very quick anyway and we were soon back on our journey, singing and laughing. We enjoyed ourselves so much I didn't notice we'd arrived at the seaside until we parked. I peeked over Kana's shoulder and looked at palm trees, white sand and beach huts. Although I couldn't wait to get out, I had to stop at the door for a second when hot and salty sea air came rushing in and hit me in the face. Kana and I followed Dad to the beach and took off our flip-flops.

"Give me those before you lose them," he said and put them in a bag.

We already had swimsuits on under our clothes so we took off our shorts and tops and gave them to him as well.

"Can we go in the sea now?"

He laughed. "We've just got here but all right. Come on you two. And anybody else who's ready."

He climbed over the sand bank and down the other side. The children followed him and we all ran into the bright blue water. I'd been to the seaside a few times in England; the sea was dirty there and you couldn't swim in it. We splashed about and threw water on each other while older boys and girls played cricket on the sand. Tara Aunty wouldn't let Uncle Sohan join in with them. She wouldn't let him play with us either, she made him sit next to her and be quiet. The water came up to our waists and we were allowed to swim where it was deeper if we stayed close to a grown-up. Uncle Theo stayed out the farthest so he could shout at anyone who tried to go past him. We had so much fun jumping and playing in the sea that we stayed there until the sun got high in the sky and the ladies called us to eat. All of us were hungry and ran to the shore.

We had a *lampries* packet each, with not so hot ones for the kids, and a bottle of Cream Soda with our meal instead of water. I loved eating rice and curry on a banana leaf with my fingers. I was supposed to wash my hands first but had already started when Mum got a bottle of water out so she said never mind. I ate everything and would have licked the leaf clean if she hadn't been watching. After I finished my *lampries*, I had food all over the palm of my eating hand, like the other children. When I was grown-up, I'd be able to eat without getting my hand dirty. For pudding, Kana and I shared a fresh mango. She didn't like the sour taste of the seed so I sucked it on my own. I was drinking the last of my Cream Soda when she whispered, "Shall we take Victor over there to talk about our secret club?"

"You ask him," I told her while sucking the mango seed until there wasn't any more juice.

"Where are you going?" Mum asked when the three of us started walking away.

"To that palm tree," I said.

"Alright, but stay where I can see you."

We sat under the branches, away from the sun. I could feel her looking at us so I sat with my back to her.

"We want you to join our club," Kana told Victor.

"What do you do in it?"

"We play Veddhas," I said, "and climb trees. It has to be a secret."

"Don't tell my sister then. She tells Mum everything."

Dad called my name. "I'm taking photos. Hurry up, if you want a picture with your friends."

We got up to return to the others before anyone guessed we were up to something. Uncle Sohan watched us then when Tara Aunty looked away to talk to another uncle, he escaped from her and came to meet us.

"Sohan," she shouted. "Come back."

He ignored her and kept walking, holding out his arms to me.

"Rohini, give your favourite uncle a kiss."

Kana stood between him and me and put her hands out to stop him getting closer. Dad came running, his camera swinging around his neck. He grabbed Uncle's wrist.

"Sohan, I told you to leave my family alone. Why the hell couldn't you stay in India?"

"Don't you want to know what I was doing there, Nathan?"

"Nothing you do is of any concern to me."

"I was with government officials. You know, the kind who like to trade in animal rugs and wall hangings."

Their faces were close and they stared at each other. Even though Dad was twisting Uncle's wrist, it didn't seem to hurt him. Two other uncles took Uncle Sohan away and stayed near him for the rest of the picnic. My father had to sit with Mum and my grandparents until he stopped saying swear words. I counted three bloodys and another word beginning with F that I couldn't hear properly because Appa coughed over it.

"He's into poaching. I'm sure of it," Dad said.

"Don't be foolish," Mum said. "Sohan would never go against my father's wishes."

When Dad was back in a good mood, he started taking pictures again. He couldn't get everyone in one photo and had to take lots of small groups. It took forever with the children because the boys pulled funny faces instead of saying cheese. After he finished with us, he walked round taking photos of grown-ups and even got one of Uncle Sohan staring at Tara Aunty's bosom.

Kana and I played with the others until the sun started to go down in the sky and we had to return to Colombo. We didn't want to go home and tried to be the last to get on the coach. Mum made us climb in, saying, "I want to count twenty-six kids." Victor called us to sit by him but his sister,

Leela, pushed past and got there first. She poked her tongue out at us and his mother stared at Kana and me until we sat in another seat. I didn't know why they were being so horrible. Amma said later that Aunty Indra was jealous of other people's happiness and we should feel sorry for her. I tried but couldn't think nice thoughts about her. I was sorry instead that Victor had her as a mother. Buddha would have been all right about me feeling like that, because if you have to be sorry for someone, it doesn't matter who it is so long as they're in the same family.

We'd only just driven away when the coach driver stopped by a stream around the corner for the men to go to the toilet by the road. Uncle Sohan was the first to get off. When he stepped down, his hat flew away in the wind and into the water. "I'm not giving that up without a fight," he said and got ready to jump in after it. Dad and Uncle Theo stood behind him and laughed as they cracked a joke.

Tara Aunty didn't take her eyes off them. In a cross voice, she told the driver, "Get that hook you use to get cases from the hold, will you? And hurry before the fool jumps in or is pushed."

"Do you think my dad or yours will push him in?" I asked Kana.

"Both. But Buddha will forgive them."

I leaned into the aisle to look through the windscreen and see if Dad threw Uncle in. Tara Aunty got down with the driver and waited until the hat was fished out of the stream. Although it was dripping, Uncle put it on, saying he'd never take it off again. Tara Aunty pulled it off his head, stuffed it into a blue carrier bag and scolded him for being a nuisance. I wished he'd stop being a handful. He was as badly behaved as I was when I was tired.

Aunties passed bags of jujubes down the coach. They were like fruit pastilles and I looked for one in my favourite red colour. I forgot it was hard to chew and it glued my mouth together. A boy a few rows in front started the children singing, *She'll be coming round the mountain*. I had to wait until I swallowed my sweet before I could sing too. I chewed as quickly as I could and joined in the second verse. I'd only finished the first line when the uncles started to sing, *Roll me over in the clover*, louder than us. The aunties shouted, "*Aiyo*, there are children present." Kana and I didn't know the words to *Roll me over* and Mum wouldn't let Dad teach them to us either.

Uncle Theo asked the driver to switch on the radio so he could find out who'd won the cricket match against Pakistan. Sri Lanka had lost by a few runs. He told Dad, "We may not have won but the way we're playing it won't be long before we get Test status."

"What's that?" I asked Kana.

Her head was resting on my shoulder and she'd fallen asleep. I thought it must mean the team had to pass a test in sums to see if they could add up cricket scores.

Back at St Vincent's college, Amma and the aunties made us pick up empty bottles and jujube packets and put them in plastic carrier bags. Everybody sang, *For he's a jolly good fellow* to the coach driver. Appa tipped him a bunch of rupee notes and refused to take money from the uncles, saying no, it was all right, he'd take care of it. When I grew up, I was going to be kind like him. I was also going to swear and take the Lord's name in vain if my husband wasn't listening.

None of the children wanted to get off the coach and end the outing but our parents made us get down. Dad told Kana and me to say goodbye to each other in the playground. We hugged and held hands but wouldn't let go. Uncle Theo stood over us. "Come along, girls. You'll be together again in a few days." We carried on holding hands until Mum and Dad started walking without me to the car. They didn't even look back to see if I was following. I got frightened at being left behind, gave Kana a kiss and ran to catch them up.


In the morning, Appa took me for a walk to the beach and taught me the first verse and chorus of *Roll me over in the clover*; though I had to promise to keep it as our secret. The words were easy to understand, except for a few.

"What does lay me down, do it again, mean?"

"It's about . . . a man tickling his girlfriend."

"Tickling's not rude."

"We'd better get back."

Even if *Roll me over in the clover* wasn't as rude as I wished, I felt so much older because my grandfather had taught me part of a rugby song.


In the height of Sri Lanka's monsoon season, when north-east winds blew across Yala National Park, Sohan stepped down from a jeep, dressed in the khaki shirt and shorts that Uncle Alagar insisted they wore while in the jungle. The ground was waterlogged and his every footstep squelched in mud that was soft from days of rain. Keen as he was to hunt leopards, he knew the Veddhas wouldn't take him out in the wet because vehicles would ruin dirt roads in that weather. Besides, he had yet to find a tracker to help him flush out the big cats. His first choice was Herath, one of the best, as was his father, Chief Aruma, men who could detect animal scents in the wind and spoor under fallen leaves. Yet he couldn't ask the Palar household to release Herath from his duties, having only just installed him there. He'd have to take whomever the Veddhas offered. He felt bad about deceiving these people but if they knew what he wanted the leopards for, or that he wanted more than one, not even the business-minded would help. Some had grown up with him on his many visits to their village, after Uncle told him to cancel whatever plans he'd made and come on a trip to the jungle. "I want you to understand the Veddhas," the old man used to say, "before their culture vanishes for good." And they'd shown him how to distinguish between the footprints of leopards, wild pig and sloth bears, even where to look for pythons in marshes and hollow trees. Lessons given out of respect for the world in which they lived, not so he could make a profit; which was why Uncle Alagar kept bringing him there, to give him the wisdom of their simple life, another signpost to show him the way home.

Chief Aruma and men from his tribe were waiting at the fork in the road. No tourist welcome dance for him, just recognition in their eyes.

"You have news of Herath?" the chief asked.

Sohan knew that would be the first question yet he hadn't bothered to find out how the boy was doing. "I heard he is well," was all he could come up with.

The chief took a piece of betel from the pouch around his waist, tossed it into his mouth and chewed on it. "His brother will be with him in a few days. He will tell me how my son is keeping."

"Are the loggers still bothering you? I can pay for more rangers, if you need."

His face blank, Chief Aruma spat out red betel juice. "We put up a tent for you near the village." His voice took on a softer tone. "Same place your Uncle liked."

# THE FOX AND THE CAT

Christmas was only a few days away and I was getting excited about my big present that my parents had bought in London. I knew what I wanted because I'd talked with friends to see what they were getting and I'd watched the ads on TV to see what new toys there were. Mum hid my gift and even though I asked nicely she still wouldn't let me play with it until Christmas Day.

One morning, while Appa and Dad were on the front veranda playing chess, Mum and Amma joined them too because they liked to sit outside while gossiping. I stayed inside, in the sitting area and pretended to read my book.

My father called me. "Come outside and get some sun."

"I can't read out there. It's too bright."

I knelt on the sofa by the front window and peeped outside. While Dad and Appa played chess, Mum and Amma talked about relations: which ones were nice, which ones weren't, what they thought my cousins would grow up to be like and who would marry whom.

They'd forgotten about me.

I crept into Appa's bedroom. I'd already tried my parents' and Amma's but my grandfather didn't like his things being disturbed and he always knew when I'd been in his room. Remembering that the door creaked, I pushed it open slowly and tiptoed to Mum's favourite hiding place, the almeira. I was about to open it when a voice from the front of the room said, "Good morning." I jumped out of my skin. Who had found me out and would they tell Appa? He didn't lose his temper a lot but when he did, he shouted and waved his arms about. I turned round and saw Herath collecting laundry for the dhobi man. My heart thumping, I whispered, "I'm looking for my present."

"Naga."

I put my hands together, like in a prayer. "Please, Herath. I already know what it is."

He pointed to the chest at the foot of the bed. "Your grandfather told me to put it in there. Only a look and no playing with it."

I stopped for a second just in case someone had come in without me noticing. When nobody spoke or made a noise, I knew it was safe to lift the chest lid. There in a plastic bag, not yet gift-wrapped, was my baby doll. I was about to lift her out when Amma coughed outside. I shut the lid quickly. It would have been dangerous to take her then. I'd have to wait until there was a better chance of not being found out.

Putting a finger to my lips, I said to Herath, "Don't tell anyone."

"Our secret."

My heart still beating fast, I hurried onto the veranda. The only free seat was next to Mum and I sat by her, wondering if she could guess what I'd been up to but she carried on gossiping as if nothing had happened.

Herath came onto the veranda with a tray of cold mango juice and glasses. His hair was loose; it fell on his face as he put the tray on a side table. Amma watched him pour drinks while she spoke about the money Tara Aunty had borrowed.

"And don't shake your head at me, Roshan. I can see you out of the corner of my eye."

"It's the eye at the back of the head that worries me."

Oh my gosh. I always thought her Evil Eye was one of the two on her face. If she had another one at the back, she'd have seen me looking for my present. I waited for a scolding but she only went on and on about Tara Aunty. I'd got away with it. That really was my lucky day.

Herath pushed his hair away from his face and went back to the kitchen. "I wish I had curly hair like his," I said.

Amma smiled at me. "You have Veddha blood in you, from my side. Maybe it'll grow like that when you're older. And you know, there aren't many Veddha families left. You should learn more about your culture, child."

Appa picked up a bishop, changed his mind, and put it back. Then he lifted a pawn and put it down with a thump, farther along the board. "Come to me after I beat your father and I'll tell you about Sri Lanka."

Dad kept looking at the chess pieces. He pushed a knight forward. "Check."

Appa sat up in his chair. "What the - ?"

The squeaky wheels of the dhobi man's rickshaw came down the road and into our front garden. Herath must have heard them too because he brought two bags of laundry down the veranda steps. Poor Herath. His family was disappearing. I was going to ask Kana if he could be the other boy in our club. He was almost a grown-up but it didn't matter.

Mum looked at my father and grandfather who were bent over the chessboard. "That's going to be a long game, Amma. Shall we go shopping? I need to get earrings for Rohini and a gold chain for me."

Appa grunted. "You're going to drive the Mercedes? The sky's full of rain clouds and these roads get slippery in wet weather."

Dad laughed. "He's afraid you'll smash his car."

"If you prefer, we can stay and talk while you play chess."

Appa got up. "I'll fetch you the keys."

I was allowed to sit in the back of the car on my own and away from the doors. Mum drove slowly out of the gates and down the road, stopping for people who waited at crossings.

"You're a much better driver than Nathan," my grandmother said. "He should take lessons from you."

"Amma, it's no use. Dad doesn't listen to Mum when she tries to teach him while he's driving."

We went to my grandparents' jeweller, where my father bought the gold *thali* necklace he gave Mum at their wedding. She didn't wear it much in England because people thought she was showing off so he bought her a wedding ring to put on instead. The jeweller man brought out a tray of star-shaped earrings. My mother called me over to choose a pair. I had to stand on tiptoe to see the counter so was allowed to stand on a chair.

"Can I have the ones with the blue stone?"

"Good choice," the man said. "Sri Lankan sapphires are best in the world."

He put them in a small box then wanted to know what kind of chain Mum was after. She said twenty-two carat and not too long, in an unusual design. "I have something you will like," he told her, showing her a pretty chain of gold beads with links in-between. When the phone rang in the back of the shop he went to answer it, leaving us with the jewellery. Soon as he'd gone, Mum pulled the chain with both hands.

"What are you doing?" I asked. "You'll break it."

"I'm seeing how strong it is."

"That's a good test," Amma said.

My mother was still pulling the chain when the man returned. I was afraid he might ring the police because she was acting like a hooligan, then thought that if she wasn't going to set a better example for me, it wouldn't matter if I was sometimes naughty too.

"I'll take this necklace and the earrings," she told him.

"Good choice, good choice," he said.

It was too hot to do more shopping and the sky was getting darker so Amma decided we should go home. We made it to the front garden just as the thunderstorm started. Huge raindrops splashed on the roof of the carport and by the veranda steps. Creepy-crawlies were washed out of their hiding places under bushes and ran all over the place. The *kadillai* seller hurried in from the road to take shelter under the Temple tree but he was already soaking wet. Appa told him to dry off in the servants' quarters and have a cup of tea and something to eat. I stood on my bed and opened the shutters to stick my hand out of the window and feel warm rain on my skin. The water ran down my arm, onto my shoulder and dripped onto the pillows. Saras caught me and told me to shut the window. By the time the rain stopped, the *kadillai* seller's sarong was still wet so he borrowed one from Herath. He thanked my grandfather for letting him stay and have something to eat and drink, then he pushed his cart back up the road.

After the sun came out, Dad showed me a rainbow of soft colours that stretched across the road. He couldn't take his eyes off it. "When that happens," he said, "a fox and a cat are getting married to each other."

"I don't understand."

"Something so beautiful can only happen when enemies are at peace."

I wished for a rainbow every day in Sri Lanka, only without the monsoon so I could play outside and climb trees.


My parents and grandparents were going to a party that evening. Children weren't invited so I was left behind with Saras and Herath. I was allowed to stay up for half an hour after my eight-thirty bedtime, but had to change into pyjamas first. Dad told me to be good.

"I will."

I waved goodbye to them from the veranda. They argued on the steps because Amma wanted Mum to drive and Appa and Dad said no. The men got into the front seats and wouldn't get out again even after my grandmother scolded them. After they left, I wanted to play with my present but Herath and Saras were standing guard.

"Why don't you have an early night?" I asked Saras.

"What are you up to, kunju?"

"Nothing."

I sat on a rattan sofa and read my book until bedtime when I pretended to yawn and went to my room straight away. Saras listened to me saying my prayers then she tucked me in. "Go to sleep, small one. If you want anything, Herath will wait in the sitting area until your Mum and Dad come back." I closed my eyes and acted like I was trying to sleep.

She talked to Herath in Tamil then laughed. I heard footsteps going to the back veranda and waited a few minutes to get out of bed. If I was caught, I was going to pretend to want a glass of water. Opening the door a little, I crept out. Herath had nodded off. Keeping one eye on him, I ran to Appa's room and switched on the bedside lamp. After slowly opening the heavy chest lid, I took my present out. My doll wouldn't come out of the front of the cardboard box because she was strapped in with plastic ties so I pulled and pulled the back until it tore. It was only a small tear so Mum might not have noticed it when she wrapped my present. Herath snored loudly outside. I'd forgotten about him and that he could wake up. I was frightened of being found out but carried on anyway, careful not to crinkle the plastic at the front because I wanted to open a brand new gift on Christmas Day. I fed my baby with a bottle then put her against my shoulders to burp her. When she'd brought up all her wind, I quietly sang her a lullaby until Herath coughed in the sitting room. He could have caught me at any time. I pushed my doll back into the box, couldn't do up the ties again so threw them in the bin and put my present back in the chest, shutting the lid softly.

After coming out of my grandfather's room, I stood by Herath to make sure he was still asleep. His eyes were closed and his chest went up and down as he breathed. When he yawned, I ran past and jumped into bed. I thought I heard him laugh softly but wasn't sure.

"What are we doing tomorrow?" I asked Dad on Christmas Eve.
"Church in the morning. Then back here for lunch."
"Just us?"
"Afraid so, girl."
"Nathan, don't tease," Mum said. "Uncle Theo is coming here with Kana and his mother. The Fonsekas are coming as well because Uncle Mahen needs to be in Colombo over Christmas."

I jumped up and down. "Appa, I'm starting an earthquake."

He chased me across the room and caught me then picked me up and pretended to throw me down the back veranda steps. I giggled as he swung me backwards and forwards. After a few swings, he put me down, saying, "I'm getting too old for this horseplay."

I sat next to Saras who was squatting on the back veranda, making the day's curry powders: one for biriani, one for fish and one for prawns. The smell of seeds she was roasting to grind made my mouth water. I could hardly wait for the Christmas Eve dinner she was preparing. It was the one meal each year when servants were allowed to be like family and eat at table with us. Amma was in the kitchen with cooks she'd asked to come in and make rotis and shorteats for the next day. One of the cooks was Saras' sister, who made the best rotis in Colombo; everybody wanted her and she'd walk from house to house, cooking for people.

"Your sister's staying here for Christmas," I told Saras.

"I like to have family close."

"And Herath's brother is coming, too."

"He finished boarding school yesterday and will spend a few days here."

"I didn't know Veddhas celebrated Christmas. I thought they only had yaku."

"You are right, small one, but Herath likes to see his family."

I felt sorry for poor people who didn't have good jobs so they had to live in someone else's house and be a servant. When I grew up, I was going to buy a big house so all my servants could live with their families.

Appa had been to market to get king prawns and fish for the next couple of days. He used to live by the sea in Trinco and knew the best seafood to get, so he liked to choose it himself when he had the time. Sri Lankan king prawns were my favourite food. They were half as big as my hand and really tasty. Servants didn't get to eat nice food often, so that night was to be a treat for everybody.

I went to see what was going on in the kitchen. Saras' sister was beating dough and flattening it to make rotis, which she covered with damp cloths and put in the fridge ready to fry later. My grandmother was making curries on the stove and spotted me by the door. "Rohini, please don't come in. We're cooking and I don't want you running about and hurting yourself."

"Can I stay here and watch?"

She raised her voice, "I told you - "

I ran for my life and sat next to Mum on the sofa. She stopped chatting to Dad and Appa and put an arm around me.

"Stay out of the kitchen, darling. Amma's busy."

"I know. That's why I ran to you."

I'd just recovered from my lucky escape when Herath came in the room and served us an iced lime juice drink. I took a sip and watched him as he went out of the sitting area onto the back veranda. "Dad, why doesn't Herath have a good job if his father can afford to send his brother to boarding school?"

"Appa pays the school fees."

"If more people helped others," my grandfather said, "we could halve this world's problems."

"Amen," Mum said.

I wondered what I could do to make life better for servants. Saras' room was dark and needed an electric light bulb even during the day, but then I remembered the thin mattresses she and Herath put on the hard floor to sleep on. Although they were used to it, I wanted to get them beds. I couldn't do much on my own, grown-ups wouldn't listen to me, and God was back in hospital having a new knee put in because he broke the last one playing cricket. Maybe if I asked nicely, Buddha would make Appa buy beds for Saras and Herath.

"I'm going to my room," I said to no-one special.

My father folded his arms. "What are you up to?"

I wished I hadn't said anything. I nearly told a lie but didn't like lying to him. "I'm going to pray to Buddha."

"What's wrong with God? We're Christians."

I didn't know what to do. Amma didn't mind me speaking with Buddha, but she was far away in the kitchen and had just shouted at me for getting in the way.

"Tell you what," Dad said. "Pray at bedtime and we'll go for a walk on the beach now."

I felt guilty, wanting to play on the sand, also not wanting to let Saras and Herath down. My father might have got cross if I asked for a few minutes to pray. I ran to my room, kissed my Buddha statue, said I'd see him later and rushed out again.

Dad pretended to smack my bottom. "Finish your prayer, monkey?"

Mum scolded him. "Don't harass her, Nathan."

She always looked after me.

He laughed. "Anybody else coming for a walk?"

"Count me out," Mum said. "I'll be needed in the kitchen."

Appa got up. "I'll come. It's not too hot to be outside."

The three of us set off down the road, my father and grandfather chatting to each other, me skipping between them to the whoosh of waves, and enjoying the smell of salt in the air.

I asked a question I already knew the answer to, but had to ask in case something had changed in the world that only grown-ups knew about. "Dad, when will things get better in Sri Lanka so we can move back here?"

"Not yet, girl. Not yet."

He sounded sad so I held his hand.

"Appa? Do you know?"

My grandfather coughed, blinked a few times then shook his head.

"I miss you all too."

His voice sounded funny so I held his hand as well. I hoped he and

Dad cheered up soon so I could let go of them and play. Something pushed against my back then a dog's head shoved itself between the three of us, nosing around my leg. My father took a close look at it.

"Doesn't seem to be a mongrel. All the same, don't pet it, Rohini."

Appa also looked at it.

"No need to worry. It's Selva's. It's not rabid or diseased."

The dog stayed with us until we got to the railway line then it went back up the road when someone called it.

"Whistle for it to come back, Dad."

He wasn't listening to me but checking left and right for trains. "Nothing coming. Let's go."

I stood on the sand the other side of the track and looked behind. The dog had disappeared. I was going to ask Appa about it later so I could make friends with it. I pointed to a rocky part of the beach and told my father, "I'm going there."

"Okay," he said then chatted to my grandfather about the Sri Lankan cricket team, and when they'd be allowed to play in Test matches.

Mum said he forgot to do things when he talked about sports. I tugged his arm. "You have to keep an eye on me to make sure I don't wander off."

"I will."

I collected seashells and filled my dress pockets to the top. When I couldn't get any more in, I asked my father to carry some. He held out his hands and I piled them high. He didn't notice what I was doing and chatted to Appa. "Making the move to English law was harder than I expected. Even if Sri Lankan law is based on the same principles."

"You've never mentioned that before. I still think you should have kept up the family tradition and taken up accountancy."

"Numbers and I don't get along, as you know. Anyway, I won't switch career." He smiled. "As you also know."

I collected as many shells as I could and came back, my hands full. "Appa, can you take these to the house for me while I get some more?"

"Those dirty things. Are you mad?"

"Dad?"

"One more. You take the rest."

My grandfather looked at his watch. Amma told him off if he was late for a meal. "It's nearly dinner-time," he said. "Better go back."

I put my hands around my shells, careful not to break any. We waited at the railway track and Appa put an arm on my shoulder. He looked both ways then said, "Come, girl." The three of us walked across and back up the road. My father and grandfather took long steps and I had to hurry to keep up with them.

"Can you go slowly? I don't want to drop anything."

Appa stopped, rolled his eyes at me and held out his hands. While he talked to Dad he took all the shells I carried without looking at how many there were. I jiggled the shells in my pockets. I'd collected loads more than Mum would have let me bring back, and knew I'd have to hide them from her.

Herath and his brother were chasing each other and playing the fool in the side garden. They ran away laughing and joking when they saw us, their curly hair flying about. Nobody was in the sitting area but I could hear my mother talking near the kitchen. Luckily my room was near the front door so I hurried indoors and emptied everything from my pockets onto the bed. Dad and Appa put all they carried onto to my pile. My father gave me a plastic carrier bag, told me to put the shells in it and wash off the sand.

I filled the bag with water in the bathroom but it was so heavy it slipped and my dress got soaked. I thought Mum might not notice if I changed clothes or might let me get away with it if I said I got wet at the beach. After swishing the shells around, I poured water out of the bag then ran through the dining area towards my bedroom. My mother was watching Saras pound spices on the side veranda and saw me across the courtyard. I acted like I hadn't seen her and rushed into my room. I'd only just pushed the bag under the bed when the door opened. Mum looked at my wet dress then at my feet where a pool of water was getting bigger and bigger. I looked back at her as if there was nothing wrong.

"Change your dress," she told me, bending down to pick up the bag, "or you'll catch cold." She dried the shells in a towel. "I don't know who's worse, you or your father for letting you bring all these to the house. What were you going to do with them?"

"Take them to London."

"Not all, sweetheart. You can give some to Kana."

I shook my head.

"Aren't you friends with her anymore?"

"I want to take some of Sri Lanka to London, in case we can't live here again."

She stroked my cheek. "We'll see."

I was sure I could squeeze all my shells into our suitcases, even if I had to put them in one by one, between clothes.

Mum held my hand as we went back to the sitting area where Appa was talking on the phone. Amma stood by, listening to everything. My parents always told me it was rude to eavesdrop, but it's different for grandmothers who are allowed to know everything.

"Tara sounded disappointed we couldn't be at her party tonight,"

Appa said as he put the phone down.

Amma tutted. "That woman and her parties. Who does she think she is, inviting us a few hours beforehand?"

"I'm sure she didn't mean to be rude."

"Enough, Roshan. One of us knows what we're talking about and it's not you."

It sounded like they were going to start an argument. I waited to hear what happened next but Amma went to the kitchen to see if dinner was ready. My grandfather had had a lucky escape.

Because there were still a few minutes until we ate, I did handstands against a wall. When Dad called me for dinner I couldn't find the sandals I'd thrown off so as not to mark the paint, so washed my hands and came running barefoot.

The servants had already brought the food from the kitchen and were sitting at table. My eyes nearly popped out of my head when I saw what we had to eat: fried prawns, rotis, yellow rice, mutton biriani, fish *sodhi*, *murunga*, *paripoo*, all served on Amma's china. My mouth watered as steam from the food carried the spicy smells to me. While we held hands round the table and Appa said Grace, my thoughts weren't about thanking God but about what to eat first. Eyes half-open, I peeped at the food. Herath saw me looking and winked. After my grandfather had finished speaking to the Lord, I said, "Amen," the loudest so He'd know I was thankful. Soon as we stopped holding hands, Herath's brother dug into the food. Not knowing what to start with, or how I was going to eat as much as I wanted to, I served rice and vegetables then took a piece of fish. I looked to see what was on my plate and what was in the dishes on the table. I didn't have any prawns.

Mum saw me looking at them. "Shall I put one on your plate?"

"I'll wait."

I wanted Saras and the other servants to take some first. I tried not to look while everybody grabbed prawns but couldn't help myself. Soon there were hardly any left in the dish then Herath's brother took the last one. I couldn't believe I wasn't going to get any, thought others would think about me the way I had about them and leave me something. Mum smiled kindly at me and gave me one as big as the palm of my hand from her plate. I should have known she'd look after me. I cut it up into pieces then took my first mouthful of rice, vegetables and prawn. Wow. It was the best I'd ever had. Even Mum's cooking didn't taste like that. When Dad asked if I was excited about Christmas Day, I didn't answer him: I'd just taken a bite of fried prawn and was enjoying the sweet and salty fish flavour that was spiced with ginger and garlic.

"Small one is busy," he said.

He left me alone after that and so did the others. We were all busy with the feast that Buddha had given us. Herath and his brother giggled a lot; Saras and her sister didn't talk much anyway, but were even quieter then because they missed their family most at Christmas. I asked Buddha in a silent prayer to find them nice husbands and give them at least two children each, because you should always have a brother or sister to play with.

After dinner, when I'd changed into pyjamas and brushed my teeth, I was allowed to stay up with the grown-ups to wait for Christmas. Taking *Swallows and Amazons* with me, I sat next to Mum by the Christmas tree, which looked pretty with tinsel, baubles and white fairy lights. I really wanted to stay awake but put my book down after a page. My head fell forward and I nodded off for a few seconds. Dad kept watching me. I knew he'd put me to bed if I wasn't careful. I pushed my eyelids up with my fingers and looked at him so he'd see my eyes were open and I was wide awake. It didn't work. Mum would have waited until I fell asleep on her lap. He didn't take any of my nonsense, came over, picked me up and carried me to my room.

# CHRISTMAS DAY

**Jaffna parade (Saras' tale)**

On Christmas morning you wandered alone,
your shoulders hunched, the stance of survival.
In bare feet you trudged to the old rice mill
and paused to bow at a funeral pyre.

All over my land, bells ring for the dead.
They always peal twice. The sound of revenge.

Each Christmas morning, I hold your last gift;
more precious than gold, frankincense and myrrh,
is burnt paddy husk in woven palm leaves.
Ashes of Jaffna. Black powder that's home.

Amma was murdered; the soldiers used guns.
Afraid for my life, you urged me to run.

Yet on both sides of Elephant Pass, march
the sovereigns of war, ransacking our homes.
They journey to ravage our infant peace,
with missiles for presents, knives in their hands.

I placed my trust in God and his wisdom,
sang hymns, read psalms, each book in the bible.
His stories are false. Hope died on the cross.
A counterfeit faith is all that I have.

In the silken light of dawn, cockerels crowed, dogs barked and Perth Avenue woke up. Sohan crept into Roshan Uncle's garden, a cardboard box under his arm. He'd have to be quick delivering his Christmas gift: a clatter of pots and pans at the back of the house meant Saras, Herath or a servant hired for the holiday season was awake. He paused by the front gates to think about years when he too was invited to share the annual feast with the Palars. Arul Aunty once made Christmas pudding at his request, although she spiced it with cardamom and would have added black pepper if she hadn't run out of the seasoning. He left his gift on the veranda and waited. Nothing happened so he glanced at his watch and peered down the side garden until Herath appeared.

"Nathan *mahathya* is here?" Sohan asked.

Herath nodded.

"You know what he is doing for the rest of his holidays?"

The young man nodded again, didn't volunteer more information. Sohan pulled a wad of notes from his wallet and held it out.

Herath flinched and retreated a step. "No money."

"So why did you agree to meet me?"

"My father told me to come."

As long as he lived, Sohan would never understand the Veddhas. If not for money why did Chief Aruma let his son who was training to be a shaman, work as a servant in the Palar household? All the same, he knew better than to try and persuade the stubborn young man to change his mind and spy on Nathan. He could only hope the next stop on his journey would show him how to end the turbulence in his life.

He strode up the aisle of the empty church to a front pew. At that time of day, he could escape the congregation who were Christians in the house of God, money-grabbers and social climbers outside. While reciting the Lord's Prayer, he listened for the footsteps of the other worshipper who also came in early for peace and quiet. Yet all that disturbed the calm that Christmas morning was a draught, lifting dust from forgotten corners of the aisles and transept, creating a faint, musty smell. He waited for what seemed like a lifetime. If he stayed any longer it meant a risk of being seen by the caretaker, who'd known him from short trousers to long and who'd want to wish him Happy Christmas. Sohan was in no mood for season's greetings; he wanted to speak about Uma, to stop thinking about his plan to sell leopard skins. And why wouldn't Herath help him? Above all, he wanted to find peace with Nathan. So he entered into another dialogue with the Lord, making it last until footsteps strode up the aisle towards him. At last, he felt the tap on the shoulder he'd hoped for.

"Sohan. It's been a long time, my son. You know you're always welcome."

"Thank you, Father, but you know how I feel about these people."

Father Woodgate patted him on the back. "Did you come to pray?"

"I was wondering."

"If I was going to choose hymn thirty-five? I had to. It was Uma's favourite before she lost her family. It helps to remember, son, even if it pains us. Will you come to the morning service?"

"She'll have her family with her."

"Uma needs you, too."

"It's not easy, Father."

"I know about your falling out with Nathan. I also know love shows itself in many ways. I don't judge you, son."

"You don't know what you're talking about. None of you do."

He stormed out of church, the slap of his leather soles on clay tiles echoing from floor to ceiling. Standing briefly outside at the entrance, he knew without a backward glance that Father Woodgate was kneeling in front of the altar, making the sign of the cross and praying for his soul, as he had since his baptism, through confirmation, teenage years and every day since.


On Christmas Day, I jumped out of bed and shot past the red and white stocking that my parents had put at the end of the mattress. Where was my big present? I ran to see Mum and Dad but their room was empty. Appa laughed loudly in the sitting room. He must have been joking in there with the others. After giving everyone a good morning hug, I looked under the Christmas tree. There was nothing.

"Where is it please?"

"We forgot to bring it," my father said. "You'll have to wait until we get back to London."

Then I saw it under his chair. I tore off the shiny gold wrapping paper and kissed my baby doll.

Appa said, "The box had already been opened. Do you know how that could have happened?"

"I did it. I found it in your chest, after I'd looked everywhere."

"At least you're honest."

I put my doll against my shoulder then went to show her to Saras and Herath in the servants' quarters where they were opening presents from my parents and grandparents. Saras was trying on a green silk sari Amma had given her. Her sister was holding up a blue one against herself, to see what it looked like. Herath's brother felt the material for school shirts and trousers he'd been given and said what good quality they were. Herath preferred Sri Lankan clothes because he liked to dress more like a Veddha so his presents were sarongs in a grey check and short-sleeved shirts. He put his things in a cardboard box to sell later and give the money to his family. I really wanted him to have something new to wear on Christmas Day but he liked to help his family more than keeping gifts. And I couldn't understand why Appa and Amma had only given servants clothes when they could have given them beds as well, instead of mattresses on the floor. I also felt sorry that Saras used burnt paddy husk to clean her teeth. My grandparents tried to give her a toothbrush and toothpaste once but she said, "No, thank you," she didn't want to change what her father had taught her in Jaffna.

"I got this doll for Christmas," I told her.

"Lucky girl."

I nodded.

Herath took a quick look at my present but didn't say anything. I didn't mind that he wasn't interested. I just wanted him to see my new doll. Cuddling my baby, I skipped back to the dining area.

Everybody else had eaten breakfast while I was asleep so I took the chance to sit in Appa's chair at the top of the empty dining table. I lifted the muslin cloth from a bowl of mashed purple yam and ate while Mum stroked my hair. Chickens clucked in the courtyard; Saras and her sister clanged pans in the kitchen and talked to each other; Herath and his brother laughed and joked while they swept the outside corridors with scratchy brooms. Those were Sri Lankan noises I loved and was always going to remember, especially at breakfast-time.

After I finished eating, Dad told me to get washed and dressed, we were going to leave soon for church. I hurried to the bathroom then my bedroom, excited about wearing the new dress we'd bought in London for today. I'd chosen a pink one and like all my other dresses, it had pockets so I could carry a hanky. I gave my new doll a kiss then put her on a chair next to my statue of Buddha and joined the others on the veranda.

Appa was going to drive us all to church. "Even though my wife wants Uma at the wheel." I looked at Amma to see if she was going to start a fight with him because he wasn't obeying her. She reached for my hand. "Come help me, child. That man is driving me up the wall." I'd seen her going up and down steps on her own when nobody was looking so knew she just wanted everyone to feel sorry for her. I was glad she didn't lean on me as much as she did when grown-ups helped her, or she might have squashed me. While opening the car door to let her climb in, I looked behind to see if the others were following. Appa winked at Mum and Dad as he watched me help Amma. She saw him with the Evil Eye at the back of her head. "Roshan, just as well for you it's Christmas Day." Nobody talked while we all got into the car. I tried to sit by the window but had to stay between Amma and Mum in the back. The smell of my grandmother's Eau de Cologne reminded me a bit of being ill because when I had a fever, Mum sprinkled it on a hanky, which she put on my forehead. Amma's face was covered in the powder she wore when she went out. She didn't wear lipstick because, "It's for young women." Her only other make-up was a *pottu* on her forehead.

At the end of our road, I asked if we were going left or right. Dad said we were going right: the church was past Mount Lavinia. I'd have to see kite-flying at Galle Face Green another time. All the shops were open, *kadillai* and ice *palaam* sellers were everywhere, pushing carts by the side of the road; families walked along the streets, as if it was an ordinary day and they were going to school or work or just shopping for groceries.

"Why aren't those people at church, Mum?"

"Most Sri Lankans are Buddhists or Hindus so today doesn't mean much to them."

I was going to say a prayer that night for children who didn't get Christmas presents because there weren't any Christians in their family.

We passed a shrine on the roadside, which was a small altar with a gold Buddha dressed in a red sarong. A coach driver had stopped to make an offering and was bowing while we drove past. I wondered if Buddha would mind me going to church to sing Christmas carols and thought he'd be all right about it because it was like a party for Jesus' birthday.

The sun shone into our car, making me so hot that my legs stuck to the leather seat. To keep cool, Amma used her special occasion fan made of silk with embroidered flowers. When I was old enough to look after it properly, she was going to give it to me. "You'll lose or tear it if I give it to you now," she said. I turned towards her so she could fan me too, the air gently blowing my hair and cooling my face.

At church we parked behind a grey car, which Dad said was Uncle Mahen's. When I saw Victor going up the church steps, I waved to him and tried to run across the road. My father put a hand across my shoulders. Even though I wriggled, I couldn't get free. The Fonsekas waited for us and as soon as we reached them, I got the smell of mothballs from Aunty Indra's sari. She should have had it washed by the dhobi man before she wore it to service.

"Sunday school is cancelled," Uncle said. "The teacher has a cold so we have to take the kids in with us." I liked it when children were allowed into church because priests sometimes let us have a piece of bread and sip of wine with the grown-ups.

We'd got there early so most of the seats were empty. Instead of sitting at the back to escape quickly after the service finished, we went all the way to the front pews so Amma wouldn't have far to walk to receive communion. Uncle and Leela went into their seats first. Victor waited for Aunty Indra to go in next so he and I could sit together.

Aunty said, "You next, son."

He didn't budge.

Uncle snapped his fingers. "Do as you're told."

Victor went in and didn't look back at me. Once we sat, we'd have to stay where we were for the whole service and I wanted to chat to him. I tried to squeeze past my aunt as she walked into the pew. She wouldn't let me through. I pushed and pushed. She pressed back harder, her hard body stopping me. I put my head down like a bull and charged but her sari was slippery and I nearly fell over. Dad grabbed me and tried not to laugh. I told him, "We want to sit together. We'll be good." It was too late anyway. Aunty had sat on the bench between Victor and me. She folded her hands in her lap, looking pleased with herself. I didn't know why she was being nasty. In my best voice, I asked her, "Please can Victor sit next to me?"

"We are here to worship our Lord."

I didn't think she was a nice person.

Dad put an arm around me. "Aunty's right. You two can speak later."

I still didn't think she was nice.

A lady with grey hair turned round to see who was making a noise in a holy place. My father and aunt had been talking too so she couldn't scold only me. Amma tapped the lady's shoulder.

"How are you keeping, Mrs Jegarajah?"

"What?"

Amma spoke louder. "Merry Christmas, Mrs Jegarajah."

The old lady fiddled with her hearing aid. "There's no need to shout. I'm not deaf."

There were other people in her pew but nobody was next to her, poor thing. "Mum, can we take Mrs Jegarajah home for lunch? She's on her own."

"Her family are at the Hindu temple. They're coming to ours for drinks before lunch."

Amma whispered to my mother, "I hope she behaves. She won't win prizes for diplomacy."

I didn't know what diplomacy was and thought it might mean Mrs Jegarajah told rude jokes that weren't funny. I was going to listen closely to her in case she said the word beginning with F that I couldn't hear at the picnic. I'd learned bastard as a swear word the other night, when Dad thought I was asleep while he talked to Appa about Uncle Sohan. I still had to learn more to grow up quickly but didn't dare lean over Victor's mum to ask if he knew the F word. And Aunty Indra's sari still smelt of mothballs.

The sun shone through stained-glass windows, onto a picture of Jesus. He must have been happy to see so many people in church, candles burning, the tables by the altar covered in lace tablecloths and Temple and Lotus flowers all over the place.

On a pillar to my left was the wooden board that had hymn numbers on it. At the top in white letters was 157. "Look, Mum. My favourite," I said, showing her my hymn book. I waited for the organist to play the first part of the music so we could begin *Away in a manger*. I loved to hear everybody sing together. God must like the sound of voices too, which is why he makes us sing in church. I held the hymn book but didn't need to read it because I knew the words by heart. I sang loudly so deaf Mrs Jegarajah could hear. She liked me doing that because she turned round to see who was singing for her. After the first verse was over, she had trouble standing and leaned on her walking stick. When we got to the end of the carol, she rubbed her legs as if they were hurting then she bent her knees to sit, and oh my goodness, she broke wind. She should have waited until she was at home instead of doing it in God's house. I put my hymn book down, pinched my nose with my fingers and hoped that breathing smells through my mouth wouldn't kill me. Mum and Dad were looking away, trying not to laugh. When they stopped smiling, I thought the smell must have gone away or Mrs Jegarajah had broken wind again. I let go of my nose and sniffed the air. It only smelt of mothballs.

The priest asked us all to come for communion. I stayed as far away from Mrs Jegarajah as I could, knelt at the front and stuck my tongue out for the bread. I was at the end of the line and had to wait for such a long time that my mouth went dry. As the priest put the goblet to my lips, I held onto it with both hands so I could take a gulp of wine and get drunk. All I got was a small sip before he tugged it away. Victor tried the same trick. He didn't get away with it either. We walked back together to our seats thinking Aunty Indra hadn't noticed but she followed us down the aisle and pushed between us. Dad put a hand on my shoulder before I had a chance to charge her again.

After the bread and wine, we had to kneel on cushions to say thanks to God for the snacks and please give us a nice lunch too. As I closed my eyes, I looked at the board again so I could be ready for the next hymn. When I saw it was thirty-five, I got a shock. Mum hadn't seen it yet. She was kneeling with her head bowed and eyes closed. I didn't know what to do.

That number made her cry. My parents had never explained why she was afraid of it and I didn't keep asking in case she got upset. She couldn't have been afraid of getting old because she was already twenty-six. I leaned forward and around her to get Dad's attention but his eyes were shut tight while he prayed. I crossed my fingers and toes and wished that God would change the hymn number. He must have gone to the pub for a Christmas drink because it stayed the same. I was about to try speaking to Buddha when the priest spoke. "Now for the next hymn, number thirty-five." Mum didn't move and her eyes went shiny. Dad was worried about her too and put an arm around her shoulders as she sniffed. She wiped her nose with the hanky I gave her from my dress pocket then opened her mouth to start singing *Once in Royal David's City*. I put my hymn book on the shelf in front of me and pulled hers down to share it so she wouldn't have to sing on her own. After getting some loving from Dad and me, she stopped crying halfway through the carol and sang with the rest of us, although I could hardly hear her until we got to the last verse, when she sang a bit louder. She tried to give me back my hanky afterwards but I let her keep it because she'd made it wet.

The priest told us in his sermon that we had to be kind to everybody, especially people we didn't like. He can't have known Aunty Indra very well or he wouldn't have said that. He spoke about the Troubles, said we had to pray for prisoners in jail, and it didn't matter if they were Sinhalese, Tamils or Muslims. He went on forever, his voice was slow and I watched his mouth as his lips moved. He told us about the Jaffna village he lived in when he was growing up and farmers who had lost everything in the war. Tired from staying up late last night, I yawned and started to nod off. I dreamt I was on a beach with Uncle Sohan. We ran about laughing and chasing each other then decided to play catch. He threw a ball to me but Dad snatched it and wouldn't give it back. I was about to tell my father not to be silly when someone shouted, "God be with you and Merry Christmas." I didn't know why the Lord was on the beach as well until I rubbed my eyes and saw other people sit up too. The priest was in his pulpit, looking at me. I thought he'd be angry because I'd had a nap while he gave his sermon but he smiled at me. Jesus must have told him not to get cross with children for falling asleep in church.

A silver collection bowl was passed along our bench, the coins making a chink, chink sound as they dropped in. Amma turned in her seat to see how much Uncle Mahen was giving but Appa bent forward so she couldn't get a look.

"Roshan," she said. She was cross with him.

He folded his arms. "Yes, dear?"

"I was trying to - "

"I know."

The bowl moved to the pew behind. At last, we were free to go. Appa and Uncle went down the aisle first to unlock the cars. Mrs Jegarajah leaned on her seat to push herself up and stared at me. I thought she was going to ask me to help her walk so I looked away. She was a big lady.

"Rohini," Amma said. "Help Mrs Jegarajah."

I pretended I hadn't heard.

Dad said, "Go ahead, girl. I'll give her a hand."

I didn't hang about and hurried out of the pew to catch up with Appa and Uncle Mahen. Victor sneaked past his mother and joined me as soon as he could. We couldn't go fast because God doesn't like anyone running in his house. When I couldn't smell Aunty Indra's sari anymore I knew we were safe. We ran down the church steps to catch up with Appa and Uncle. They were so busy gossiping they didn't notice us come up behind them.

"That's church over with until Easter," Uncle told my grandfather. "If it weren't for the children, I'd let Indra go on her own. But you have to set an example."

"I know what you mean. God knows I had little enough free time when Nathan was young, without having to get up early on Sundays."

"Appa," I said, "church is a good place to pray."

"Child, you're not to repeat what you heard or I'll be in trouble with your grandmother."

"I promise."

"You too, son," Uncle said. "Your mother will never let me hear the last of it."

"I swear on my sister's life."

"Considering you two fight like cat and dog, that means nothing."

I smelt the flowery scent of mothballs coming at us. "Uncle, can Victor come in our car?"

"Our family will come together," Aunty said from behind me.

Uncle was feeling brave and took no notice of her. "Go with Rohini if you want, son. We'll follow right behind."

Victor shot into our car. As soon as his family drove off, I looked behind and saw Aunty Indra put on red lipstick while starting a row with her husband. She wouldn't let him speak and was only interested in what she wanted. Her red lipstick mouth moved for the whole journey. Uncle Mahen watched the road ahead and smiled a bit because he'd stood up to her.

When we arrived back at Perth Avenue, Kana was having a drink and shorteats on the front veranda with her dad and grandmother. "Fine way to treat your guests," Uncle Theo said, "leaving us to entertain ourselves."

"Nathan was supposed to tell you we wouldn't be back from church till gone eleven," Mum told him.

"Ah, yes. That's right, he did. I must have forgotten."

Amma tutted at Dad. "Forgotten, my foot."

While Appa served the grown-ups alcohol, Herath put a jug of mango juice on a table for the children and served us a glass each. We all thanked him, except Leela. She just took hers and drank. Even after Victor told her off for not having manners, she still didn't say thank you and her parents didn't scold her. Kana gave her a funny look and came to sit with me. Leela got nasty and asked Kana why she was having Christmas lunch with us if she was a Buddhist. Uncle Mahen scolded her for being rude to guests but he didn't say anything about her being rude to Herath.

Poor Herath looked tired, like he'd been working hard. I felt bad about being with friends on Christmas Day while servants had to work.

"Can you bend down, Mum? I want to say something in your ear."

After I asked my question, she said, "I don't see why not."

Amma watched as I whispered and knew I was up to something. I sat with the children at the other end of the veranda and acted like I hadn't noticed her looking at me. Even from there, I could feel her staring at me, trying to guess what I was going to do.

Aunty Indra lifted her glass and called out, "Hey, another sherry please."

Uncle Mahen said, "That'll be her third and my good wife can't handle more than two."

Mrs Jegarajah and her family rolled up in their car, parking on the road because there wasn't enough space in the front garden. She didn't have any children for me to play with: only a tall man and her husband got out of the car. They helped her walk to the bottom of the veranda, where she stopped and looked at the steps. I turned away in case she asked to lean on me but her husband brought her up. The children had to get off their chairs to make room for her and her family so we played chase in the carport, not knowing where else to go that wouldn't get our best clothes dirty. When I heard Mrs Jegarajah say something, I stopped playing and listened to her in case she told a rude joke.

"Uma, child," she said. "How are you coping after the service? *Aiyo*, I don't mean to upset you but it was a terrible day when you lost your family in the riots."

"It's Christmas," Appa said. "Let's talk of the happy times we have ahead."

"Oh, of course, Roshan. But you know, Uma, it was a loss for me too.

I have many happy memories of your family's parties at number thirty-five and whatever pain we suffer, what is the point of being alive, if we can't be remembered? Isn't that right, Roshan?"

My grandfather grunted.

Mum held Dad's hand. "Thank you both, for thinking about me and my family."

I knew that when she came back from a school trip to Kandy, her family had run away from a house fire and was too scared to come back. I never knew she used to live at number thirty-five and that was why it made her sad. I felt older after I found out and it was all I could think about until Victor pulled my arm.

"Come on, Rohini. The grown-ups have forgotten about us. We're sneaking off to play chase."

I followed him down the side of the house to the back garden. Leela said her new shoes were hurting, she didn't want to be the first chaser and she'd tell her mum if she was. When she bent down to loosen her shoe buckles, Victor crept behind to push her over. Kana grabbed him and took him away before he got us all in trouble. I followed behind, still thinking about what Mrs Jegarajah had said.

Victor laughed. "I nearly got away with it. Anyway, Kana, why are you being nice to my sister when you don't want her in our secret club?"

Leela came running and wanted to know what we were talking about.

"Nothing," Victor said.

"I'm telling on you."

They stared at each other, pulling faces and poking their tongues out.

"Come on," Kana said, taking me by the arm. "Let's play chase. You're *It*, Victor."

He came running to touch me. Kana touched him back for me, took my hand then we ran away together. We all raced around the yard, up and down veranda steps and along outside corridors, only stopping to catch our breath after we'd each had a turn at being *It*.

I'd been so busy running that I'd forgotten about number thirty-five. It didn't worry me anymore and so I let go of Kana's hand. She said, "I'm glad you're feeling better, Rohini."

Amma came out of the dining area on her way to the kitchen. The Jegarajahs had gone to relations for Christmas lunch and we were going to have ours soon. "Wash your hands," she said. "I don't want ragamuffins at my table." Even Leela did as she was told by my grandmother and we took it in turns to use the bathroom sink. Kana was younger than Victor but before he even tried, she warned him about splashing us. We were hungry so instead of using towels we wiped our hands on our clothes as we hurried to the dining table.

I tugged my mother's sari. "Did you remember what I asked?"

"Rohini, you and Kana sit here. Theo, do you mind sitting next to your daughter?"

"What's going on?" Dad said.

"Nothing, Nathan. Put yourself over there please."

When Victor tried to get on a chair next to Kana and me, Mum told him to sit with the men. I wouldn't have minded him being with us but he was happy to move and make faces at Leela. I watched as my mother put everyone where I'd asked her to.

The table was laid with a lace tablecloth and my grandmother's best blue and white china, which had been a wedding present from England. She scolded Appa for two whole days the year before, because he accidentally broke a saucer. They didn't make that design anymore so she couldn't get another one. I pushed Kana's and my plates farther up the table.

"What's for lunch?" Dad asked.

"Special biriani," Amma said.

"I'd have liked roast turkey," he told her.

"Nathan, don't be difficult," Mum said. "In England you want rice and curry and in Sri Lanka you want roasts."

Dad laughed.

Herath and his brother brought in a silver tray of chicken biriani with chopped cashew nuts on top, and in dishes that matched the blue and white plates: poppadum, fried prawns, rotis, mutton curry, brinjal curry, *paripoo*, *seeni* sambal, *pol* sambal, *idli* and fried fish. There was so much they could hardly fit it all onto the table. I went to push a china dish away from the edge of the table.

"Ouch."

"Careful. The dishes are hot," my grandmother said. "Did you burn yourself?"

"No, Amma."

"Hold it under cold water anyway."

When I came back from the bathroom, Herath had stopped bringing in food and was standing by the table with his brother. Appa told us all to hold hands for Grace.

Aunty Indra said, "I have to powder my nose."

She was away for so long the plates got cold.

Uncle Mahen said, "Arul and Roshan, I apologise for my dear wife. She must be powdering her whole body, not just the nose."

The children giggled. The grown-ups didn't. We waited and waited for Aunty. Dad and Uncle Theo joked they'd be dead from starving if she didn't hurry up. Herath and his brother were still standing by the table, ready to start serving wine. At last, the bathroom door opened. Victor clapped his hands and shouted, "Hurray."

Aunty Indra was a bit wobbly and fell off her chair as soon as she sat on it. Nobody rushed to help her so she tried to pull herself up by grabbing the tablecloth. Amma's dishes moved towards her. Oh my gosh. They were going to crash onto the floor.

Uncle Mahen put a hand on his forehead. "*Aiyo kadivillai*, Indra. Let go of the bloody tablecloth. You'll pull everything off."

"Don't use that tone with me. Help me up."

Uncle didn't budge at all. Aunty sat on the floor, one hand on the tablecloth, one on her chair, like she didn't know what to do next. If my grandmother's best plates and dishes broke, we'd have all got a scolding for at least a week. Herath saved us by twisting Aunty's hand off the tablecloth and pushing her up and onto a chair. She didn't look at anyone and picked up her napkin, which she then dropped on the floor, so we had to wait again while Herath fetched a clean one. Even though he was the only one who helped her, she didn't say thank you to him and his poor brother was standing there, falling asleep.

I didn't know if my plan would work but it was all I could think of. I looked to my left. Mum had done what I'd asked and put the Buddhists together: Uncle Theo, Kana, her grandmother and me. I counted the Christians around the table: Uncle Mahen, Victor, Leela, Appa, Mum, Dad and Aunty Indra. There were more of them than of us. Amma was Buddhist before she married so must still have been half of one. Four of us and my grandmother were enough to speak to Buddha while there were so many Christians around. We all held hands, ready for Appa to thank the Lord. I tapped my mother on the arm.

"Ask him now. Quickly. Before he starts."

"Appa, Rohini wants to say a special Grace, if you don't mind."

"Go ahead, child."

"This should be interesting," Amma said.

I closed my eyes and took a deep breath. "Thank you Jesus for giving us enough food for everyone. I don't know how you keep doing it." I stopped for a second. I was going to have to be brave and say my prayer out loud. "And Buddha can you fix it so Appa doesn't make servants work on Christmas Day? God can't sort it out because he's on sick leave again. Amen." I opened my eyes and sneaked a peek at my grandfather. He coughed as if he was choking. He looked like he was trying not to laugh. I didn't think he was angry but didn't dare look at him again.

Dad said, "My daughter wants servants to have the day off and us to still have a meal."

"Leave her be, Nathan," Amma said. "The child means well. That was kind of you, Rohini."

I wanted to cry until Kana gave me a kiss and Mum told Dad off for being mean. He said sorry for upsetting me, he was only trying to be funny.

"It's all right," I said. "I know you can't help it."

Everybody laughed.

Herath and his brother smiled at me as they served wine and water. Even if my prayer hadn't worked, at least they weren't looking so tired.

We all ate quickly and had seconds of everything. After we stuffed ourselves, there was still lots of food left in the dishes for the servants and I had room for pudding. I was putting a spoonful of *wattalappam* in my mouth when a car pulled up outside. As sandals slapped up the front veranda steps I turned to see who had come. Wearing a tee-shirt and jeans, Uncle Sohan walked into the sitting area as if it was his house. He hadn't even dressed in his best clothes for Christmas Day. Dad stood up and made a fist of his right hand. If he started a boxing fight, I was going to join in. Mum caught me when I jumped down and she wouldn't let go. Dad tried to go to Uncle but she stopped him too.

"Please, Nathan, let your father sort it out."

Appa was going red in the face. He went over to Uncle. "Sohan, I told you not to come here today."

"What's the matter, Nathan? Not man enough to see me off yourself?"

"That's enough," my grandfather said. "You'd better leave."

Uncle sat on one of the rattan sofas. "I'll have a Christmas drink first, if you don't mind." He picked up a cricket magazine from a side table, flicked through it then patted the seat next to him. "Hey, Uma. Come and tell me your news."

Appa stood over him. "You'll leave now."

"What's wrong with you? Can't a chap have a quiet drink with his friends?" He tried to push past to get to Dad. "I'll just wish Nathan Happy Christmas before I go."

"I won't have you upsetting the family like this."

My grandfather marched him outside. I didn't hear any shouting or screaming so Uncle must have behaved himself. He reversed out of the carport and drove up the road. I listened for a car engine coming back but didn't hear anything. I stared at the sofa he'd sat in.

"I hope he goes away forever and we never see him again."

Amma said, "Be careful what you wish for, child. We don't always want what we ask for."

Sohan's hope for a quiet drive home was dashed by cars and tuk-tuks zigzagging around bicycles and rickshaws. Didn't he have enough on his mind without having to deal with maniacs in traffic as well? Even if Hindus and Buddhists didn't celebrate Christmas, they should have been at someone's house for lunch: aunts, uncles, cousins or friends, any of them. He drummed his fingers on the steering wheel. He too, should have been with relations but he'd turned down the invitation from his mother.

"Look, Mum, you know I can't stand that husband of yours. I warned you before you married Arjun you'd have to choose between us."

"*Aiyo* come, please. Otherwise it will just be his family here."

"I'm spending the day with Tara," he lied. "I'll be with you on Boxing Day."

He pulled up by Galle Face Green and strolled across the grass until he reached a bench facing the sea. The place was deserted except for a few street vendors selling *kotthu roti*. Crowds would no doubt pour onto the green later to fly kites, meet and gossip. A light breeze brushed his cheeks and blew sea spray on his face. He cracked his knuckles, a solitary sound in the empty space around him. Damn Roshan Uncle. Damn Nathan.

He wished he hadn't taken the trouble to release a Loten's sunbird in their garden at dawn as a Christmas present. How often had he done that for them as a boy, climbing trees in Jaffna to catch the creatures, which he then brought south to Perth Avenue? All because Roshan Uncle was superstitious, believing the family would stay together if a sunbird roosted nearby. One year, Uncle paid him for his efforts with a cricket ball, the same make used by professionals. Sohan hadn't even dropped a hint about what he wanted. Uncle knew small gifts meant more to him than rupees.

A gust of sea wind swept over blades of grass on the green, bent them flat. Sohan raised a hand to comb the hair he'd parted that morning with a straight line. At least he wasn't with family and didn't have to worry about busybodies wishing him Happy Christmas. The last thing he needed was for his stepfather, a police officer, to sniff out the reason for his visits to Yala. God knows, he shouldn't have had to resort to poaching. Uncle Alagar's belief in him should have kept him on the straight and narrow. While elderly aunts were concerned about him drinking his life away and betting on horses, the old man had said, "You'll turn out fine, son." Yet there he was, plotting to hunt leopards, working out how to smuggle skins abroad.

And a few months before Uncle died, as if he had a hunch of what lay ahead, he asked Sohan to marry Uma and take care of her. Sohan didn't have a passion for her but didn't love anyone else either so when she turned eighteen they got engaged and planned their wedding day, down to ordering a Manipuri sari from India for her. All went as expected until she fell in love with Nathan. He'd let Uncle down, and it hadn't been his fault. At least the end of his engagement spurred him on to stop being a drunken gambler or gambling drunkard, depending on which of his relations was lecturing him. It had taken a few years to shake off the lifestyle he'd led since Uncle died, yet he'd done it and built up an import-export business. The old man would have been proud of him.

He leaned forward and rested his arms on his legs. People he loved had come into his life then vanished, first his father then Uncle Alagar. And when someone dies, they're gone and you can't bring them back to sit on your bed at night, comfort you over nightmares or give you a warm cup of milk to help you sleep.

The sun slipped lower in the sky, tinting all around him pink and gold. He must have seen a thousand sunsets like that one, each holding him in awe. In the distance, a passenger ship sailed west, taking families away from the mess that was Sri Lanka. Maybe he should also go abroad and join the mass exodus, although if he did that he would betray everything that Uncle Alagar, rightly or wrongly, had stood for.

A shadow fell over him, a scent of jasmine floated above his head and someone laid a hand on his shoulder from behind, the touch so faint he only just felt it.

"How did you know I'd be here?" he asked, without turning to see who had disturbed him.

Tara sat on the arm of the bench. "Sohan, I know you better than you realise. Roshan Uncle gave me a call and said you'd paid him a visit."

"I have a score to settle with Nathan."

"*Chee*, Sohan. On Christmas Day?"

"As good a day as any."

Tara cupped his face with her hand. "Come to my place. My family have eaten and gone home."

He'd rather have stayed where he was, deciding which tracker to hire at Yala, though he couldn't resist the allure of her perfume. "Okay. I've nothing else to do."

"I say, you're not exactly flattering me but come, anyway, darling." She waved at her driver to go away. "Now, where is your car?"

"I nearly took you to Delhi with me."

"Ah yes. Your mysterious business trip. But I don't want to talk about that now. Let's go and relax."

At her place, she poured him a glass of arrack, topping it up with ginger beer. "Drink this. It won't solve your problems but at least you're good company when you've had a few."

He couldn't help laughing.

"That's better," she said. "Now, open this."

"What is it?"

"It's a box, wrapped in Christmas paper. What do you think it is?"

He felt his cheeks getting hot. "I am so sorry. I've - "

"- been getting into knots over Nathan. I know. Presents don't bother me anyway."

That wasn't true. He'd forgotten her birthday last year and she'd gone to the Maldives for a week without telling him.

"Okay," she said. "I punished you over my birthday but it's serious with Nathan. You two need to fix what went wrong."

"You think I don't know? He needs to be told where to go."

Tara lifted the piano lid and sat on the double stool Sohan had bought her because she sometimes liked to play duets at parties. Glass in hand, he listened as she played a piece of up tempo classical music, which could have been written by Chopin or Bach or any of that motley crew. He'd told her once how much he liked its rapid pace and the fact that it drove out his demons. Her back swayed from side to side as she moved her fingers across the keys, making felt hammers hit notes that rose from the soundboard. Nathan's long fingers had also flowed across the piano to prolonged applause at school recitals, yet in spite of his music teacher's encouragement to follow his dream and become a professional musician, he'd opted for a safer career and become a lawyer. Sohan downed a swig of arrack in one go. Their friendship would have survived if Nathan had made the most of his talent and not turned bitter because of regrets.

The phone rang and he lifted a hand to answer it. Tara said, "Leave it," and continued playing. Unlike her, he was not yet lost to music and his hand hovered over the receiver. When the ringing stopped a few bars later, he switched to listening to the piano again, leaving his arm stretched across the back of the sofa. Tara finished the tune and started another one, a slower melody that lulled him into a light sleep just as the phone started again. This time he picked it up.

"Hello?"

"You have to leave my Dad alone."

"Rohini?"

The phone went dead.

"Who was that?" Tara asked as she carried on playing.

"Nathan's daughter."

Tara closed the piano lid, came to him. "Make it up with him, darling."

"And that's why you haven't repaid his father's loan, is it? You and I are two of a kind."

"I am a widow. My husband left me with this house and not very much to live on. Roshan Uncle knew when he lent me the money he wouldn't get it back. That's why he only gave me half of what I asked for."

"You could work."

"All right. Hire me in your business."

"Touché. But not on your life. I don't want the madness of my affairs to spoil what we have."

"You don't want me to stick my nose into what you're up to, you mean."

He put an arm around her, pulled her close and kissed the nape of her neck. "Some things you're better off not knowing."

Tara drew back. "Now you're scaring me."

He kissed her, a peck on the cheek. "It'll be over soon."

She pushed him away. "Give me your word it's nothing to do with guns or the Tigers."

"What kind of man do you take me for?"

In the early hours of daylight, the weight of her body across his woke him up. With him living half in Colombo, half in Kandy, they didn't often get the chance to be together like this. He smiled as he thought of the gossip they caused among aunts. "*Aiyo,* you must marry her, you know. This affair thing is not good for her reputation." He stroked her shoulders, the tops of her arms. They'd been dating since the end of his engagement to Uma, while he was a layabout and before he turned his life around, yet Tara had been impatient for her future, wasn't interested in a bum; she wanted someone to buy her twenty-two carat gold jewellery and a house in Cinnamon Gardens. And she wanted it with a click of her fingers. So she'd married Jehan.

After Sohan had built up a wealth that matched her husband's, when she saw the mansion he lived in, the Mercedes he drove, she came to him one evening and they became lovers again. Yet after a night of conscience, he confided in Roshan Uncle who told him, "You must respect marriage vows, son, even if they're not yours." So Sohan stepped back from the romance, picking it up again only after Tara was widowed.

He watched her as she slept, her long black hair spread over a pillow. He loved her and over the last few years had often wanted to propose to her. He'd even bought her a twenty-two carat *thali* for their wedding day. Yet whenever he opened the safe in his house, his hand floated over the heavy gold pendant and chain, then passed over it. For he couldn't forget that along the way she'd given him up to be the wife of a surgeon.

# FIRST STEPS

Mum and Dad visited a friend, leaving Kana and me with my grandparents. We were allowed to play in the front garden on our own, so long as we promised not to go into the road. I wanted to see what would happen if we were disobedient. Kana said she wasn't going to upset the grown-ups.

"Or I might not be allowed to visit you anymore."

"I don't think they'll stop you coming."

"It isn't just that. Bad Buddhists are born again as insects and worms and have to live in the ground."

Using twigs to poke the earth, we explored the front garden, under shoeflower bushes, around the Temple tree and by the gateposts.

"See. They're everywhere," she said.

"Will I be born an insect because I can't find peace?"

"No. And anyway, if you keep practising, you'll find it."

I didn't believe her. There must have been a million insects just in Appa's garden. Some of them can't have found peace either. "Can I come back as a shoeflower?"

"It has to be an animal."

"But they're so pretty. Saras melts the petals in coconut shells to make *pottus*."

"Mum makes a dot on her forehead with red lipstick. At least, she did when she lived with us."

"Do you still love her?"

"Yes. But she was only interested in her boyfriends."

She stopped talking as she remembered her mum didn't love her much. To help cheer her up, I showed her a yellow butterfly by the front gate. "Look, Kana." She smiled a little and waved to it.

We carried on digging the earth, hoping that what we found wasn't going to be anything hairy, then we made a deep hole and jumped back when a long worm wriggled out of it.

I said, "Victor says if you cut them in half, they grow into two."

"I don't believe him."

"We can ask him to cut one when we see him again."

"He's gone back to Kandy. Only Uncle Mahen is in Colombo now."

"What about our secret club?"

"We'll have to wait until he comes back."

I knew we could play Veddhas with or without Victor, and we didn't need the secret club for that, anyway. I just wished he hadn't left Colombo.

We watched the worm crawl away and didn't notice Herath come down the side garden until he was by us, carrying his clothes in a cloth bundle. He was going to spend a week in Nilgala to live like a Veddha again. He'd be away while we needed servants to look after visitors but Amma said it was important for him to be with his family. Saras' sister was going to stay with us instead to help. Their parents had died long ago and they didn't have any other relations in Colombo whose Christmas parties they could go to.

I wished Kana and I could travel with Herath to the jungle and hunt deer with a bow and arrows. We could have done dangerous things like climb down cliffs on ladders made out of plant ropes, using burning torches to scare away bees, so we could take their honey and give it to the King of Sri Lanka. We'd tug on the ropes to tell the Veddhas at the top of the cliff to pull up the pot of honey first, then to pull us up.

"Herath, will you learn the Dola Yaka [3] ceremony at Nilgala?"

"Maybe, naga."

"I think you should then you can call spirits for help before we climb rocks and trees for honey."

"I have to go or the truck will leave without me."

"Can we come with you to Nilgala?"

"Another time."

"Then can we come with you to the end of the road?"

"Rohini," Kana said. "We're not allowed."

Herath waved goodbye and went up the field side of the road. I stood by the gate and watched him, afraid a spitting cobra might come out of the grass and bite him but he walked with his head up, not looking out for snakes. Being a Veddha must have made him brave. I was his cousin on Amma's side so perhaps one day I could also walk near the field without being scared. He stopped to talk to the *kadillai* seller halfway up the road and bought a packet of *kadillai* to take on his journey. I leaned forward, jealous he was on his way to the jungle and I had to stay in Colombo. When I tried to go outside the gate to follow him, Kana pulled me back by my dress. "You promised your Amma and Appa you'd stay here." I'd only wanted to go to the top of the road, where a truck would pick up Herath and take him to his village then I could walk back on my own, show I could be responsible.

"I want to do something grown-up."

"We can. It just has to be safe."

"We're old enough to go for a walk without grown-ups."

"No."

"My mum will still love you."

"We shouldn't disobey."

"It's not disobeying, it's growing up."

Kana played with the bottom of her dress. "We shouldn't do it alone."

"We can go with the dog from the house up the road."

"Which one?"

"The one that followed Dad, Appa and me to the beach the other day."

"It has to be a big dog to look after us."

"It's a Labrador." I pointed to her shoulders. "This high."

"How will we get it to come with us?"

I couldn't believe that at last, Kana might do something dangerous. I grabbed her hand before she changed her mind. "Let's have a secret club meeting to decide."

To plan our first outing without grown-ups, I wanted to have a proper meeting in a wigwam made out of an old sari. I searched my mother's suitcase and almeira but she'd only brought new or nice clothes on holiday and she'd have been cross if I used those. Kana and I looked for my grandmother and found her lying on her bed, reading a bible. I hoped she wasn't going to read me a God and Jesus story. I didn't enjoy them, even at Sunday school.

"Amma, can I borrow an old sari?" I asked, trying not to look at her bible.

"You want to wear it?"

"We want to make a wigwam."

"Take the green one in the bottom drawer of my almeira. I kept it for you to practise wearing when you're older."

The drawer was too wide for me to open on my own. Kana had to take one handle while I pulled the other. The wood was so heavy, we nearly fell backwards. I took out a sari that was lying on top.

"This one?"

"Yes. Don't tear it."

I gave her a quick kiss, and rushed to leave before she read the bible to me. Kana stood by the bed. I thought she was going to tell Amma I tried to be disobedient in the garden. I waited by the door, hoping my friend wouldn't let me down, knowing even if she did, I'd still love her. All she did was kiss my grandmother in a shy way.

"Leave the door open, child," Amma told her. "I want to hear what you two get up to."

We made two piles on my bed using my parents' pillows and mine. They still weren't high enough for a wigwam.

"We'll have to ask Appa for his," I said.

My grandfather was lounging on his armchair in the sitting area, a newspaper over his face. He didn't move at all when I touched his arm to see if he was asleep. I lifted the paper and put my head underneath to see what he was doing. His eyes were open.

"Appa, can we borrow your pillows?"

"No."

"We'll have to talk to you if we can't play."

"Like that, is it?" He rolled up the paper, pretended to smack me with it and laughed. "Go on, take them."

We added his pillows to the piles on the bed and spread Amma's sari on top. The wigwam was just high enough for us to sit under and have a meeting. We talked fast about our first outing without grown-ups and came up with a plan for making friends with the dog from up the road, then we decided that the more we did on our own, the more the grown-ups would have to let us do without them, like living in the jungle in a Veddha village or going to toy shops by ourselves to spend pocket money. After we'd run out of ideas and things to do, we stopped talking and realised it was dark and stuffy in the wigwam.

"I'm hot," I said.

"Me too, and I can't breathe."

Trying not to get caught up in Amma's sari, we folded the long piece of material as best we could and went to return it to her. Appa was speaking on the phone in the sitting area, with his back to us. "No, Sohan, you can't visit us now. I don't want any more trouble while Nathan is here. You two obviously can't patch it up so come and see us after they've returned to England."

"What's happening, Appa?" I asked when he finished the call.

"What? Oh. It's just your Uncle Sohan being a nuisance."

He was frowning and didn't ask why I was carrying a crushed sari. Amma was fast asleep so we opened the drawer quietly and put her sari back. When we were in my room again, I shut the door to talk to Kana.

"What do you think Appa was talking about?"

"Uncle Sohan must be trying to make your mum his girlfriend."

"I won't let him. I'll bite his knee and you can help."

"Buddhists aren't supposed to fight."

"If you only pull his leg while I bite it, you won't be fighting."

"I might not be here to help you. *Thathi* won't let me cut school so I have to go back on Monday."

"I'm going to miss you."

"Me too."

"Let's do something special before you go back."

"Like what?"

"We can go for a walk with the dog."

"My dad's police friend told him there could be riots any day."

"We can take a look first and see if it's safe."

Appa was on the front veranda, wearing a *verti*. He could have worn trousers instead of the white sarong and shawl, but sometimes he liked to be Sri Lankan while drinking his afternoon cup of tea. He blew on it to cool it down and sat alone, enjoying the quiet. Kana and I walked past him, pretended he wasn't there, and managed to reach the bottom veranda step before he asked, "Where do you two think you're going?"

"To the gate," I said. "We won't go out."

"That's correct. You won't."

We poked our heads past the gate pillars, looked left and right but I couldn't see as much from there as I could have from the grass pavement. I felt Appa watching so didn't dare put a foot outside the garden and bent forwards to get a better look. Kana grabbed me from the back to stop me falling over. The road was empty, no cars, *kadillai* or ice *palaam* sellers, only an old man with a walking stick on his way to the beach.

"I can't see any riots," I said.

"They start suddenly."

"Have you ever seen any?"

"I wasn't born when they happened before."

"If there are any again, they'll be the last ones."

"How do you know, Rohini?"

"Buddha told me."

"He doesn't make promises like that."

"He felt sorry for me because I can't find peace so he told me a secret. He asked Jesus to talk to me about it."

"I thought you spoke to God."

"God's on a package holiday in Spain, so Jesus does his talking while he's away. What do rioters do?"

"They fight in the road and start fires."

I remembered how Mum's family got frightened and ran away in the last riots. "We don't have to go on our own for a walk yet. Though I'd still like to make friends with the dog."

"Me too. Do you think your Appa will help us like we talked about in our pow-wow?"

"Let's ask him."

My grandfather was still on the veranda, sipping his tea made with warm milk.

"Appa," I asked in a nice voice, "can you take us for a walk?"

"To the beach?"

"Up the road, the other way."

"And what is up the road the other way that could be of interest to you two?"

I opened my mouth to tell a lie but couldn't. "We want to get to know the dog that followed us."

He thought about it. "Why not? It won't hurt for you two to have something else to guard you."

Kana and I looked at each other. We hadn't thought it would be this easy. Appa picked up his cup and saucer and walked to the dining table. We followed behind, in case he disappeared without taking us out. He turned round and bumped into us.

"My God. I've grown two tails. And if you want to go out with me, you won't tell my wife I took the Lord's name in vain."

"I promise," I said.

"And me."

He changed into a shirt and pair of trousers and we set off, Kana and I walking along the grass pavement on the left of the road. "You'll fall down the ditch if you get too near," he said. We carried on walking where we were. I couldn't see any snakes in the field but didn't want to take a chance one might be close by. "That reminds me," Appa said, "of what your father and Sohan got up to when they were about your age."

"Dad was naughty?"

"Oh yes. They were on a train, going through Jaffna. They waited for the train to go slowly then when they saw a villager, they opened the window and shouted, *pambu, pambu*."

"It means snake," Kana told me.

"Poor chap pulled up his sarong and ran."

Kana and I looked at each other, giggled and ran ahead, shouting *pambu* at my grandfather. He pulled up his trouser legs and chased us. We ran away from him, laughing so loudly that people came out of their houses to see what was going on. I thought he was going to tell us to be quiet but he waved to everybody and carried on chasing. I'd never had so much fun with him before. We ran up the road until he shouted at us to stop by a big white house and wait for him. Through iron gates we saw rose bushes, their branches sticking out all over the place.

"Why doesn't Uncle Selva take care of his garden?" I asked Appa when he got to the house. "The ground is full of leaves and rose petals."

He was out of puff and I had to wait for him to get his breath back before I got an answer.

"My God. I haven't run. So far. For so long. His wife passed away. A few years ago. He'll take an interest. When he's ready."

"Are the gates closed to keep the dog in?"

"And to keep out. Those Colombo women. Who want to marry him."

I wondered what had made Uncle Selva so frightened of ladies he wanted to shut them out, and thought his wife must have scolded him like Amma.

A tall, thin man in sarong and *banyan* came down the veranda steps and opened the gates for us. "Roshan. I say, come in, *machan*. Don't stand there like a stranger."

"Long time no see, Selva."

They hugged and patted each other on the back for ages then Uncle called a maid to serve drinks and shorteats. She hurried over with a tray of passion fruit squash, *vadai* and napkins. The drinks were warm but I didn't ask for ice in case Uncle thought I was rude.

The dog came and lay down by Kana and me. We tried to see if it was a boy or a girl by tickling it until it rolled over then we had a good look between its legs. She stayed on her back looking at the food. We fed her pieces of *vadai* and let her lick our hands after we finished eating. Mum would have scolded us for doing that but we knew Appa wouldn't tell her what we'd done.

Uncle asked, "What brings you here, Roshan? Not that you are not welcome, of course."

"My granddaughter and her friend want to make friends with your dog."

"Ah, yes. Good. Shelala doesn't get as much exercise as she needs so it will be fun for her also."

"Can we come here to play with her?" Kana asked.

"Yes, child. Whenever you want. If I am not here, the maid will let you in."

Appa shook his head. "If you don't mind, Selva, I'll be happier if the girls are at my place where I can keep an eye on them."

"Of course," Uncle said, looking at my grandfather. "The way things are in Colombo and all. Just give a ring and I will ask one of the servants to bring her to your house."

"Can she come now?" I asked.

"Take her. I'll send someone for her before dark."

Kana stroked Shelala. "Her fur's got twigs and leaves in it."

"Remove them if you want. I'll give you a brush."

Appa said to wait until we got back home to groom her. He told Uncle, "It'll keep them out of mischief at my place."

We finished our drinks and said thank you and goodbye to Uncle. Appa followed behind while Kana and I ran down the road with Shelala between us.

When Mum and Dad returned from visiting their friend, Kana and I waved to them then carried on taking turns to brush Shelala's fur. We only stopped after she went round in circles, chasing her tail. My grandmother looked at me over her crochet when I went inside to ask for a pair of scissors.

"Honestly, child. Now what do you want to do?"

"Give Shelala a haircut."

Appa looked up from his late afternoon cup of tea. "Selva will stop you from playing with his dog if you return her in a sorry state."

"No scissors," Amma said. "Selva will cut her fur if he needs to."

Mum whispered to Dad as I went back to the garden. "How long before Rohini asks for a dog in London?"

I hadn't thought of that. I was already hoping for a palmyrah tree for my birthday and wondered if they'd get me a dog before then. It could look after me the evenings they went out so they wouldn't have to bother with babysitters.

I ran back in. "Can I?"

"Can you what?" Dad said and smiled.

I jumped up and down. "A dog. Can I have one?"

"They need a lot of care and exercise."

"I'll do it."

"We'll see."


When Herath came back from Nilgala, he didn't want to talk much to Kana or me. He wouldn't tell us what he did in the jungle or if he went hunting or anything. All he said was that he had to fix the broken fence in the back yard. We followed him around anyway until Appa told us off.

"Leave him be. His heart is with his people especially when he's just returned from his village."

"Then can we go with Uncle Selva when he takes Shelala for a walk?"

"Another day. Selva isn't ready to look after two imps."

Kana and I had to play on my bed. The sun went behind clouds and the grey sky made the room darker. I felt like I was back in England and switched on the light but it wasn't the same as sunshine. I hoped it wasn't going to rain on Uncle and Shelala while they were out. Kana took my Russian dolls out of each other, lined them up on the pillow then put them back in again. "They're pretty," she said. I pretended to read my book while watching her. She was always happy and I would have been too if Mum and Dad treated me like a grown-up. When the clouds floated away and the sky turned blue, I moved along the bed to sit in a sunbeam.

"We need special help to make Colombo safe, Kana, or we'll never be allowed out alone."

"Help from God?"

"He's no good, and Jesus isn't either. They let the last riots happen."

"What about Buddha?"

"I'm saving my Buddha wishes for later."

"Then what can we do, Rohini?"

"We could ask the yaku to stop the Troubles. We'll have to dance to make them appear."

"We can do the leaf dance."

"That's to have fun. It isn't talking to Veddha spirits and angels."

Herath came in, carrying a laundry bag to collect clothes for the dhobi man.

"Can you teach us Kiri Koraha, please?" I asked him.

"Only a shaman should do it, naga."

"Then what can we do? We want to talk to the yaku."

"The answer will come to you."

I didn't know what he was talking about or why he wouldn't teach me how to be a shaman. After he'd gone out of the room, Kana said, "Calling yaku might be like finding peace." But I'd never been able to find that. I tried hard to think of a way to stop the riots and just couldn't. By evening, I still hadn't come up with an idea. Kana was thinking hard too and when we went to the table for dinner, she clapped her hands and whispered in my ear. "I know what we can do. We can make up a Veddha dance to say thank you for the food like you do with Grace. Then we can talk to the yaku when they show up to watch us dancing." I jumped up and down, whispering back, "We can dance round our plates like Herath does in Kiri Koraha."

After Saras put the last dish of food on the table and went back to the kitchen, we served ourselves rice and chicken *porial* with *keerai*, making sure we each took the same amount. Kana accidentally served herself a spoonful more rice than I had, so we shared the extra. Dad looked at us.

"What are you two up to?"

"We want to do something," I told him.

"Which is?"

"Can I ask Amma instead?"

"Do you want to say a Buddhist prayer?"

"No, Daddy."

Amma told him off for making a fuss. "Let the child decide her religion."

"I think you're forgetting Buddhists were involved in the last riots."

"Son, more of them helped the Tamils than were against. What do you want to do, Rohini?"

I looked away from my father and wanted him to stop looking at me. "Kana and I want to do a dance to say thank you to the yaku for our food."

"That's why we say Grace," he said.

I was doing my best to help grown-ups stop the fights and he was spoiling it for me. I put my hands together, like in a prayer. "Please Daddy?"

He took a deep breath and let it out again slowly. "All right, then."

We got down from the table and took our plates to the sitting area.

"What the - ?" he said.

Appa patted him on the shoulder. "Let them get it over and done with. Besides, this should be good to watch."

We put our plates on the floor.

"Put your food on the coffee table, girls," Mum said. "I don't want insects crawling over it."

I wished she wouldn't keep telling us what to do but Kana picked up her plate so I did the same.

"What shall we do now?" I asked my friend.

"Let's do the Twist."

Although we didn't have music to dance to, we twisted like Uncle Theo at Tara Aunty's party. We went down, all the way to the ground then up again, then down on one leg. The grown-ups turned to watch us. They must have swallowed food without chewing and choked on it because they kept coughing. After we twisted up and down a few times, I looked up but couldn't see any yaku or angels. I wondered if they only flew down from Heaven during the day, though Herath sometimes danced at night for them so I knew they could see in the dark. I twisted up and down again. All I could see above was the white ceiling.

"It's not working," I told Kana.

"Let's try the *Baila*."

With our hands behind our backs, we danced without falling over but still couldn't see anything. I was starting to think Sri Lanka would never be safe enough for us to go out alone for a walk when Kana had a brainwave.

"Are all yaku men?" she asked.

I didn't know if all of them were but nodded anyway.

"We could wiggle our bottoms," she said, "like Tara Aunty does when she wants men to look at her."

I clapped my hands. "And we can make up a song for them."

"When I skip, I sing boom di di boom."

"Are there any other words?"

"No. Just that."

We sang boom di di boom over and over and wiggled our bottoms as much as we could. We danced fast, like Herath did in Kiri Koraha, and looked around the room for angels and yaku. I wasn't sure which dance they'd like best so did a bit of the Twist as well, in case they missed it before.

Saras and Herath came in from the back of the house and watched from the dining area. Saras wiped her hands on her sarong. My lovely ayah had left her meal and washed her hands to come and look at us. Herath folded his arms and smiled. With the whole house watching Kana and me, I was sure the Veddha spirits would appear.

Appa was eating too quickly and coughed a lot. Amma had to thump him on the back to stop him choking to death. "My God," he said, reaching for a glass of water. "I've never seen anything like it."

"Kana, I think Appa's seen yaku."

"I can't see anything."

"Maybe they only appear to grown-ups, to scold them for rioting."

She wiggled her bottom quicker and looked around the room. "I wish I knew where they were."

"They must be over us. Let's wave to them."

We raised our hands above our heads and waved at the air. "Hello. We're over here."

"Now I've seen everything," my grandmother said.

"I told you, Kana. Amma's seen them too."

I'd have liked yaku to show themselves to me as well, but was happy they'd come down to Earth from Heaven and seen us dance. I was sure they'd stop the riots or at least make them the last ones ever. My legs were shaking from going up and down while doing the Twist so I told Kana we could stop dancing. She kept going for a little longer and waved above her then stopped too.

Our work done, we took our food to the dining table. Saras and

Herath were still by the back veranda, smiling. My parents and grandparents hadn't finished their meal and still had their hands over their plates because they'd stopped eating to watch us. They must have been proud we'd done something grown-up and made yaku appear. Not caring that our dinner was cold, we said, "No thank you," when Amma asked if we wanted Saras to warm it up.

Even though Kana and I were supposed to spend the weekend together, Uncle Theo picked her up that evening. Her grandmother in Matara had broken her ankle and wanted all her family to make a fuss about it. Monday was the start of Kana's school so I had to wait a whole week to see her.

"It's a long time until I can play again with Kana," I told Dad.

"Perhaps Uncle will let you see her in the afternoons, after she's done her homework."

"Can we pick her up from school?"

"I don't see why not. When we're free."

At least I had something to look forward to, but it wasn't the same as playing with her every day. I felt like my holiday had ended.

One day, Mum and Dad went out to visit friends and Amma had a late afternoon nap. I sat on the front veranda with my grandfather, both of us reading books. We were waiting for the sun to set so we could watch the sky change colour.

"Will it turn pink or orange today, Appa?"

"Hard to tell, small one."

"But what do you think?"

He put his book down and looked up at the sky. "Orange."

I didn't care if he was right or wrong. I just wanted to know what my Appa thought.

A small bird landed on the floor, looking for crumbs to eat, so I fed it a piece of *vadai* I'd left on my plate. I liked being out there on a hot day, next to my grandfather. I could smell the shoeflower tree at the front and the only noise was a dog barking far away. I felt as cosy as when I'm snuggled in bed at night while it's raining outside.

I'd just started reading my book again when a neighbour's servant jumped over the garden wall and ran to us. "*Boru kakul* is coming," he said then ran to the next house. He kicked up a lot of dust in the garden as he ran. Appa shut his book.

"Rohini, come inside with me. Quickly."

"Are the riots happening?"

"Nothing like that, child."

"I'll get your house keys."

"No need to lock up. We'll just shut the doors."

"Shall we wake Amma so she knows what's happening?"

"We'll leave her alone."

I followed him as he hurried to the servants' quarters, calling for Saraswathie. "*Boru kakul* is nearby," he told her when she came out of the kitchen. Saras wiped her hands on her sarong then ran into the bathroom.

"What's she doing, Appa?"

"Closing the window shutters," he said as he hurried to the other side of the house. "Help her by doing your room, while I do over here."

I tried and tried to close the shutters in my room but couldn't line up the wood. Dad told me it had been like that when he was a child too. I wished Appa had fixed it long ago. Using both hands, I lifted one shutter to meet the other one but didn't have a free hand to do the bolts. "Saras, Saras," I called. She hurried in and helped me.

"Rohini," my grandfather called from the sitting area. "Come quickly. Stay on the sofa," he said, walking away. "And don't make a noise."

"Where are you going?"

"To the side room off the front veranda. I don't want any noise out front so you'd better be quiet."

"Will you stay with me, Saras?"

"I have to go the servants' quarters, kunju, to look after the back of the house."

They left me on the sofa and disappeared out of the room. After Appa shut the front door with a loud click, I heard his footsteps go along the front veranda to the side room then couldn't hear him anymore. The whole house went quiet and I didn't know what was going to happen. I couldn't even hear the chickens cluck in their coop. They must have hidden too. I was scared to be alone and scared to move in case the rattan seat creaked and a burglar heard me. He might have burst in from one of the bedrooms and grabbed me. I didn't know which room he'd jump out of. I wished Amma hadn't sent Herath to the market. He'd have sat with me and looked after me. I nearly ran to be with my grandmother in her bedroom but she might have got cross if I woke her from a nap. My heart thumped. I looked up at the picture of Jesus. He looked worried. I didn't think he was going to take care of me because I was praying to Buddha more than God.

A man outside shouted in Sinhalese, saying the same words again and again. He sounded like he was down the road, then his voice got louder until he was right outside our house. I thought he'd break in, snatch or hurt me. A tiny caterpillar crawled along the side of the wall and hid in a small crack. I tried to pull the sofa forward so I could hide behind it as well but it was too heavy for me. There was nowhere else to go in the sitting and dining areas. I got scared, forgot what Appa said about staying in the room and ran out of the front door to go to him. When I got to the veranda, I suddenly stopped. A man on stilts in the garden smiled at me, showing red teeth that made him look like the devil.

"Appa, Appa," I shouted.

He didn't come to rescue me so I shouted again.

"Appa, Appa."

He came stomping out of his room, had a row with the man and yelled at a small boy who was trying to sneak down the side garden, past the Temple tree. He shouted at them again then gave the man some money and waved at them to go away, keeping an eye on them as they went out of the gates to the next house.

"I told you to stay inside," he said to me.

I started crying. "I was frightened."

He sat down and let me sit next to him, while he put an arm around me. "I suppose I shouldn't have left you on your own. Do you remember what a *boru kakul* is?"

I wiped my eyes and shook my head.

"It means false legs. They're crooks. If you don't shut the doors and windows, they get someone, probably the boy he had with him, to steal from the back of the house while they keep you talking at the front. And if they know the master is in they never go away and come back, day after day, to beg for money."

"I didn't know."

"All right, all right. Come. Let's tell Saraswathie they've gone."

Afterwards, he let me follow him around until Amma woke up. She drank a glass of warm water then let me sit with her the rest of the afternoon and didn't get cross with me once. When my parents returned, I ran to my mother and pushed my head into her sari.

"We were burgled in the riots," I said.

"What?"

Appa rolled his eyes. "*Boru kakul*. No riots."

"Did they get anything?"

"Nothing. Small one got a scare and I gave him some money. That's all."

My father patted my head. "Let's hope they don't come back again."

I had nightmares that night because I thought the *boru kakul* was in the front garden, so Dad asked Uncle Theo if I could stay over at his house.

The next day, Uncle picked me up after Kana came out of school and took me to their place. I had to play with toys in her room while she did her sums and spelling homework in the dining room. When she finished, she ran upstairs.

"We can play together now," she said.

"The *boru kakul* came to Appa's house yesterday."

"Did you pray to Buddha?"

I shook my head and looked at her.

"You'll feel better if you find peace," she said.

"I don't know where to look."

"Do what I do."

I copied the way she sat, legs crossed, hands on my knees with palms facing up then shut my eyes tight.

"Think about your breathing," she said.

I started breathing loudly.

"Now make your mind go empty."

"I've emptied it."

I waited for her to tell me what to do next, but she'd gone quiet. I opened my eyes a bit and peeped at her. Her face was still, as if she was asleep. I thought she'd forgotten about me. "Where are you looking for peace?" I asked, in case it was in the room and I hadn't seen it.

Kana sighed. "It's in your head."

"I've emptied mine."

She jumped down and took a doll out of her toy chest. "You have to practise at home."

Even if she couldn't show me peace, she let me sleep with her and hugged me all night. In the morning, I wasn't afraid the *boru kakul* might be in the garden and little by little, I stopped being frightened of him then I forgot about him.

I still missed seeing Kana while she was at school so Mum and Dad let me ring her every day to say goodnight. Sometimes the exchange was busy, I couldn't get through and had to wait to speak to her the next day, and then we couldn't have a long chat because she went to bed early to be up in time for school.

"Dad, can you talk to Uncle Theo and see if he'll let Kana cut school? We can all go to Sigiriya and see the frescoes."

"No chance."

"It'll be good for her."

"I'll see if she can come at the weekend, but I think Uncle is taking her to see her mother."

I tried to imagine Jyoti's face. I'd never seen photos of her and thought she must have been ugly with black teeth.

"Dad, I think we should take Kana and Uncle Theo to London to live with us."

"I've already suggested it to him. He says he'd rather be here."


My holiday stopped being fun. I didn't even enjoy the parties we went to because Kana had to visit her grandmother instead of coming with us. Once, I shut myself in my room and tried to meditate, sitting cross-legged on the bed the way my friend did. When peace didn't come, I squeezed my eyes tight to force it into my head. Nothing happened even though I did my best. So I gave up.

"Amma," I said, showing her the statue of Buddha she'd given me, "this is no good. He doesn't like living in a Christian house."

"Child, you may be right."

I couldn't believe it. I'd just been rude to my grandmother about the gift she'd given me and she was telling me I was right. She took the statue and closed her hands around it, as if she were praying.

"There was a time when we used to respect each others' religions. Now we fight and use different gods as an excuse for making trouble."

I didn't know what she was talking about. I kissed her cheek anyway, because she seemed sad. She gave Buddha back to me and I put him on my bedside table.


Sohan set up a meeting in Pettah market, to pay a bribe that would keep his accomplice's family in rice, *paripoo* and ghee for a week, and if they could stretch it that far, a couple of meals with fish or chicken; for Tara and him, it would have bought a single dinner at a hotel near Galle Face Green.

He arrived early for the appointment and blended into the hustle and bustle of the indoor market. Stall holders ignored him while they invited passing servant boys and girls to feel their produce for ripeness. Leaning against a wall, he watched money changing hands and baskets being filled with mangosteens, snake beans, *goraka* and green, red and yellow plantains. Then among the raised voices of market trade, someone called his name. He inched round, as if he had all the time in the world and the meeting meant little to him. His accomplice was a good head shorter with bloodshot eyes, no doubt caused by a night of drinking *toddy* and playing cards. The man's khaki shirt was creased and smelt like he hadn't changed it for days.

Before Sohan handed over a wad of rupee notes, he stepped back from the chap's stale breath and looked him in the eye. It wasn't too late to walk away from his plan. He'd still have to pass over some cash for the other man's troubles, but this wasn't about money. The fellow stretched out a greedy hand and nodded at a police jeep. "My driver is waiting." Sohan hesitated before passing the bribe into a warm, moist palm. The chap slid the notes into his trouser pocket with the ease of someone who had been bought before, saying, "I will take care of business for you." Without a backward glance, he slipped into a passing crowd and towards his vehicle.

Sohan watched the plans he had sculpted, walk away and out of his control. Worse still, there was nothing he could do about it. Then again, he'd thought it through, step by step, he had nothing to be concerned about. All his accomplice had to do was keep his side of the bargain. Besides, what was the worst that could happen? What were the chances of it happening?

Struck by fear, he raced after the fellow, bumping into market traders and their customers as he ran, all the while shouting he'd changed his mind, he wanted to do this Uncle Alagar's way. "Come back. Come back. Come back." He'd never know if the fellow didn't hear him or couldn't care less. Either way, he was too late. The jeep sped off and disappeared into a mass of buses, cars and tuk-tuks, carrying with it the greatest risk he'd ever taken.

Mum and Dad went out to play tennis, leaving me with my grandparents. When I was bored with reading my book and if nobody was looking, I bothered Herath while he was sweeping floors. He didn't mind me following him around except when Appa caught me chatting about nothing.

"Rohini," my grandfather said, "what have you been told about interfering with servants?"

"I'm learning about Veddhas."

"All right, but don't keep him long."

"Come, Herath. Let's sit and talk."

Appa went to the sitting area by a window to read a paper. The room was a bit dark even with the sun shining through the doors and windows. I took Herath to the dining table and sat at the top in my grandfather's chair. I wasn't allowed to be in charge during meals but nobody minded me sitting there at other times. Herath was on my right by the back veranda and chickens clucked behind him in the courtyard. On the outside corridor by the kitchen, Saras talked to the rice-pounding woman who'd made flour for my grandparents since Dad was at school. Her long pole smashed rice with a soft thud and ground it into flour for *kolkotta* and *stringhoppers*.

"There are two types of Veddha, remember?" Herath said. "Gam Veddhas who are farmers and live in villages, growing *chena* and crops."

"I forgot. What's the other kind?"

I already knew the answer, I just couldn't think of anything else to say. Appa was watching us through his newspaper, his eyes never leaving me.

"I am a Gal Veddha," Herath said. "We live in rocks and the forest and hunt with bows and arrows."

"Like the Red Indians."

"Veddhas are different."

"How many scalps have you got?"

"We hunt for food, not people."

"Can you show me your bow and arrows?"

Appa shook his paper.

Herath stood up, saying, "I have to sweep the kitchen."

My grandfather called me. I hurried over to him. "Yes, Appa?"

"Gal Veddhas don't hunt much these days. Their hunting grounds have been stolen from them."

"Okay. Can I play in the garden?"

"Go ahead but - "

"- don't go on the road."

I ran outside and headed for the Temple tree at the side of the house. Putting one foot on the trunk, I grabbed a thick branch and pulled myself up, climbing higher than my bedroom window. A few flowers fell on the ground from where I'd disturbed them. I looked around the tree, couldn't see anything in reach then spotted a thick, strong branch. I leaned over to pull it down, but couldn't hold it steady. It flew up, the leaves flicking my face as it sprung up.

"Ouch."

"Rohini, what are you doing?" Appa shouted from inside the house.

"Nothing."

He came outside but didn't see me up the tree. I stayed quiet, thinking he might go back in.

"Good God," he said. "How did you get up that high?"

"How did you know I was here?"

"This many petals on the ground mean there's a child in the tree. Today, you. When he was your age, your father. What are you doing there?"

"I wanted a branch to make a bow and arrows."

"Come down, child. I'll buy you a set."

"I want to make my own."

"Down. Now."

When I was halfway down, he held out his hand to me. I didn't take any notice of him and jumped to the ground on my own, like a Real Veddha.

"I have to make arrows out of this tree, Appa. Toy ones don't have points, they have rubber ends."

"Exactly."

We went inside and told Amma we were going to Cargills in Fort, to buy me a bow and arrows. I thought she was going to scold my grandfather for spoiling me but she picked up her crochet hook and ball of cotton to carry on with a half-made doily. She looked at me as if she wanted to give me a crochet lesson. She'd already taught me to knit the year before. I ran onto the veranda and said I'd wait for Appa there. I heard them laughing then he came out and told me to get in the Mercedes. He let me sit in the front and drove slowly to Fort, waiting for people to cross roads.

"Go fast like Dad," I said.

"If I have an accident with you in the car, your grandmother will give me hell."

Parking in Sri Lanka was easy. You didn't have to worry about meters, yellow lines or rushing out of a shop before a traffic warden gave you a ticket, you left the car where you wanted and gave a poor man money to look after it. We left ours outside Cargills on the main road. The shop was old with wooden counters, not like Selfridges that looked brand new. It was much smaller too. I really wanted to carve my hunting tools out of a tree branch. I wasn't allowed to use sharp knives but Mum and Dad would have to let me if I was going to cut wood.

"Are you sure they'll have bows and arrows, Appa?"

"If it's anywhere in Colombo, it'll be here." He looked around the toy section. "Good. We're lucky, there are two sets left."

"I can make a better one."

He held back a smile and told me to choose one. The plastic wrappings were dusty, not like toys in England that came in new boxes.

"If I practise with these, can Herath make me real ones from a tree?"

"When you're older."

"When will that be? I'm growing up every day."

"Hurry, girl, or Amma will think we're lost."

Before the end of my holiday, I was going to show him and all the others just how grown-up I was, so they'd see it was safe for me to live in Sri Lanka again.

"Thank you for buying this for me. Is it next year's birthday present?"

He laughed. "Call it a special extra."

He paid the man, gave me the bag with my gift then another man came to see our receipt and make sure we'd paid. I held my hunting tools to my chest. I was going to be the best Veddha ever. On the way home, Appa let me sit in the front of the car again so long as I promised not to touch the handbrake or gear stick. I wasn't going to do anything like that. I was more interested in my bow and arrows, even if I wasn't allowed to open the packet until we got back to the house.

We'd just driven past Galle Face Green when we had to stop. Right in front of us were police cars and past them, the air was black.

"Where's the smoke coming from, Appa? There aren't any buses or tuk-tuks."

"That place over there is on fire."

I stood up and followed his finger to where a crowd of people were standing. A little smoke got into the car and burned my nose so my grandfather wound down the window to let clean air in. He saw his policeman friend, Joseph Mendis, and called him over to talk. They spoke in Sinhalese then Appa turned left and took us home through back roads. He didn't say very much on the way. Soon as he stopped in the carport, I ran out to show Amma my bow and arrows.

"Did your grandfather drive carefully?" she asked.

I nodded. "And on the way back we saw a fire." I ran to the servants' quarters to show Herath my new toy. He was in the kitchen, eating a late lunch. "Look. I've got hunting tools."

"Naga wants to be a Veddha."

I felt so proud and was going to do my best to be just like him.

I spent the rest of the afternoon hunting and firing arrows at the trunk of the Temple tree, while my grandfather sat on the front veranda, drinking tea and reading a book. I accidentally knocked off a few pieces of bark and hid them on a branch so Amma wouldn't notice they'd fallen off. She came out after her afternoon nap, saw what I was doing and told me to respect a tree of worship. "Aim for the garden wall," she said. "And keep an eye on her," she told my grandfather. I shot at the wall but sometimes missed so the arrows went over the top and into next door's garden. A servant boy brought the first two back then told me his *mahathya* had asked if I could stop playing for the day.

I ran up the veranda steps. "Appa, can I shoot at your chickens? I promise not to hit them."

He lifted the cup of tea to his mouth, blew on it to cool it down, then took a sip. All I could see over the top of the cup were his eyes. He slowly licked tea off his lips as if he had forgotten I was waiting.

"And you expect the answer to be yes?"

"Hunters need to practise."

"I'll move my car. Aim at the carport."

I shot arrows at the holes in the patterned bricks and was still practising when my grandmother told me to come inside.

"A few more minutes, Amma. Please?"

Mum and Dad came home just then. It was getting dark and they definitely wouldn't have let me stay outside so I followed them in. I showed them my bow and arrows.

"What's this?" Dad said as he took them from me.

"I'm now a Veddha." I grabbed my hunting tools back, ran to the door, turned round and aimed for him.

"Not inside, girl," Appa said.

For a short while I stood as I was, ready to fire my bow and arrow. Dad sometimes let me be naughty but it wasn't our house and Amma was watching. Herath and Saras started bringing dinner to the table.

"Tomorrow, I'm going to hunt you down," I told my father.

"You bet. Now come and eat."

I'd run about so much in the sun I started to feel tired during dinner and my eyes kept closing after I'd only eaten a few mouthfuls. Dad helped me wash and brush my teeth then carried me to bed. I didn't mind having an early night because he let me sleep next to my bow and arrows. As I nodded off, Appa talked to the others about the fire we'd seen.

"Joseph Mendis was there as we drove past. He said the police knew a Tamil shop was going to be burnt and they did nothing about it."


The next day, we were all sitting in the shade on the front veranda, drinking passion fruit juice when Mum asked Dad to get her a piece of love cake from a shop on Galle Road. He was going down the steps when I saw my chance. I aimed to miss because I didn't want to hurt him but accidentally shot him on the bottom. I stood laughing then ran to Mum as he pretended to chase me.

"I'll get you later," he said and went up the garden and out the gate. When he came back, he'd forgotten about being fired at and was eating an ice *palaam* in a paper cone. He'd also brought one back for me.

Mum put down the newspaper she was reading and said to nobody, "There are only six thousand Veddhas left in Anuradhapura. Much less if you count those who survive by hunting and fishing."

"Herath is a Gal Veddha," I told her.

"You've been busy."

"I'm learning about Sri Lanka."

"You should know as much as you can about your culture," Appa said.

"Herath's just finished sweeping."

He laughed. "All right, go."

I ran to the kitchen where Herath was chatting to Saras. He said he'd come in a minute to the dining table to give me a lesson about Veddhas. I brought my bow and arrows and sat in Appa's chair, swinging my legs. Herath sat on my right, by the back veranda. The sun shone behind his hair and he looked like the picture of Jesus in the sitting area. He put his arms on the table, like he always did to give me lessons. I touched the teardrop birthmark on his hand. I wanted one like it too and when nobody was looking, I was going to colour one on me with a black felt pen.

He began his story. "I'm going to tell you how my people came to live in Sri Lanka, a long time ago."

"How long?"

"Thousands of years. Before Buddhism . . ."

I'd never counted that high so it must have been a lot.

". . . my people walked here from India."

"You can walk on the sea?"

"Naga, you must let me finish then ask questions."

"Okay."

"It was mostly land then. We are talked about in the Mahawamsa as ghosts."

I touched his arm. "I can feel you. You can't be a ghost."

"What they meant was we lived in the forest and we'd come and go without anyone knowing we'd been there. Many years later in India, a lion fell in love with a princess. They married and had two children."

I giggled. "You're pulling my leg. Lions can't marry people."

He winked. "It's true. The lion and princess had a very bad grandson, Vijaya, who was banished from India. He and seven hundred of his friends were sent away from their homeland."

"Where did they go?"

"To Sri Lanka, where Vijaya married one of my people."

"The ghosts?"

"Yes. Their children became Sinhalese and Veddhas."

I'd been good and listened quietly without asking questions so felt I could ask one then.

"When did Red Indians come here?"

"They didn't."

"So how do Veddhas know about bows and arrows?"

My grandmother came onto the back veranda and looked at us. "You can tell her more tomorrow, Herath. Saraswathie is working alone."

"A few more minutes, Amma, please?"

"Tomorrow," she said and took Herath away to the kitchen before he'd finished his story. I slid off my chair and ran to complain to my grandfather.

"I was learning and Amma stopped me."

"Saras has a bad headache. She needs help with the cooking today."

"Then will you tell me more about Veddhas?"

"Herath should. It's the history of his people."

I remembered what my mother said about Appa being rich and not having a TV in the house because he liked to live simply. "I think you can afford to pay for another cook to help."

He messed up my hair. "Your grandmother likes to make your meals."

"Why doesn't Saras have a husband to look after her?"

"The man she was engaged to died."

My poor ayah. She should have been married and had children but only had me to love her. I wanted Herath to carry on helping her so even though she was feeling better the next day, I decided to wait until later in my holiday for another of his lessons.

Mum and Dad took me to meet aunts and uncles even if there weren't children for me to play with because they were at school. I'd sit quietly on a sofa, picking cashew nuts out of *murukku* and reading my book. I was missing Kana loads. One evening, I rang her without asking Appa first if I could use his phone.

Uncle Theo answered and said, "She's gone to bed, darling."

"I haven't seen her for ages. Can I go to school with her one day?"

Dad took the phone from me, patted my bottom and told me to run along. He laughed and joked with Uncle then called me after he finished the call.

"Am I in trouble?" I asked.

"Not at all. Kana is going to sleep here Saturday night."

"Yeahhh."

"Rohini, is there something you want to tell me?" Appa asked.

"Sorry. I'll ask if I want to use the phone again."

Uncle rang to say he was leaving his place and would be with us in ten minutes to drop off Kana and pick up Dad and Appa for cricket. I stood by the front gate and looked down the road for them. The sky was a light grey so I wasn't sure if it was just a sea breeze that was making palm trees sway or if it was the start of monsoon rains. It didn't matter anyway. I was going to see my friend again and for a whole weekend. When her dad's car came down the road, I ran into the garden and up the veranda steps. As soon as they parked in the front, Kana jumped out and we hugged each other.

Uncle Theo asked Appa, "Are we going to the cricket in your Merc or my Austin?"

"If I'm coming, we are not going in your car. Red is for hooligans."

"I thought you'd say that. Couldn't resist asking though."

If my grandfather hadn't been excited about going to watch cricket, he'd have scolded Uncle for playing a joke on him. Instead, he said, "I've invited Selva too. He doesn't go out much since his wife died."

"The more the merrier."

Shelala came down the road with Uncle Selva. She ran around Kana and me, wagging her tail fast.

Amma's arthritis was playing up and Saras had gone down with a fever so Mum stayed at home with them instead of going to the cricket like she was supposed to. Dad gave her a quick kiss on the mouth. "Are you sure? I can get someone else to look in on them."

"You know I can't leave them when they need me."

"All right. We'll be back early evening."

He started the engine and drove off. After they'd gone, Kana and I ran about in the garden with Shelala. I heard the bristles on Herath's brush scratch the back veranda as he swept. He'd clean the kitchen next.

"Shall we do it now, Kana?"

"Do what?"

"Go for a walk on our own with Shelala."

"Your mum will stop us."

"She's in the kitchen with Amma. Saras is having a nap and Herath is at the back."

"It's not safe."

"There can't be any riots or Appa wouldn't have gone out."

"We shouldn't."

"We won't go far. Just to the beach."

Carrying a bottle of water and drinking bowl for Shelala, and my bow and arrows in case the Troubles started while we were on our walk, we sneaked out of the front gate.

# TAKING CHANCES

Sohan took a risk going to the beach by Perth Avenue, sitting on the same flat-topped boulder he'd sat on in his youth, facing the ocean while sea spray caressed his cheeks and lips. He fancied a swim to cool down but not only did currents in those parts carry away the strongest swimmers, there was a hidden drop beyond the shoreline that would suck him in. If he wanted to plunge into waves, he'd have to travel south to Mount Lavinia. Unwilling to move from his boyhood refuge, he sprawled on the warm rock and mulled over his plan to resolve the quarrel with Nathan. His scheme was still in place, even though he'd tried to chicken out of it at Pettah market. In twenty-four hours they'd be buddies again. Strong words would have been spoken, perhaps he'd have a few bruises but they'd be worth it if he won back his friend.

Behind him, children laughed, their chatter drifting along the beach.

"Shelala can take us over the railway line," a young girl said. "Like a guide dog."

"Rohini, she's waiting for us to tell her what to do," Theo's daughter said. "You look to the right and I'll look to the left."

"No trains this way."

"Or here. Let's go."

Rohini jumped up and down on the sand, a few boulders away. "We did it, we did it."

Sohan took sunglasses out of his shirt pocket, put them on as the small ones came into closer view. He lifted himself on his elbows and looked around. He couldn't see an adult with the children. What were they doing alone on the beach? Why wasn't Uma with them? The three playmates ran about and chased each other up and down the sand, the dog wagging its tail before it chose which of the girls to run after.

Rohini picked up a piece of driftwood and threw it for Shelala to catch. "It's more exciting without grown-ups. We can even touch dirty wood without being told to put it down."

"I'm going to look for crabs," Kana said. She squatted by a pool of water and poked the sand with washed-up twigs. "There's one."

"It's really small. It must be a baby."

"They're all this size."

The girls carried on looking for crabs. Sohan thought they couldn't come to any harm while playing on the sand. He still wasn't happy that they should be unattended on the beach. Perhaps Herath or Saraswathie was on the way to watch over them; it wasn't like Uma to let her daughter go out alone.

"Look, Kana," Rohini said. "That family's playing cricket. Let's ask if we can join in."

Theo's daughter shaded her eyes with her hand to gaze down the beach. "We're not supposed to talk to strangers."

"They look like nice people."

"I'm not going."

Rohini started to walk towards the cricket players while Kana shouted, "I'm going back with Shelala if you go on your own."

"She's my dog. Come on, Shelala."

The dog stayed where it was.

Rohini came running back. "I only want to make friends."

"You can't, unless your mum and dad know who they are."

"Then what can we do? We've already played chase."

"We can go back."

"But I haven't put my foot in the sea."

Sohan sat up with a jolt. Surely Nathan had warned his daughter to stay away from the water? He pictured the small one being dragged away by currents into the swirling ocean. He edged off the boulder, inch by inch. The girls were several paces away, out of touching distance.

Kana stared at him, as if she might have recognised him, then fidgeted on the sand. "We have to go back."

"Not yet," Rohini said, taking off her sandals and leaving her bow and arrows with her friend. "Don't let Shelala take those."

She ran to the sea and dipped her foot in the water. Sohan strolled towards her, keen not to frighten the youngster. She was about to put her foot in again when Kana shrieked, "He's coming." Rohini turned round to look at him, slipped on a cluster of green algae and fell towards the water. He skidded across pebbles as he raced towards her. Jesus Christ, why didn't children listen to their parents and keep out of harm's way? Kana screamed, then so did Rohini before she slid ankle deep into the sea. For God's sake, she's going in. He'd dive in after her, if he had to. He couldn't let her die. He wouldn't. She slid in up to her knees and screamed again. Adrenaline coursed through his muscles, made them work faster, giving him the speed and power he needed to reach her. He lunged forward onto the sand. Would he make it in time? He had to. He stretched as far as he could. Nearly there. Oh my God. She was sinking deeper, up to her thighs. He reached out and grabbed her arm. She slipped away. All he had was a split second before the current dragged her into the ocean. He wasn't sure he could do it. He stretched out again, extended his arm until it hurt. The gap between them was lengthening. More. He needed to stretch more. Just as she slid in up to her waist, she reached out to him. He grabbed her by the wrist and yanked her out of the water into his arms.

She was safe. He'd saved her. He couldn't believe it. I nearly lost you. I nearly lost you. His temples throbbing, he carried her away from danger, holding her tight. She was still screaming and crying, as was Kana, who came to him and sobbed into his legs. The dog joined them at the shoreline, wagged its tail and dropped a piece of driftwood at their feet, nudging their legs when nobody picked up the wood to play. Sohan held the girls close and soothed them until they quietened. Never before had he known such fear and never again did he want to feel so desperate or helpless. The two small ones calmed down before his own breathing settled and only when his heart stopped pounding did he loosen his grip on them.


Uncle Sohan took us back to Appa's house and walked behind us all the way. When we got to the front gate, there was shouting and crying coming from inside. Something terrible must have happened. I grabbed Kana's hand. "I think the riots have started." I didn't understand why they'd begun in my grandfather's home. He was a good man and liked the Sinhalese. Herath came running up the side garden and saw us.

"*Inghe, inghe*," he yelled.

Mum ran out of the front door and down the veranda steps, her eyes redder than I'd ever seen them. "Where have you two been? We looked everywhere."

"We went for a walk," I said. "Shelala was taking care of us."

Uncle Sohan stepped forward. "These two were on the beach. Rohini dipped her foot in the sea and slipped. I had to pull her out."

"You foolish girl. You could have drowned."

I grabbed her skirt and cried, so did Kana then we cried louder. We'd been grown-up and gone for a walk on our own, but ended up being scared and upsetting people we loved.

Amma came onto the veranda. "Let's go in, Uma. The girls are safe, praise the Lord. Sohan, I can't thank you enough. Will you come in?"

"I'll go now if it's all the same to you, Aunty."

"Up to you, son."

Mum put me in dry clothes then sat in the middle of Kana and me on a sofa. We kept saying sorry to her. She wiped our eyes with her hanky before she wiped her own. "Promise me you'll never run off like that again. I didn't know what had happened to you."

"Promise, Mum."

"Cross my heart, Aunty Uma."

"All right. Now go and play in Rohini's room. I have to help Saras with the cooking."

I wanted to know that everything was going to be the same as before my adventure. "Are you still going to make yellow rice like you said you would this morning?"

"I'm going to cook country rice instead."

Kana cried again and pushed her face into my mother's body. "I don't want you to stop liking me, like my mum did."

"That'll never happen, sweetheart. And your mother does love you."

Wanting to cheer up my friend, I took her to my room and said, "Now that Mum feels sorry for you we might get yellow rice."

Shelala followed us in and lay down for a little while then went to the back veranda, leaving hairs on the floor. I didn't know if Herath would make me sweep them up for misbehaving, so I picked them up with my hands anyway and put them in the bin.

Kana and I took my dolls to the front veranda to wait for the others to return from cricket so we could have dinner. We didn't dare go down the steps or into the garden because Amma or Herath always watched us. Soon after the sun had set, my stomach rumbled and Mum said we didn't have to wait any longer. I hurried to the table, taking Kana with me in case my mother changed her mind and didn't give us anything to eat. She'd never done anything like that before but I'd never been so disobedient.

While we had our meal, Amma rang friends to see if the men had gone to someone's house for a drink and forgotten to come home. After a few calls, she joined us at the table.

"Nobody's heard anything," she said.

"They'll be back soon," Mum told her.

Kana and I finished our rice and curry and waited to see if we'd get pudding when a car pulled up outside. Uncle Sohan came into the house. I didn't look at him.

"It's nothing to worry about," he told Amma, "but I need to speak to you."

He went to a side room with her and shut the door softly. When she came out, her eyes were red and she was wiping them. She called Mum into the room and they stayed there for ages. Herath brought us fresh rambutan and took our dinner plates away. I said sorry and thank you to him.

"It's finished now," he said.

I was glad we were friends again. I hadn't wanted to upset anybody.

The grown-ups came out of the side room and sat at the table. Amma told Saras to put Kana and me to bed.

"When's Dad coming home?" I asked.

Mum looked at Uncle Sohan. "Soon."

"Did the cricket match go on late?"

"Yes."

"But it's after curfew. They'll get in trouble with the police."

"Uncle Sohan will make sure they're all right. Your dad will kiss you both goodnight while you're asleep."

Kana had forgotten to bring pyjamas so I gave her my new red pair with white hearts, which fitted her the same as they did me. I told her she could keep them and hoped Mum wouldn't mind me giving away my clothes. Saras tucked us in like she used to when we lived there and as she bent over me, I smelt coconut oil in her hair then my beloved ayah told us in her gentle voice to go to sleep.

Sohan joined Uma and Aunty at the table. Laid out on a blue gingham tablecloth were dishes of country rice, mutton curry, fried fish, bone *rasam*, tomato *kulambu*, and *vaarai*. A typical Jaffna meal and on any other day, one that would have made his mouth water. If he hadn't gone to the beach that afternoon to remember old times, he could have made a few phone calls, put a stop to his plan and if he had, he wouldn't have felt like he was eating the Last Supper. Yet if he hadn't been on a boulder by the shore. . .

"Eat something," Aunty said.

A gathering of spices and flavours lay on his tongue but he couldn't enjoy them until he reassured her. "They'll be released soon. My stepfather, Arjun, has guaranteed it."

"So you told me." She stared at him, as if talking to a servant who'd been caught stealing. She served herself a spoonful of *rasam*, wincing as she tilted her hand to pour the gravy over her rice. "Uma, fetch me my painkillers from my room please."

He couldn't look her in the eyes. She knew. He was sure of it. He'd only arranged for Nathan to be arrested at a checkpoint so he could rescue him, be his saviour and recover their friendship. How was he to know the damn police would get carried away, throw Roshan Uncle and Uncle Selva into jail too? Theo had left cricket early to work on an engineering project so had escaped being picked up.

Aunty asked, "How did you find out about the arrest?"

"The fellows at the station rang Arjun because he's the Superintendent of Police on duty tonight."

She fixed him with that look of hers. "If I find out you had anything to do with this, you'll have me to answer to."

"Amma," Uma said, coming back with the painkillers, "he's doing all he can to help. Isn't that right, Sohan? You'll get them out safely. Promise me you won't let anything happen to them."

Her voice trembled and it was all he could do, not to break down as well. Aunty however, was still insisting on answers. "Sohan, why did Tara ring earlier to say you were going out of town? That woman never rings unless she wants something."

He couldn't reply. He didn't want to lie to her anymore and felt bad enough that he'd deceived Tara by asking her to call the Palar household, and give him an alibi. Stupid to think it would work, but he'd run out of ruses and it was all he could come up with.

"Whatever has gone wrong between you and my son," Aunty continued, "you have to put it right."

Yet Nathan was trapped in a corkscrew of anger so Sohan couldn't put it right, just like that. He got up from his chair, averting his eyes from his aunt's stare. "I'll see what's taking Arjun so long."

"And you had better pray none of them come to any harm."


At the police station, a servant boy cleaned red stains off a wall. A whiff of disinfectant made Sohan feel sick to the point where he had to lean against the counter to steady himself. While he tried to regain his senses, a hand gripped the back of his neck and spun him around. Jesus, they weren't going to arrest him too, were they?

"You took your time," his stepfather said, staring him in the eyes.

"I didn't know you were here."

"Phone calls weren't enough."

Sohan looked again at the station wall that was being cleaned. "How long before you can get them released?"

"The minister I know is in the Maldives on vacation. Pulling strings tonight has been hard."

The smell of disinfectant hit Sohan again. He wanted to retch and the scar on his thigh seared through his trousers. "I need to get them out straight away."

Arjun took him aside, out of earshot of the police and the men in sarongs who sat on wooden benches, having been picked up for one spurious reason or another. "The police here tell me you had something to do with this. What the bloody hell were you up to? And don't bullshit me."

"I was trying to put something right."

"Next time, choose another way. I won't help like this again, and then you take the chance of your friends becoming statistics."

Sohan's every nerve trembled. While resting on a beach or in his sitting room, his plan had seemed nothing more than a game of cops and robbers.

"Can you do anything?"

". . . It's not always possible to get everyone out. Sometimes, sacrifices have to be made. You have to let me know priority."

Jesus, Jesus, Jesus. How was Sohan to choose? All three men had treated him well and none had deserved this. Should he ask for the life of his best friend first or Roshan Uncle, a man who had been a father to him, or Uncle Selva, who waited in the background to catch him when he fell? It was impossible to decide between them. "I can't play God."

Arjun looked him in the irises. "You already have."

Sohan dragged his hand through his hair. His eyes became moist and his voice shook. "Please. I beg you. You have to save them all." He couldn't tell if his stepfather stared at him with pity or disgust.

Arjun clicked his teeth. "It's in hand. They're all being released."

The servant boy finished his cleaning, took his bucket and rags and retreated to the back of the station, leaving behind a faint pink trail that he couldn't remove from the wall. A policeman, one hand on his baton, nodded at the boy in passing then looked Sohan up and down. A door along the corridor opened. The policeman beckoned Arjun.

"Your friends are free to go," he said, his hand clenching his baton.

"Thank you. I'll make sure the minister knows of your personal co-operation." Arjun strolled towards Sohan and whispered, "Let's get them out of here before these bastards change their minds."


Kana was awake before me and playing with my Russian dolls, which she'd arranged in a line on her pillow.

"Did my dad kiss us goodnight?" I asked.

"I don't know. I was fast asleep all night."

"I dreamt I heard shouting."

"I didn't hear anything."

We'd both been told off the day before and I'd had a bad dream while she forgot everything. I didn't want to ask her again to show me how to meditate so I knelt on the floor by the foot of the bed and prayed to Buddha. Sunlight shone through the window and onto my head. My head still didn't go quiet. I finished praying and sat next to Kana, hoping her peace would rub off on me. Although I waited for ages, nothing happened and I thought it never happened for anyone, she just pretended it did to make me jealous of her. The dog next door barked outside, but I couldn't hear the rooster. I tiptoed to my parents' bedroom door, opened it softly and peeped in.

"It must be early," I told Kana. "They're not up."

"Saras and Herath are awake. I went to give them a good morning hug."

"You shouldn't have gone without me."

"You were asleep."

"You never do anything with me. You won't even show me how to find your peace."

She took my hands. "You can't be angry or it won't work."

We sat cross-legged but instead of putting our hands on our laps, she carried on holding mine. It was like the first time we met at her house when I felt blessed to be near her. I remembered to close my eyes and relax my arms and legs. I started with my toes then rushed up my body until I got to my mouth.

"I've forgotten what comes next."

"Breathe and think about air going in and out of your nose."

"Now what?"

"Empty your head."

I giggled.

"Rohini."

I opened my eyes. "Was that it?"

"It can't be. You're laughing."

Still giggling, I put my hands over my mouth then she giggled too. I was glad she wasn't being strict anymore.

We went looking for a grown-up to give us breakfast. I thought I'd find my grandparents in the sitting and dining areas, but the whole room all the way to the back veranda was empty. Saras and Herath were eating in the kitchen and looked surprised to see us.

"Small ones are up," Saras said.

"Everybody else is sleeping," I told her.

"Your Dad and Appa got back late last night. They're still tired."

I yawned. "I think they must have gone to a party."

Herath looked at Saras then got up to give us something to eat and drink. His plate was still full of food so I said we'd wait for him to finish breakfast. He told Kana and me to sit at the dining table. He'd bring us something.

The smell of jackfruit white curry that he brought made me hungrier. After going for a walk on our own I didn't think I'd get anything like this again so couldn't believe my luck. I ate quickly in case Mum came out of her bedroom and scolded me for eating nice food instead of country rice.

After Herath saw we'd started eating, he left us so he could finish his breakfast. Kana and I ate everything on our plates then served ourselves seconds. I hadn't left much space for lunch but was enjoying myself too much to stop. When I only had one mouthful left on my plate, I waited for my friend to catch up then we ate our last mouthful together. Appa came out of his room and wanted to know how long we'd been up.

"We've finished breakfast," I told him. I'd forgotten to say Grace but he didn't ask me about it. "Did you fall over?" I asked, touching my right eye. "You've scratched yourself here."

"That was those bas - it's nothing. I bumped into a door."

"Were you drunk?"

"Enough questions, girl. Is your father awake?"

"Not yet."

He told us to get washed and dressed and play in the back garden where Saras and Herath could see us.

"We want to climb the Temple tree," I said.

"You'll have to make do with the back garden for now."

I didn't know why he was being so grumpy but didn't think I should argue or play with my bow and arrows, in case I shot him by accident. To help Herath with clearing the table, Kana and I took our plates to the kitchen.

"Appa's in a bad mood," I whispered to Saras.

"He's had a hard night."

"We have to play where you and Herath can see us. Is he cross because we went to the beach on our own?"

"You two have already been scolded for that."

"I wish I could take you and Herath to England."

"Get dressed, kunju, then play in the back garden."

Although Kana and I tried to pet the chickens, they wouldn't stay still for us. I held one by the back so she could stroke its head but it pecked her because it was tired from laying eggs. When Uncle Selva and Uncle Theo turned up for breakfast, Kana ran to hug her father then was sent away to play with me. The grown-ups talked in whispers and we couldn't hear what they were saying.

"They must be speaking about us going for a walk," I said.

"They're talking about Uncle Sohan. I heard my dad say his name."

We moved a little closer to the back veranda then sat on the steps to listen better. Saras told us to come and help her in the kitchen. "The grown-ups are having a serious talk."

"Did Uncle Sohan try to kiss Mum?"

"No, kunju, but he's upset your family."

Herath went into his room and brought out two old rattan dining chairs that had been repaired to put in the servants' quarters. "Stay here, small ones. I'm going to sweep outside."

I looked around the kitchen while Saras washed up pots and pans. Even though morning light brightened the room, it was still grey stone on the floor and walls. When we got back to England, I was going to save my pocket money and buy a picture for her to hang. It'd have to be new savings because Dad made me keep the money I already had for when I was older. I watched Saras wash and wipe plates, dishes, pots and *chatties*.

"What can Kana and I do?"

"I forgot you can't sit still for long."

She wasn't smiling at me like she usually did. She looked worried as she gave me a small pot and showed me the shelf to put it on. Kana jumped down too, asking for something to do. We got everything back in its place, except the heavy pans, which Saras put away, then we sat on our chairs and waited to be told what to do next.

Herath finished sweeping but couldn't do any housework in the sitting and dining areas while the grown-ups talked there. "Come," he said to Kana and me. "I'll stay with you while you climb the Temple tree."

"Appa said we can't."

"Your grandfather just didn't want you two to be alone. *Vanghal*."

We jumped off our chairs and ran down the kitchen steps. As we passed the back veranda, I saw my father stomping up and down the dining area. Appa and Mum put an arm each on his shoulders and talked to him. He was really angry.

"I'll kill the bastard. Give me back the car keys, Uma."

I tried to run in to help him. Herath grabbed me and carried me to the side garden. "I am a hunter and you are the deer I have hunted."

"I want my Dad. You let Kana hug Uncle Theo."

"No more lessons if you don't listen to me, naga."

"I hate Uncle Sohan."

"You mustn't hate anyone. Now. You want to climb the tree or sit in the kitchen again?"

Kana ran ahead to the Temple tree and pulled herself up. "Quick, Rohini. Before we have to go back inside."

"I want to say hello to Dad. He didn't kiss me goodnight."

Herath put his hand under my chin and looked me in the eyes. "All right, small one, but you come straight back."

"I promise."

I sat on my father's lap and pointed at the bandage on his cheek.

"You've hurt your face."

"It's nothing, sweetheart."

He and Appa must've been drunk if they both walked into a door, or perhaps Uncle Sohan had shut it on them. Although I wanted to stay and protect my father, I remembered my promise to Herath. I didn't know what to do until Dad put me on the floor and said he'd play with me later.

I rushed back into the side garden. "I came as fast as I could."

"A Veddha always keeps her word," Herath said, messing up my hair.

I didn't feel like a Real Veddha. I hadn't been able to keep my father safe from Uncle Sohan, and hoped yaku would understand that sometimes children don't know what to do for the best.

Kana and I climbed up the tree to play at being angels and yaku in Heaven. We flew over Colombo to stop grown-ups fighting. Our wings took us higher and higher until we were in the clouds with God then we flew to the sun to talk to Buddha. We asked him if he really had to turn people into worms if they misbehaved in this life, because we'd like to become shoeflowers after we died. I was about to ask him what he was going to turn Shelala into when Dad marched down the front veranda steps and got into the Mercedes. Appa came running behind him.

"Wait, son. I'll come with you."

Uncle Theo wanted to join in too but Appa said he could only handle one argument a day, so please go home and he'd let him know what happens.

"Where are they going, Herath?"

"To talk to your Uncle Sohan."

"Why does Appa have to go with my dad?"

"To stop any fighting. This must come to an end."

A crow hopped on the roof of my grandfather's car and flew over it as Appa and Dad drove off. I hoped it followed them to Uncle Sohan's house and did its business all over him.

Uncle Theo called Kana to come home with him because her cousins hadn't seen a lot of her lately. She held my hand and we wouldn't let go until Herath told us we had to be brave Veddhas and do the right thing.

"I don't want to be brave. I want Kana."

"And I want to stay with Rohini."

He climbed up the tree and gently made us come down. Amma put an arm around me and took me up the veranda steps.

"Come inside, girl. You two will see each other soon."

I started crying and so did Kana when her dad put her in his car.

"It's not our fault," I told my grandmother, "and you're punishing us."

Even while hot-headed teenagers, Nathan and Sohan had never come close to hitting each other, quarrels had been resolved with one or the other surrendering. Yet when Sohan had rung Roshan Uncle's place that morning and offered to make peace, Nathan wanted to meet him alone, to talk, he claimed. Sohan refused. "Bring your father," he said.

He waited at Tara's for the showdown, not exactly neutral territory, all the same a safer place to meet than his own house, which his friend would have enjoyed wrecking. He pictured Tara's reaction if her silk cushions ripped or if anything landed on her lacquered piano.

He'd forever have nightmares of that servant boy cleaning blood off the station wall. If not for Arjun, the three men who meant the most to him would still be locked up and God knows in what condition. Uncles Selva and Roshan knew enough government ministers to set them free, yet the police refused to believe they had connections or more likely, had chosen instead to have a party of violence, mild as it was by their *thadiyan* standards. Sohan held his head in both hands. How stupid he'd been in his mission to repair his friendship with Nathan. And Tara's reaction, when he'd admitted all to her, was not exactly supportive.

"You certainly get yourself into a mess. It's why I wouldn't marry you. I needed a man who wasn't going to give me trouble and . . ."

"And what?"

"And who'd put an expensive roof over my head."

"So finally you come clean that you married for money."

"Face it, buddy, you were a bum but I never stopped loving you."

Sohan kissed her hard until their lips bruised. Tara was the first to pull away.

"Nathan and Roshan Uncle will be here soon. I'd better leave."

"Where are you going?"

"I'll be at Jyoti's. Ring when you are finished."

He opened his mouth to say something then changed his mind.

"I know about you and Jyoti," Tara said. "But we weren't a couple then. Now, is there anything else you want to confess to?"

"You know everything that matters."

As soon as the front door opened, Nathan pushed his way in and lunged forward, his blow catching Sohan's temple. Roshan Uncle forced himself between the young men. "You've had your punch, son. Now leave it."

Sohan knew retaliation would be wrong. Not wishing to take another hit however, he walked behind his guests to the lounge, dropped onto the sofa opposite, moved silk cushions aside. He made himself look at their bandaged wounds and winced at the suffering he had caused.

"Your stepfather rang," Nathan said. "He told us everything."

"*Machan*, last night was unforgivable. It sounds mad, but I was trying to get some reaction from you, to make you talk to me."

"Since when do you call me *machan*?"

Sohan felt a rush of blood to his head. He'd forgotten how easy it was to hate Nathan. Everybody's favourite, captain of the school cricket team, prizes for coming first in exams, a mother who cared more about him than money, scoring winning runs in the Royal-Thomian match. Nathan bloody Palar.

Uncle said, "Why can't you both put the past behind you?"

Nathan rushed to his feet. "That will never happen. I want nothing more to do with him."

"Son, please."

"I'm leaving. You can stay if you want."

A weary look on his face, Uncle got up too. "I've done all I can," he said to Sohan. "I have nothing left."

Reluctant as he was to give up on his friendship, Sohan wondered if it truly had ended and if it had, he knew he was responsible for setting it on fire until not even embers of affection remained.

On a side table lay a Schumann LP, its sleeve a picture of a grand piano against a maroon background. He slid the record out, held it by the edges, blew off a speck of dust, placed it on the hi-fi unit. Leaning back on the sofa, he shut his eyes and braced himself for the barrage of drums and violins that introduced the piece. Then came the part he waited for: piano notes floating through the air, music as white as innocence, soothing, calming. He was supposed to have been godfather to Rohini. "We'll be blood brothers and look after each other," he and Nathan had promised each other while at school. Sohan had needed the reassurance of the vow more than his friend, yet both swore allegiance. The orchestra hammered out a noise as passionate as Nathan's rage. Sohan steeled himself at the start of each crescendo and held his breath until he heard piano notes, pretty as Tara. Clutching a silk cushion, he breathed in the scent of jasmine that came from flower arrangements scattered around the room. He imagined she was on the duet stool, smiling at him, playing for him. Stretching out an arm, his hand brushed the side table where the LP had been, where she'd left pages of sheet music. If she left the house in a mess, her servants were allowed to put everything back in its place except her music. By running his finger along the staves, he felt her next to him, her soft skin sliding against his naked body.

He didn't want to be alone any longer, couldn't abide the loneliness of his actions; without thinking twice, he called her at Jyoti's and asked her to come home.


When Dad and Appa returned from visiting Uncle Sohan, they stomped about the house. My father picked up a newspaper, pretended to read it then put it down. The last time I'd seen him this angry was when Sri Lanka lost a cricket match against India.

"Was it Uncle or cricket that upset you?"

He looked at me like he'd never seen me before.

"Shall we get him drunk?" I whispered to Mum.

"That won't help, sweetheart. Come and sit on my lap."

Herath brought a pot of broken orange pekoe tea that Amma usually kept for special guests. He put the tray down on the coffee table and left it to brew. The smell of warm milk in the jug made me feel sick and I hoped nobody was going to make me drink some, even in tea. We all went quiet while my grandmother kept checking to see if the water in the pot had turned brown. After lifting the lid a few times, she poured a cup for everyone, except me. She must have remembered from the year before that I didn't like it. When she gave Dad his tea, she asked him what had happened with Uncle Sohan. He didn't answer her so she tried my grandfather.

"Roshan?"

Appa grunted. "Let it be, Arul."

She wasn't having any of their nonsense. "I'm losing my patience. Sohan is part of this family and this has to be put right."

Dad said, "I've made up my mind. You can do what you like."

She watched him rub his right hand. "You should get that X-rayed, Nathan. It may be a hairline fracture."

"Don't fuss. I'll go tomorrow if it isn't any better."

Herath brought him some ice in a napkin to put on it. My family was always getting hurt by Uncle Sohan and nobody could do anything about it.

Appa said he was going to spend the rest of the day at Uncle Selva's place. Dad said he'd go too.

"Bring him for dinner," Amma told them. "But don't come back in a worse mood."

When they did return, I was on the veranda watching the sun set with Mum. A sea wind made me shiver and the sky was dark grey; it wasn't the pink or orange I loved to watch with Appa. I couldn't smell shoeflowers in the front bush either because the wind blew the scent away. Dad came up the steps and asked me for a hug. I wasn't sure if he was still in a temper so shook my head and moved closer to Mum, holding tight to her dress. He stood still for a second, held his arms out to me then said, "Sorry, for being a grouch, darling. My hand and head have been hurting all day."

I couldn't help myself, I ran to him for a kiss.

# CROSSROADS

Kana came to stay at my grandfather's house for a few days because Uncle Theo was going to Bombay to build a bridge for the government.

"Does he hang off the side and screw it together?" I asked her.

"He's an engineer. He draws the pictures and the builders make the bridge."

I liked drawing. When I grew up, I was going to be an engineer too.

"Does he go away a lot?"

"No. But I miss him when he goes."

Mum was listening to us and went to her bedroom. She came out with two small boxes. "I've got a surprise for you girls." She gave us a pair of gold star earrings each, which had a ruby in the middle and a back that screwed on. We asked her to put them on us. I'd tried to do it myself once but couldn't find the hole in my ear.

Kana touched the rubies. "They're the same colour. We're like sisters."

"I wish we were."


Even though my family had been invited to parties, we stayed at home because Appa and Dad were still in bad moods. They didn't want anyone visiting, didn't want to go anywhere and didn't want to talk or play. Instead, they lounged around the house, reading newspapers and the same cricket magazines. Kana and I stayed in the garden to keep out of their way and kept close to Mum if they were in the room. Amma only spoke to them if they were rude to her and then she'd give them one of her looks.

One day we were all in the sitting area, Kana and I reading *Swallows and Amazons*. She read faster than I did and waited for me to finish before she turned a page. I lifted my head to talk to her about Peggy and Nancy in the book, and who we thought was going to win the race to capture a boat, when Appa said, "For God's sake." I grabbed my friend's hand and we ran to my mother, knowing trouble was on the way, not wanting to be on our own when the shouting started. Appa looked at the two of us and kept quiet. Out of the corner of my eye, I saw the picture of Jesus and asked him silently to stop the fights. He wasn't smiling so I guessed he wasn't going to do anything. It'd be up to Amma to give a blackguarding if it was needed. Appa watched her crochet a doily then threw the newspaper he was reading onto a side table. It slipped off, onto the floor. Amma carried on with the doily as if she wasn't watching him but I knew she was. He picked up the newspaper from the floor, rolled it up, tapped it against his leg and threw it on the table again.

"For God's sake," he said. "We've got hundreds of crochet mats. How many more do we need?"

"This is exactly why I sent you to patch things up with Sohan, and you bring your son back with an injured hand." Dad gave her an angry look. She stared right back at him. "And don't think you can take it out on me, Nathan." He opened his mouth to say something but she wouldn't let him talk. "I haven't finished. This has gone on long enough. You and your father had better go to Selva's and see if he can talk sense into you."

"This is my house," Appa shouted. "I'll do what I like."

I watched Amma to see what she did. Her eyes went mad, like she was about to explode but she said nothing until my father and grandfather went out of the front door. She picked up her crochet and moved her hook in and out of the cotton like a madwoman. Her eyes calmed down with every stitch then she carried on with the doily as if she had nothing else to do. "If you two hadn't been here," she told Kana and me, "I'd have given him what for."

Suddenly I had a brainwave. All I had to do to stop grown-ups having quarrels was to be in the same room as them. Though with Appa and Amma, Dad and Uncle Sohan and Kana's mum, I didn't know how I could be everywhere at once until I remembered my Sunday School teacher said Jesus would always show the way. With him and Buddha on my side, I was sure I could show the grown-ups how to stop sulking.

"I'm going into the garden," Kana told me.

"Wait for me," I said, running after her.

She picked a shoeflower, rubbed the petals in her fingers, smelt the perfume.

"I know how to stop the fights," I said.

"Smell this."

"I know how to stop the fights."

"I found peace this morning."

"I can't find it," I said in a funny voice. "I have to do something else."

"What do we have to do?"

I put my hands over her ears and whispered my plan.

Later on, we were sitting in the Temple tree, pulling petals off flowers and watching them float to the ground when Dad and Appa returned for lunch. We jumped down, ran inside and sat on a sofa, ready to do our best to stop quarrels, just by being there. Appa plonked himself at the dining table and folded his arms.

"You've come back for lunch," my grandmother said.

"Where else am I to eat?"

"With the chickens, if you don't behave."

"I'm here, Amma," I said from the sitting area.

"Just as well, child, or your grandfather will be looking for another wife."

I knew she didn't mean it but when we joined Appa at the dining table, I listened for the start of a row. With the tips of his fingers, my grandfather made a ball of rice, *keerai* and fish curry, and opened his lips wider. Was he going to say something rude to Amma before he pushed the food in with his thumb? I stopped eating and waited.

Mum stroked my cheek. "Eat, girl."

"I'm watching Appa," I whispered, "in case he starts a fight."

He finished chewing then looked down at the table. "There'll be no more arguments, child. Eat."

Mum looked across the table at my father. "Enough, Nathan. Please?"

"Eat, girl," he said.

I wished I'd kept an eye on the grown-ups before. So long as I was in the room, I didn't have to worry about them fighting.

Amma still sent Dad and Appa to Uncle Selva's for the afternoon. "Come back when you've stopped scowling for good," she told them. "Not just when the small ones are around."

Now that I knew how to sort out the grown-ups squabbling, it meant Kana and I didn't have to worry about them anymore, except when we were stopping their fights.

We played at being Veddhas in the garden and took it in turns to use my bow and arrows to hunt wildlife. There wasn't a bird nearby and we weren't allowed to shoot at Appa's chickens, even if we shot to miss, so we had to aim at pretend wild pigs. Then we lay down on the front veranda, like we were sleeping in the middle of a jungle, putting branches and twigs at the bottom of the steps so if the wood cracked while we slept, we'd know a sloth bear was near and we could get ready to cut its throat. I told Kana it was all right to kill an animal if it was to save our lives. Just as we lay down to rest, a small brown bird flew down and picked up a twig for its nest. I reached for my bow and an arrow to see if I could aim to miss it.

Kana said, "You'll hit it, Rohini."

So I didn't fire.

When we woke up from our sleep, the sun was setting and my father and grandfather still hadn't returned. I wanted to watch the sky change colour with Appa and ask him if it would turn pink, gold or orange. Amma said, "If he isn't back soon, I'll sit with you, child, and have my cup of tea." She didn't enjoy sunsets as much as he did though. "Orange, pink, what's the difference? The Colombo sun will rise in the mornings and set in the evenings if you watch it or not." Kana and I sat with her anyway on the veranda and looked at the field across the road. Above us were pink and blue lines in the sky, some of the prettiest I'd seen, but it wasn't the same without Appa. After it got dark, he came back for dinner with Dad and Uncle Selva. My grandmother told Saras to set an extra place at table for Uncle. In Sri Lanka, anyone could turn up for a meal and you could have a party if lots of people came.

I don't remember what we had for dinner. I watched brown moths, bigger than butterflies, fly around the light above the dining table. Nobody else seemed to mind or notice the noise they made as they flapped around. I dodged from side to side as they flew to and from the light shade. I was sure one was going to land on me and make holes in my skin like they did in clothes.

That night, I dreamt I was sailing alone on a ship back to England because I hadn't been able to stop fights. Mum and Dad stayed in Sri Lanka and told me not to return until I learned to behave. As I sailed away, the land got smaller and smaller until I couldn't see the people I loved, waving me goodbye.

In the morning, I cried softly. I turned to my side and looked at Kana sleeping in sunshine. I rubbed my eyes and listened to noises I'd got used to on holiday: chickens clucking in their hen house, Saras banging pots and pans in the kitchen and Herath's scratchy broom on the outside corridors. I started to forget my bad dream. I was in Colombo with my family and Kana. I'd have *hoppers* for breakfast, not cornflakes. If I did have to go back to London, it'd be with my mum and dad, not on my own and if I was lucky, my best friend and her dad would come with us.

At breakfast, Kana and I broke off the lacy top of our egg *hoppers* and dipped it in *sodhi* because the coconut sambal was too hot for us. Herath looked at me for a long while. "Naga is tired." I nodded at him. He was taking good care of me, even if none of the other grown-ups had noticed I wasn't feeling myself.

Amma's arthritis couldn't have been bad in her hands that morning because she ate with her fingers, taking small mouthfuls while looking at Appa. She asked him, "What are you planning to do after breakfast?"

"Nothing."

"Then it's back to Selva's for you two until this foolishness is over."

"Dad, will you send Shelala to us when you get to Uncle's house?"

He stroked my face but I didn't know if that meant yes or no, it just meant he still loved me.

Kana and I stood by the front gate to watch him and Appa go up the road, my father walking by the grass verge the way I did, as if he'd become afraid a cobra might crawl out of the field and bite him.

"Do you think he'll let Shelala play with us?" I asked my friend.

"I don't know. He's still in a bad mood."

Appa held his hands together behind his back, like he did when he was thinking. He must have been trying to find a way to stop Uncle Sohan rowing with Dad.

We hung around the garden wall watching my father and grandfather get farther and farther away, while a crow shouting *caw caw* flew over my head and landed on a palm tree across the road. We waved hello to the *kadillai* seller and his daughter as they walked by, pushing his wooden cart. The wheels were wonky and he had to hold it with both hands to stop it rocking. His daughter hid behind him and peeped at us. I tried to give back a small packet of *kadillai* he gave Kana and me.

"I don't have any pocket money left."

He shook his head. "It is present for you."

I said, "Thank you," and shared the spicy chickpeas with Kana. We'd only had a few when Appa and Dad disappeared into Uncle Selva's garden. I still didn't know if my father was in a temper or if he was going to let Shelala out. I had to wait until I'd eaten my last *kadillai* to see her run down the road to us. I held my arms open to hug her and looked up the road, hoping to wave to Dad but he'd gone into Uncle Selva's house without checking to see if I'd come in safely off the road. Amma said later that men are like that. They don't think.

Kana ran down the side garden with Shelala while I pushed the gates together. They didn't meet in the middle and were too heavy for me to lift and close on my own. "Kana, can you ask Herath to help me? I have to wait here to stop Shelala running out."

Herath came barefoot down the side garden, walking over the sandy earth and not feeling stones, as if he had shoes on.

He said, "One gate is broken."

"I did it. I swung on it last year and bent the hinge."

He smiled. "*Mahathya* won't repair it."

"Appa says he'll wait until I stop jumping on it, like he had to when Dad was my age."

"He keeps it like that, naga, because it reminds him of you."

I helped him lift the broken gate so he could close it. It didn't feel as heavy with two of us carrying it. He patted me on the head and went back down the side garden to the back of the house, still walking over small stones and not feeling any pain.

None of the grown-ups was around so I took off my sandals and ran around barefoot, too. Kana and I were Veddhas with our hunting dog, Shelala, and axes over our shoulders. We were in the jungle, chasing deer and wild pig for dinner, shooting them with bows and arrows.

"Look, Kana, this tree's got claw marks on it."

"Careful, Rohini, there might be a sloth bear up the tree, eating honey."

"I can't see anything up there. I think it's safe to carry on hunting."

We shot and killed a deer then dug up yams and kept them for when we couldn't catch anything to eat. Veddha women were supposed to stay in their houses, or only dig yams while the men went hunting but Kana and I were modern girls.

Mum stuck her head out her bedroom window. "Put your sandals on, Rohini. You'll cut yourself."

"Herath doesn't wear them and I'm a Veddha too, on Amma's side."

"They go on or you come in. You choose."

"Quick, Rohini," Kana said. "Or you'll have to go inside."

I didn't know why my mother had to keep bossing me around when I knew swear words and part of a rugby song so was nearly grown-up. I put my sandals back on anyway then Kana and I did a leaf dance, though we couldn't play Veddhas afterwards because Shelala kept jumping on us, so we raced around, chasing each other and trying not to bump our heads on the Temple tree as we ran past it. I stood under the tree, waiting for Shelala to get me then I reached up to pull a low branch and white and yellow petals fell on us.

"It's raining flowers," I said, laughing.

We had so much fun. Kana and I ran behind a shoeflower bush while we let Shelala lick our faces. Even if my mother could have seen us through branches, we may not have been in trouble because Uncle Selva's dog was clean and didn't have germs on her tongue.

"Rohini and Kana," Mum said from her window.

I sat on the ground and looked at her through leaves and flowers. "Hurry, Kana," I said, pulling her down to join me, "before she sees us."

"Girls. I've already told you. Don't let the dog lick. How many times? Never mind. I can't spend the rest of my life scolding you."

Dad and Appa kept going to Uncle Selva's in the morning, only coming back for their meals and to sleep. Kana and I waited for them to send Shelala to us then we played until we were tired and thirsty. I'd pour water into Shelala's bowl on the side corridor before I had a drink myself. She'd lap it up, dribble on the floor then lay in the shade under the dining table while Kana and I decided what game to play next. If Amma wasn't crocheting, she told us about her schooldays at Ladies' College in Colombo and places she used to live in, like Jaffna, Matara, and Galle. I never wanted to listen for long and looked at my mother to rescue me when I got bored. She'd tell me to go to my room and play because Amma was tired. I'd run off with Kana to hear my grandmother saying, "Now where's she going? I haven't finished."

One morning, while Kana was visiting a cousin, Amma said she'd tell me about Jaffna. I made sure Mum was around before I climbed onto the sofa, careful not to knock my grandmother's body in case I made her arthritis worse. Appa told me she didn't like people getting too close anyway: she was brought up in a strict family where nobody cuddled a lot. I felt sorry she didn't have loving when she was young and gave her a kiss. While I waited for her to start talking, I played with the fringe on her sari and made plaits out of the green threads. She saw what I was doing but didn't mind me making a mess of her clothes, and then she put an arm around me.

"Your grandfather and I lived in Jaffna when we got married. Your father was born there. I have never been so happy."

"Then why did you leave, Amma?"

"Roshan was offered a job as bank manager in Colombo. I stayed in the North with your father for a short while. Even the hill country can't match the scenery up there, but I wanted our family to be together."

What could have been better than a train journey up the mountains and through the jungle? I stopped plaiting and listened closely.

"God put all the best colours in Jaffna You can see purple flowers, blue sky, the sun, then there are green paddy fields and palm trees. Most of all, I love the red soil, which gets an even deeper colour when there are red sunsets in the sky."

I tried to imagine a land full of colours, where the earth and sky were red.

"Married and in Jaffna," Amma said. "Life couldn't have been better. You know, I was seventeen when your grandfather proposed. He was so good-looking."

"You think he's ugly now?"

"Not at all. It's just that he was the handsomest man in Colombo then."

"Was it an arranged marriage?"

"In a way. Our families knew of each other."

"When I get married, I'm going to choose my own husband."

"Oh, really?"

"Dad says I can find my own man. He doesn't know anyone who'd suit me."

"I'd heard a lot about Roshan and wanted to see for myself who this handsome man was."

"Did you visit his house?"

"My cousins and I went to Galle Face Green where he used to walk in the evenings. We had to go there a few times before I saw him." She bent down and whispered, "He used to gamble, you know. Every day he bet on horses at Racecourse Avenue."

I covered my mouth with my hands. I didn't know what she meant but it sounded like something he shouldn't have been doing. I hadn't thought of Appa being naughty before. He told me how Dad used to misbehave when he was my age, never that he'd been bad too.

Amma said, "I made sure he gave up gambling when your father was born."

Poor Appa. All his fun must have stopped after he got married. When I got a husband, I was going to let him play after work. My grandmother had a faraway look in her eyes, as if she was dreaming. I stroked her cotton sari, smooth as Shelala's fur. It made her seem kinder, that she wore soft material.

"Bring me my album, girl. I'll show you our first picture."

I fetched the dark green leather book, which was so heavy I had to carry it in both hands. She opened it slowly like it was precious. It smelt of mothballs. Inside were black and white photos tucked into pockets at the corners. With the tips of her fingers, she lifted the tissue paper that separated the pages.

"Can I turn a page?" I asked.

"All right, but be careful."

Even though I tried to do as she said, I accidentally pushed the tissue paper hard and it creased.

"I'll turn the rest," she said.

In one picture, my grandparents sat on chairs in a garden on a checked picnic rug, my father a baby on Appa's lap. There were trees and bushes around them and leaves covered the ground. Appa wore a dark suit with a tie, Amma a white sari with a border. She said it was their garden in Jaffna, when it was safe to live there.

"I didn't know you used to be this young," I told her. "Look, Mum," I said, taking the album to her. "It's Dad when he was a baby."

"I've seen that one."

"It's in Jaffna. Can we go there?"

"I don't see why not."

"Can we take Kana?"

"I don't see why not."

"I've never seen photos of you when you were small."

In a voice I could hardly hear, she said, "They burned."

"How?"

"In the house fire. I lost everything."

Her eyes started shining and I thought she was going to cry. She held me close. "Sohan was so fond of my father. All night, they looked at stars through a telescope. My dad taught us how to use them to find our way home."

"So why haven't your family used the stars to come back to Colombo? Why did they just run away and not come back?"

A car drove up outside and a lady's voice said, "Hello? Anybody home?" Tara Aunty stood in the doorway. I didn't know what she was doing there. At least she hadn't brought Uncle with her. She waited where she was for a few seconds, then when nobody invited her in, she sat on the sofa. "I came to see how you all are, after the other night and everything."

"Did you know about it, Tara?" Amma asked.

"*Aiyo*, do you honestly think I'd let the fool go ahead with it if I did?"

My grandmother grunted. "I suppose not."

Aunty looked at the photo of Dad. "I say, small one, is this your album?"

"It's Amma's. All Mum's pictures got burned."

"Is this true, Uma? You have nothing?"

Mum nodded.

Aunty had a cup of tea and piece of love cake then sniffed and said she had to get something from her house. She'd be straight back. If she wanted to wipe her nose and had forgotten her hanky, she could have borrowed one from Amma. She'd have had to bring it back, washed by the dhobi man, but my grandmother had enough hankies to last a few days without it. Aunty left anyway, and came back very soon, with a large brown envelope for Mum from Uncle Sohan. Mum didn't want to take it at first. If it was a love letter, I was going to tell her to tear it up.

"Open it, Uma," Aunty said.

Inside were photos of my mother and her family: in her swimsuit on the beach, when she was a schoolgirl, on a picnic with her sisters and playing tennis with Uncle Sohan. She let me look at the pictures then held them next to her heart. "I didn't know he had these," she said.

Aunty sat next to Mum. "He didn't either. Your families were close so I knew there had to be something in his albums."

"You don't know how much this means to me, Tara. I asked his mother when I lived there and she said she didn't have any."

"That woman would never have searched for them. Luckily, she gave the family albums to Sohan when she remarried."

Aunty left before lunch, saying it wouldn't be a good idea for Dad to see her there. She'd taken a chance on coming because she'd heard that he and Appa spent the days with Uncle Selva since the other night. Holding the photos tight, Mum saw her out and kept saying thank you, thank you.

"Come again soon," Amma said, and when my aunt had gone, "I suppose I can forgive Tara for not paying off the loan. She is a widow, after all."

I wondered if I could get a loan from Dad and use it to buy beds for Saras and Herath then pay it back out of my savings. I'd have to wait until he wasn't grumpy or he might stop all my pocket money if I asked him.

"Rohini. Come, child," my grandmother said. "I have more stories to tell you."

"In a minute, Amma." I ran outside to climb the Temple tree, slinging my bow and arrows over my shoulder to hunt deer in Jaffna.

"Now where are you going?"

I pretended I hadn't heard her.

Herath was sweeping the front veranda steps, looking ahead at the carport. I felt him watching me, making sure I was all right as I climbed the tree. Perched on a top branch was a crow that I aimed at and missed, the arrow falling to the ground, rustling leaves on the way. The crow flew away and there wasn't anything else for me to fire at, so I shot at empty branches, pretended there was a bird in there, a jungle fowl I could kill. I was Queen Rohini of the Veddhas, hunting food to feed my village. My men and women in the tribe were waiting for me to bring their dinner back. I fired at branches and watched my arrows fall to the ground. After coming down for the fifth time to pick them up, I got fed up.

"Herath, can you fetch that arrow for me please?"

"No, naga. You must get it yourself."

"Herath. Servants have to do what I say."

He didn't have a chance to answer me back. Mum came running out of the house onto the front veranda and put her hands on her hips. "Rohini, don't you dare speak to anyone like that again. Apologise now."

"Sorry, Herath."

He didn't move from where he was sitting. His face wasn't cross but he didn't say he'd forgiven me for being rude. Forgetting to take my bow and arrows with me, I went to him, not sure if I was going to get another scolding. He didn't say anything. I put a hand on his leg, said sorry again. Even though he nodded, he wasn't listening. I sat next to him on the steps, waiting for him to speak to me. When he didn't talk, I had to know if he still liked me.

"What are you thinking about?"

"My people."

The hot sun was giving me a headache. I wanted to go inside, have a cold drink and lie down but had to stay by his side until we were friends again. We sat without speaking while he thought about his Veddha family in Nilgala. I wondered if he wished he was living with them again or if he thought they were nicer than I was. My head started to pain a lot so I leaned it against him. The smell of his sweaty armpits made my headache worse, but it was his smell and I loved him. He put an arm around my shoulders.

"Come, naga, let's get your bow and arrows."


Sohan hovered in his hallway, near a photo of Rohini that had been taken by Nathan on her fourth birthday and sent to him in secret by Uma. The small one was smiling into the camera and in her hair, she wore an Alice band that matched her red dress. She never failed to touch him. He turned away from her face and thumbed through his address book, to ring every contact he had in Delhi. Yet officials neither took nor returned his calls. He thought about flying to India. Face to face conversations were easier to handle and he couldn't afford to waste time: his cousin in the USA had drooling buyers ready for exotic rugs and wall hangings and someone else would satisfy their demands if he didn't.

"Did you give him my message?" he asked the Minister of External Affairs' secretary.

"Yes, sir. And that you rang yesterday. We are busy with foreign matters. He wishes you success with your business."

He slammed the phone down. Damn those fools for taking flight when they heard about the Endangered Species Act in the USA. Those government thieves no doubt earned more by skimming overseas aid than he'd offered as bribes. He flicked through his address book again, searching contacts he'd already tried. When he'd read the last of the names in W, he threw the book onto a hall table and ran his fingers through his hair. What could he do? Should he do? The lack of co-operation from Delhi was a chance to walk away from his poaching plan and one he ought to take. He glanced at the photo of Rohini. Nathan had gone mad when he found out Uma had sent it to him and made her promise not to send any more. Sohan ran his fingers over the scar on his thigh. If India was out of the question, he'd have to export directly from Sri Lanka, which also meant speaking to the fellow who lived next door to Uncle Selva.

Amma wanted to spend a morning alone with me, and made the others go to Lakapahana, to buy batik prints for friends in London. Appa was grumpy, didn't want to go but she made him. I didn't mind staying behind with her: I could get up to mischief and even if I got caught, she might not have been cross if she'd taken her painkillers. She took them every day while we visited but didn't like taking a lot because she got a Dick Ted, and it took weeks to give them up after we'd gone back to London. I asked her who Dick and Ted were but she didn't know what I was talking about. Soon as the others had gone shopping, she sat with me in the sitting area and I let her pinch my cheeks.

"Darling, darling, girl," she said. "Your grandfather and I wait all year to see your sweet face. We've seen less of you this Christmas because of your new friend. All the same, it means a lot to us to have you here."

"I really love Kana. We'll always be best friends."

"It's good you have someone close like that."

I nodded and looked behind to make sure Dad hadn't come back from shopping and slipped into the house. "And she's teaching me about Buddha," I said softly.

"Anything else?"

"We're like twins. We do everything the same. The Veddha leaf dance is our favourite game, we share toys and books, and I even let her wear my new pink dress. Nobody else is allowed to." I let out a big sigh. "I love her most of all because her mum ran off with a boyfriend."

Amma stroked my hair. "If only the men in this family would come to their senses and show the same caring." She opened her bag of crochet and smiled as if she was going to give me a crochet lesson. "And now, I have a surprise for you."

"Shall I sing instead for you, Amma?"

She pulled an envelope from her bag.

"Later, child. I want to read this to you."

"Is it a crochet pattern?"

She took days to make a doily and I didn't want to listen for that long. Saras saved me when she came in to say the cook wanted to know what curries to make for the day.

"I'll come to the kitchen," Amma said. "Wait here, Rohini. I'll be back in a short while."

I stood on the back veranda and listened to hens clucking in the coop, telling each other what they'd got up to that morning. One scratched the ground to make a hole to lay an egg in.

Amma asked Saras to make *pittu* and fish *sodhi* for lunch and yellow rice with chicken *porial* for dinner. My mouth watered when I heard we were going to have dry chicken curry and *payasam* for pudding. My grandmother dragged a chair to the kitchen table and chatted to Saras and the cook. Last time she did that, she talked for ages. I was about to go to my bedroom when they started talking about a houseboy next door who'd been sacked for stealing.

Amma said, "It's not the bag of rice he took, it's the dishonesty."

I wanted to say it was unfair, the poor boy must have been hungry, but I'd have been scolded for listening in. All I could do was ask Buddha to find another good job for him. I wasn't going to speak to God about it because he made our neighbours sack him for stealing.

My grandmother began talking again about food and how to cook curries, so I tiptoed back into the house and when she couldn't see me from the kitchen, I ran into my bedroom. I threw off my sandals and put on a pair of white socks. Last time I skated in Appa's house, the grown-ups were on the front veranda chatting and I got caught when Mum came in to get a glass of water. Even if Amma couldn't see me from the kitchen, I crept to the front door. My socks would get dirty but if I pushed them to the bottom of the laundry bag, nobody would know.

Keeping out of the way of side tables, sofas and chairs, I slid across the house on the polished, red cement floor. I went up and down, up and down, almost making it across the room in a run and one slide. When I reached the dining area, I grabbed the edge of the table to brake and turned to slide to the front door. As I passed the picture of Jesus, I looked up to see if he was watching me. I was going to have to say an extra prayer that night asking for forgiveness, but was sure he was on my side: he'd been naughty too when he was a child, hiding in a church while Mary and Joseph looked for him.

I was skating towards the dining area when Amma came in from the back veranda. I'd been so busy having a good time I'd forgotten to look out for her. Her eyes opened wide when she saw me. I was going too fast to stop, had gone past the dining table and there was nothing else to hold onto. I slid forward and bumped into her with a thump, my face hitting her stomach. If she hadn't caught me, I'd have fallen down the steps into the back yard. To stay standing, I had to grab her sari. It was slippery and I held it tight with both hands. If I pulled it down, I'd have been in real trouble. She kept me steady then tucked her sari back into her petticoat.

"You devil child. You nearly knocked me over."

"Sorry, Amma. Did I hurt your arthritis?"

"Not this time." She looked down at my feet. "Your socks will be filthy. Give them to me before your mother sees them. Herath, take these, will you."

"Sorry, Herath."

He smiled at me on the way back to the kitchen.

I thought I was in for a blackguarding or one of my grandmother's Evil Eye looks but she did nothing, not even a twist of my ear. Buddha was taking good care of me. I was going to say a big thank you to him later. Then her sari started to unfold. There was so much material wrapped around her, she didn't notice it coming undone. First one pleat then a second then a third then the front of the sari slipped open. I said, "It's not tucked in properly." My heart was beating so loudly, I could hear it thump in my head and ears. I didn't know what would be worse, seeing Amma in her petticoat or it being my fault that her clothes fell off. Whatever happened, I was going to be for it. "You have to tuck it in," I said. She gathered the top of her sari and pushed it into her petticoat without thinking. She still didn't tell me off. I couldn't believe I'd got away with it.

"And now," she said, "your surprise. Though I'm not sure you deserve it." She held my hand and led me to the sitting area. I was in big trouble. She was going to yell at me and Saras was in the kitchen, too far away to stop me getting a long scolding. Nobody had ever smacked me but I hoped Amma had taken a lot of painkillers. We sat next to each other on a sofa and I tried not to catch her Evil Eye. The red floor I'd skated across didn't look like an ice rink anymore. She pulled the envelope from her crochet bag, held it to her bosom then kissed the top of my head and put an arm across my shoulders. I couldn't escape and to make it worse, my head was under her armpits that smelt of sweat. She can't have put talcum powder there that day but I didn't think I should tell her. It wasn't a strong smell anyway, not like Herath's armpits.

"I'm going to read you a letter Roshan wrote me," she said, "soon after your father was born. You should know how your family started."

"I'd like that, Amma."

Even though I didn't want to listen to the letter, I knew I had to be punished. She coughed and sipped a glass of warm water before she began. We only got as far as the date when a car pulled up in the front port. I wondered who had dropped in and if visitors meant I was free to play.

Appa came indoors, saying, "Lakapahana closed early for a stock-take." Amma gave him a look. He picked up a newspaper from a side table and fanned himself. "This is my house and I'm not going out again today."

Mum and Dad followed behind, carrying bags of gifts. As much as I wanted to see their shopping, I knew I'd have to wait until after my punishment to ask if they'd bought me anything. They went into the bedroom to put the presents away, leaving the door open. I waited for them to come out but they carried on gossiping.

Amma called out to Dad. "I'm reading her the letter, Nathan. You and your father should pay attention too."

Appa grunted and went outside to sit on the veranda. "I can hear you from here," he said through the open window.

Dad didn't come into the sitting area; he leaned against his bedroom door, put his hands in his pockets, and stared at the wall opposite. He wore a batik shirt I helped him choose on the last shopping trip we went on. It must have been a bad letter, if the three of us had to listen to it. Mum never misbehaved so could do what she liked and stayed in the bedroom.

*17 June 1942*

*My darling wife,*

*Only a week since I left you and our baby son in Jaffna, yet it feels like a lifetime ago that we were together as a family. Colombo has calmed down after the Japanese bombing in April so you need not be concerned for my safety. However, there are hundreds of British and American soldiers running about town. It's not a place to bring a baby so I ask that you remain in the North with Nathan until this war is over.*

*Selva has been the perfect host, picking me up from the train station himself, taking me out and about every day to view houses. We have found one in his road, by the sea and opposite palmyrah trees scattered in a field. Arul, our first home as husband and wife in Jaffna will always be special but when you see the place I have bought, you will come to love it too. There is a Temple tree full of white flowers and we can plant your favourite shoeflower bushes, so you can wake up to their scent each morning as you do now. I even saw a Loten's Sunbird on the veranda steps. Imagine that, not a fruit tree in sight and there it was, grooming itself.*

I was bored and asked Amma if she'd like to hear a Veddha lullaby that Herath was teaching me.

"It goes like this. *Ro-ro-ro, Ammi mokatada.*" [4]

She put a finger to her lips. "Shhh."

"It's the oldest in the world. Before even you were born."

"Later girl," she said and started reading again.

It was no use. I wouldn't be allowed to leave until I'd heard the whole letter.

*The journey south was uneventful. I feared the monsoon rains would drown the railway lines and delay my arrival however thankfully, they did not appear. Perhaps they will miss us altogether. Do you remember I told you I planned to travel straight to Colombo? Well, I couldn't help myself. I stopped at Kandy so I could take the train ride through the hill country. I think you suspected I would make this detour because you smiled when I said I'd come directly here. One day, Arul, when our son is old enough to enjoy this journey too, we can take a family trip so he can see mountains and jungle for himself, rather than listen to me talk about sunlight streaming through palm trees.*

*And now, my dear, I have a confession to make. The day of our engagement, I promised you I'd give up gambling. Selva had already organised a party of friends to go to the racecourse and it would have been rude of me to refuse his invitation. I hope you can find it in your heart to forgive me this one lapse. I only lost five rupees on the horses and you will be pleased to know I do not feel the urge to pick up my bachelor habits again.*

*My work at the Bank of Ceylon is going well although they need a policeman more than a Chief Accountant to watch the staff. I have had to introduce a system of signing, countersigning and counter-countersigning cash withdrawals to make sure these fellows don't get up to mischief.*

*Arul, I could write to you forever but will send this letter now so you can have some of my news at least. I have asked Dr Rajakone to keep an eye on you while we live apart and you must ask him if you need anything.*

*God willing, I will be back with you and Nathan in a month's time for a few days. Until then my dear, I remain*

*Your everloving husband*
*Roshan*

"Is that the end, Amma?"

"Yes, girl."

"I enjoyed it," I said, sliding her arm off me. "Thank you."

She rolled her eyes. "Perhaps you are too young to understand." Then, in a loud voice, "Hopefully, others will see this family was founded on love and I won't let anyone destroy that."

Dad took the letter from her. I thought he was going to tear it up until he started to read it. "Last time I saw this was on - "

"- your wedding day," Amma said. "I asked your father to show it to you."

He gave the letter back, rubbed the back of his neck, and fell into a chair. He looked like he was going to cry so I gave him a kiss. Above him was the picture of Jesus, smiling with love.

"I feel like a trip to Jaffna," Dad said.

"Yes, son," my grandmother told him. "Who knows what will happen there?"

# JOURNEY TO JAFFNA

When Amma said she didn't know what would happen in Jaffna, it wouldn't have mattered if she meant there might be riots, because I had my Buddha wishes to keep us safe.

Even though Mum wanted to take the train, Dad wanted to take the Mercedes because it needed a long run to clear the carburettor.

"What about your hand?" she asked.

"It's healed enough. If it hurts, you can change gear while I steer."

"If it hurts, I drive."

Uncle Theo let Kana come with us and cut school on Friday so we could set off early. He couldn't come as he had to go to Bombay to draw more pictures of bridges, so she made him promise to join us on our next outing. Appa had to stay in Colombo to sack one of his bank clerks for stealing and count how much money had been taken. He said if the clerk was a poor person, he'd be firm but fair. I knew he'd be nicer than God, who was too old and grumpy to help poor people. Amma was staying behind as well because she'd be uncomfortable on a long car journey.

"We'll be back in a few days," Dad said.

Apart from servants who have to work for most of the day, everybody else was in bed so there wasn't much traffic in Colombo. The sky turned from dark blue to light while we drove up Galle road. Kana and I tried to stay awake but put our heads on each other's shoulders and nodded off. Mum told Dad to stop the car so she could get out to sit in the back and stop us falling off the seat.

When I woke up, we were in the countryside and Kana was cuddling my mother. I got a bit jealous and moved closer to Mum. We drove past a paddy field where women stood in water up to their ankles, the bottom of their red saris tucked into the waist and their hair in long black plaits. They bent down to pick rice from green stalks then threw the grains into bags tied to their bodies. Their backs must have hurt if they worked like that all day. One woman wiped her forehead; the hot sun made it hard to work. She didn't have a choice though, she'd have to do it to feed her family. I said a prayer in my head for Buddha to look after them.

I hung my head out of the open window and let the wind rush past my face. Mum told me not to lean out or a passing car would knock my head off. I leaned out a little more. Nothing bad happened. We drove behind a small, open truck piled high with sacks of rice. People were hanging off its sides and I was worried they'd fall off and hurt themselves.

"They're used to it," Dad said. "Besides, the truck's going too slow for anyone to have a serious accident."

"Can I ride like that too?"

"When you're eighteen."

"Why does everything fun have to wait until I'm older?"

"Because then you'll be wise enough to choose safely."

"I can choose now."

"Uma."

"Here, girl," Mum said. "You must be hungry."

She gave us all a *kolkotta* each that Saras had put in our food bags for breakfast. I remembered the half-moon shape from before, though not what it tasted like, until I took a bite of palm sugar in soft brown paste. After *wattalappam*, it was my favourite sweet food.

We carried on driving along until the car wobbled because Dad took his right hand off the steering wheel while he changed gear with his left one. Mum wasn't happy with him.

"Nathan, you can't carry on like this. Your hand may be broken."

"It's only bruised. I can move all my fingers."

"All right, but take a break at least. We've been going five hours with just a quick breather."

"I'll stop at the next rest house we come to."

We passed one that Mum said she'd heard was no good so we went to another one called Swarna's, which was a couple of paddy fields down the road.

"That looks like a good place to stop," Dad said.

"*Chee*, Nathan. It looks run-down."

He laughed. "London's made you fancy, Uma. No grand restaurants here."

Opposite the rest house was a school where windows were holes in the wall and the playground was a yard. Inside classrooms, boys wore shorts and shirts and girls were in dresses. Seeing only brown children in class and no white ones made me feel funny, like Sri Lanka wasn't my home. After we climbed out of the car, I reached for Kana's hand and held it, pulling her near.

"London schools have glass in the windows," I told her.

"Mine does too. This one is for villagers."

I wanted the children to work hard and do their homework so they could get a good job when they were older. In one class, boys and girls were saying something out loud.

"What are they doing, Kana?"

"They're learning the Tamil alphabet. It's got nearly three hundred letters."

I'd have liked to speak Tamil properly again but didn't want to learn that many letters. ABCs were long enough. I looked behind at the children as I walked with Kana to the rest house. I was sad and didn't know why.

The rest house was dark inside and even though a light bulb was on, most of the light came from the front doorway. A girl as tall as me played cards by herself on a table. When she saw us, she ran into the back. A man in a blue and white checked sarong came out, buttoning his shirt over his string *banyan*. He grinned at us, showing yellow teeth.

"Come, come, come. Small ones eat hot food?"

"Tell him no, Mum."

"Do you have *sodhi*?" she said.

He shook his head from side to side. "Can make, can make." Then he went into the back, shouting at someone to hurry up and cook.

The girl asked my father what we wanted to drink. Her dress had a tear at the hem and looked like she'd worn it a lot. Dad ordered a beer for himself and Necto for Kana and me because they didn't have Portello. Mum had to have Fanta, the cold water she wanted came from the tap and wasn't boiled. The girl tried her best to take the tops off our bottles but wasn't strong enough, so Dad did it for her and slipped five rupees into her hand. She gave him a big smile. When I wanted to know if I could send her clothes from England, all Mum said was, "We'll see." Even though I hadn't been naughty, I wasn't being allowed to do something nice.

Dad poured his beer into a glass. Kana and I asked for two straws each so we could drink quickly. I finished half my bottle and put it on the plastic tablecloth, which was ripped at the corner and had dried curry stains on it. Dad called the man to wipe it.

"This place may not be clean," he told Mum after the man had gone, "but I bet the food tastes great."

"I hope so, for your sake."

Schoolchildren ran about in the playground, laughing and having as much fun as I did at break-time in London.

"Dad, can I show them how to play hopscotch?"

"They're at school. Teach Kana."

"You say no to everything."

"Are you feeling all right?"

"I want to go to school here," I said in a loud voice.

"Sweetheart, you'd better calm down."

"Why can't you get a good job in Sri Lanka like Uncle Theo? And why do you and Uncle Sohan always pick fights and spoil our holidays? It isn't fair."

He stroked my hair. "Life sometimes isn't."

I wanted to run away and hide so I didn't have to go back to England. I didn't care if my parents left me with Appa and Amma. Saras and Herath could look after me and some days I could live with Kana. Mum and Dad could fly back to London and live there with their friends. Thinking about them getting on a plane and me waving goodbye to them at the airport, made me frightened they might go and leave me behind.

"I'd like to learn hopscotch," Kana said.

I played with a piece of tablecloth that was hanging off the edge of the table. I didn't want to speak to anyone, not even my best friend. And she shouldn't have taken my dad's side.

"I'd really like you to show me, Rohini," she said again.

"You never show me anything."

"That's not true."

"Enough, girl," Dad said.

Kana cried softly and wiped her eyes with her hand. I hadn't meant to upset her. I was supposed to look after her because she didn't live with her mum. I took a deep breath. "I'll teach you."

"Thank God for that," my father said.

Nobody talked for a little while then smells from the kitchen filled the rest house. The man and the girl brought out the food: fluffy white rice, *murunga*, green beans and *paripoo*. Kana and I had cashew nut *sodhi*, while Mum and Dad had fish curry. I tried a mouthful of theirs and had to take gulps of Necto to wash away the hotness, though the fizzy drink made my tongue burn more. I ate everything on my plate, sucked my favourite vegetable, *murunga*, the slippery seeds sliding down my throat, and chewed it to get the last bits of juice out. I couldn't have eaten any more rice and curry but had space for pudding. The man didn't have *wattalappam* so we had to have bananas instead.

Mum paid for the meal and gave the man a fifteen rupee tip. Lunch had cost ten. He put his hands together, like in prayer, and nodded thank you to her. I wanted to give the girl a kiss goodbye but knew I wouldn't be allowed to because she was poor, so didn't ask my parents if I could.

Back in the car, we drove past more paddy fields and palmyrah trees. The ground became a pretty reddish-orange, which Dad said was because of iron. Every now and then, we passed houses separated from the road by wire fences, to keep children safe from traffic. The sun shone so bright it blinded me. Suddenly I remembered it was winter in London, cold, wet and dark. Afraid my holiday was going to end and I'd have to go back to England, I wished with all my heart to stay in Sri Lanka. I was going to pray even harder to Buddha, Jesus and God to stop the Troubles, so that one day soon we could come back to live in my beloved country.

When Dad rubbed his hand again because it was hurting, we stopped by a small and dusty village to stretch our legs. Kana asked if we could buy a *thambili* from the man by the road.

"There isn't anywhere here for us to wash it," Mum said.

"It'll be fine, Uma."

The man sliced the top off with a long knife and Kana and I took it in turns to drink the milky water inside. It tasted like lychees but nicer. Mum fanned herself with a piece of paper while she waited for us then gave in and had *thambili* too. Dad went off to get a bottle of Coke for himself. "Can't get medicines over here but there's always a Coke seller at every street corner," he said.

We stood by the car and drank while Mum and Dad looked around, as if they'd lost something and were trying to find it. All I could see were coconut trees and the red earth Amma missed seeing.

"What are you searching for?"

My mother held me close. "Not searching, darling. Remembering the old days."

"This takes me back," Dad said. "It's near where Sohan and I shouted *pambu* at some fellow. Poor chap picked up his sarong and ran for his life, thinking there was a snake nearby."

Mum laughed. "I didn't know. How old were you?"

"About nine."

"Appa already told us," I said, but they weren't listening.

"What I remember most about Jaffna," Mum said, "is *durian*. You won't get better elsewhere."

I pulled a face, Appa had once given me *durian* fruit to eat and I'd run away from the smell that was like a cesspit. I'd have tried some then if it meant we could stay.

"We don't have to go home. We can live in Sri Lanka."

My father looked sad. "Not yet, sweetheart."

I thought he was missing our country so much that he'd say yes. I didn't know what else I could do to make him change his mind, how much longer it would be to not yet or if my heart would break before then. Even when Kana held my hand and said we'd be friends forever, I didn't cheer up. I wanted to see her every day and go to the same school. And you can't hug a friend over the sea.

The drive up to Jaffna was long so we were going to spend the night near Anuradhapura Temple, and see the famous Bo tree while we were there.

"What's special about it, Kana?"

"It's the oldest in the world and it's grown from the one where Buddha found enlightenment. It means peace."

I clapped my hands, sure that if I prayed near the tree, I'd also find her peace at last. That must have been what Amma meant when she said something might happen on our journey up north.

Our guest house was on a side road, with palm trees all around, like being in the middle of a jungle. Dad told us to put socks over our shoes at night so insects didn't crawl in while we slept and no, there weren't snakes hiding in the room because they didn't come into houses.

We hired a rusty tuk-tuk to the shrine and paid the man extra to wait and take us back. Kana and I had to sit on my parents' laps as only two seats were covered with plastic and the others were dirty. As we drove over stones and potholes, I bounced up and down and Dad's bony knees dug into me.

Near the shrine was a muddy river, which wasn't deep but we weren't allowed to paddle in it, because there were tiny worms in the water that would crawl through our bodies and eat our brains until we were dead. Also, the sun was going to set soon, and we had to be at the guest house before dark. I said to Kana, "We'd better stay close to Mum and Dad or if we get left behind, we'll have to spend the night here with ghosts."

The whole place smelt of dust and made me feel like sneezing. I raised my foot to tread on a giant ant that crawled towards me.

"This is a holy place," Dad said. "Don't kill anything."

I thought he might be becoming Buddhist too, if he didn't want me to hurt an insect.

I'd never seen so many monks in one place, showing visitors their land and temple. One called us to go up steps and get closer to the Bo tree. It had a fence all around and was so tall I had to bend my head back to see the top.

"I think I can climb all the way, Kana."

"It's old. You can't go near it in case it breaks."

Above me was a low branch that had grown over the railings. I thought if I stood on tiptoe, I could pluck a leaf. I nearly reached it when a monk came rushing up to me. "Don't touch, don't touch."

He frowned and didn't take his eyes off me. I stayed close to Mum and held her hand tight until he went away. Kana grinned at him as he picked up his robe to walk down the steps. She told him she was a Buddhist but he wasn't listening. She didn't seem to mind he wasn't taking any notice of her.

"You're always happy," I told her.

"Buddha came here once upon a time."

Just then, a leaf fell on my head and slid off my hair. I caught it as it floated down my dress. Kana and I looked at each other. At the bottom of the steps was a whole bunch of fallen leaves.

"Can we go down, Mum?"

"All right, but stay where your father and I can see you."

We rushed around picking up leaves, stuffing our pockets until they were full, not caring about people staring at us. The monk who scolded me marched towards us when another one with wrinkles around his eyes pulled him back. "They are children. What harm can they do?"

Kana and I gathered a handful of leaves each then stood up together.

"Did you see that?" I asked.

"What?"

"The old monk told him to leave us alone."

"That's because he's not supposed to start fights." She held her arms out. "Are you ready?"

"Let's do it. One."

"Two."

"Three."

"Go."

We skipped and spun around, throwing the leaves up and laughing as they came floating down.

"We're Veddhas," I said.

"And Buddhists."

As leaves from Buddha's tree fell on me, I knew I was going to find peace at last. Kana and I held hands and danced in a circle until we were dizzy. I was sure that was it. After trying for days, I'd finally done it. I couldn't wait to tell my friend I was a true Buddhist like her.

"I've found your peace. My head is going round and round."

"It isn't like that. You have to be quiet and meditate."

"You're lying. You just don't want me to be happy."

"You're horrible."

"Girls, girls," Mum said, running down the steps with Dad. She stood in the middle of us and held our hands. "You're both tired. Dinner then straight to bed."

Sohan drove into Uncle Selva's front garden and left his engine running. The once pristine walls of the house were covered in peeling white paint, as if the old man wanted others to see he still grieved for his wife.

Sohan knew he couldn't put the arrest right with an apology so if there was nothing to say, he didn't see why he should stay and have a drink as he had been invited to by Uncle. He could reverse, go home and pretend he'd never arrived. With his hand over the gear stick, he pressed his foot down on the clutch, ready to make an escape. A voice barked in his head. "Shame on you, trying to run away. Are you a man or a mouse?" After the briefest of pauses, he switched off the motor and slipped the key into his shirt pocket. A rose petal from an overgrown bush floated onto the car bonnet. Every day, Uncle's wife used to fill the hallway with pink roses, red roses, gardenias and fuchsias, their scent flooding the whole house. Sohan thought he saw her scowling face in the creases of the petal, warning him not to mess her husband around. After the way he'd behaved, she must have been turning in her grave to see him at her home.

Uncle came onto the front veranda, dressed in a white *verti* and shawl. Not many Colombo Tamils wore the cloths of their fathers and forefathers, a tradition observed in Jaffna and sometimes on plantations. To see an Advocate, one who never lost a case at that, in a poor person's garment made Sohan lower his head.

"Come inside, son," the old man said, offering a hand. Always a distant figure, not interfering, he simply waited in case he was needed. That moment had never arrived for Sohan, even through all the trials of his youth, yet he took comfort from knowing that someone hovered in the background ready to help him. Uncle walked into his house with a stick and a slight limp, no doubt from the arrest. Sohan looked away in shame as he followed behind, stopping abruptly in the doorway when he thought he saw shadows moving inside.

"Is Nathan here?"

"He's gone to Jaffna with his family. I wanted to see you alone. Come and have a drink."

The teak floor of the sitting room had a satin sheen and the walls looked like they'd been painted recently. Mahogany sofas faced each other, their cushions soft to the touch, faded and comfortable. Double doors on the back wall led to a garden where greenery sparkled in daylight. Sohan couldn't take his eyes off a blue and white *Sesath* sunshade in the far corner of the room. "Beautiful, isn't it?" Uncle asked. "A *mala hate*, seven circles. You know, it's been in the Kandy Perahera." His eyes moistened. "This was my wife's favourite room."

Aunty had given Sohan maths tuition after school when he did badly in an exam. "It's not your brain that is lacking," she'd say if he couldn't solve a quadratic equation. "You're more interested in girls and cricket than your future." He rubbed his right ear, the one she used to pull if he misbehaved. A batik print of an elephant drinking from a tank of water caught his eye. He knew the picture of the man-made reservoir well; in fact, he'd studied it more than the integration problems he pored over during tutorials. In a sideways glance, he noticed Uncle watching him, preparing the case for the prosecution.

A maid brought two glasses and a jug of pomegranate juice with rose water on a silver tray. Sohan knew not to ask for the beer he hankered after. Uncle's reputation as a teetotaller was known all the way from the law courts of Hultsdorf to mansions in Cinnamon Gardens. They sipped their drinks without speaking. Gently, the older man placed his glass on a side table and wrapped his shawl around him.

"Whatever happened between you and Nathan, you have to put it behind you. It's gone too far."

The day was warm not hot, yet Sohan wiped sweat off his forehead. Blood rushed to his head, his ears. He brushed away a buzzing fly from his shirt collar and watched it settle on top of the sunshade.

"Don't worry. I can deal with it."

"Son. You don't have to do this alone."

"It's fine."

Uncle leaned forward to pick up his glass and took a slow sip before putting it down again. "That's not all. Your stepfather told me you tried to hire a tracker in Yala. Someone who can handle a gun, more of a poacher than a guide."

"How am I supposed to know the fellow's background?"

"Did you try to get Nathan involved in poaching?"

"I'm going into the safari business."

"I'll tell you this once only, son. Be honest with me and I can help you. Give me lies, I'll prosecute and let you rot in jail."

The morning after our fight at Anuradhapura temple, Kana and I forgot why we'd fallen out and were friends again. I shared my pile of leaves with her until we both had the same. Mum said to put them in a bag so as not to dirty our dresses but we'd already stuffed them into our pockets. Dad took forever in the bathroom having a wash. Kana and I were hungry and wanted to have breakfast. We sat on the bed and played Snap until he came out dressed, with his sarong over his arm. He'd taken the plaster off his face; all he had left of his fight was a red line from his eyebrow to his eye.

"My hand doesn't hurt much," he told Mum.

He didn't seem cross either. Kana said Buddha had made him more peaceful. I couldn't believe that at last my prayers were working. Buddha was so much better than God, who couldn't do anything because he had a hangover, and it was his own fault for drinking all the communion wine in a church when the priest wasn't looking. And although I loved Jesus, he was still learning to do his father's work and didn't know enough yet to help children on his own.

Kana and I ran ahead of my parents to the dining room. I had *pittu* and fish *sodhi* with a taste of red *pol* sambal. It wasn't as hot as green coconut sambal, still too hot for me. Kana helped herself to cornflakes from a side table. "*Thathi* lets me have cereal only at weekends," she said. I soaked my *pittu* with the yellow *sodhi* gravy and took a mouthful. Mum and Dad were too busy eating to notice I was swallowing without chewing much.

After breakfast, we were going to Jaffna to see my grandfather's old house, which had been built when Tamils and Sinhalese liked each other, and where he left Dad and Amma behind to start a new job in Colombo.

"Maybe I'll see a Loten's sunbird there," I said.

"I've never seen one," Kana told me. "Are its feathers really purple?"

"Appa said it's called plumage, not feathers and it's true, they're bluey-purple except their wings, which are brown. He showed me a picture."

I was proud to tell her something about Sri Lanka she didn't know and wanted to say Uncle Sohan could do a good sunbird call, but wasn't sure if I was allowed to say his name yet in front of my father. I put my hands around her ears and whispered how Uncle used to trick Mum by hiding behind the chicken shed and making bird calls.

Dad looked at us. "What are you two muttering about?"

I didn't want to start a row, didn't want to lie to him either. "Nothing bad."

"So you can tell me about it, then."

". . . Mum said Uncle Sohan can do sunbird calls."

He stopped eating. So did the rest of us. I grabbed Kana's hand, ready to run to my mother if he started shouting. He hardly ever raised his voice in London, even if I accidentally drew on his work papers.

"I remember," he said. "For extra pocket money, Sohan would trap a bird by calling it then he'd sell it to Appa and make him promise never to put it in a cage. He must have sold the same one several times over. Your uncle was fun to be around. I'll give him that."

"Are you friends again?"

He thought about it while making a ball of rice and gizzard curry. "We're not enemies anymore."

That was the same thing for me.

While Mum and Dad packed the car for the trip to Jaffna, Kana and I did a Veddha leaf dance outside the guest house, for the end of my father's fight with Uncle Sohan, for being best friends and because we wanted to. We made so much noise the owner came outside to see what was going on. We carried on dancing, making the most of it before we were blackguarded for being loud and making a mess. Mum apologised to the man and told us to pick up the leaves.

"Leave it, leave it," he said. "We mustn't forget where we came from."

# GROWING UP

Even though I tried my hardest, I couldn't think what the Jaffna house would look like. All I knew about it was the garden in the black and white photo that Amma had shown me. When I asked her how big the rooms were, what flowers there were, she said she'd tell me after she finished her bible reading for the day. I waited without asking questions but she forgot about me then she went into a day-dream, and I still didn't know any more about the house.

Although our car journey from Anuradhapura to Jaffna wasn't so far that we had to stop for a break, it still took ages. The leather seats were hot and sticky and pulled my skin when I lifted my legs. I wriggled all the way, hoping the house would be just around the corner. Dad said I'd break the suspension if I didn't sit quietly but I didn't break anything. Every now and then on country roads we passed light-coloured houses, where men who wore sarongs hitched up to their knees and women in saris or dresses sat on verandas. Kana and I waved to them as we drove past then carried on playing I-spy until we used up all the words in the car and outside. Dad talked and talked about holidays he used to have in Jaffna and told us the *pambu* story again.

"I think you're excited about seeing your old house," I said to him as we turned down a dusty lane.

"I think you might be right. And. Here we are."

I looked around, trying to make out a house I'd never seen. There were only three in the road, at the end of long drives. Dad parked at the entrance to the last one and left the engine running for a few seconds before he switched it off. Kana leaned over me to see the house better. Her warm arm pressed into mine and made me stickier. I really wanted an ice cold drink.

White with pillars and a brown roof, the house stood at the end of a long garden, in the shade of tall trees and bushes. A cyclist passed by on the road, his wheels kicking up puffs of red dust behind him. Birds twittered, rustling leaves as they landed on branches or took off. This house felt like home, even more so than Appa's place in Colombo, and it was as big as a castle in fairy stories but there weren't any wicked witches in it, only love.

"Those teak trees have doubled in height," Dad said.

"Is the town only called Jaffna?" I asked.

"In Tamil, it's known as *Yaalpaanam*, land of the harp player. Long ago, a blind lute player was given the land by kings."

I liked Jaffna better. My favourite biscuits in the whole world were Jaffa cakes. We could bring some from England and eat them under the teak trees.

I wanted to go inside and run through all the rooms. If Kana and I lived there, we could have run all over the place with the whole garden to dodge each other while playing catch. When Victor visited, he'd have to walk with an axe over his shoulder, like a Veddha man. We'd send him hunting in the teak tree forest, putting what we couldn't eat in a hollow trunk. Or we'd make him collect honey from bees that lived in the forests. Kana and I could have been Veddha mother and daughter, digging yams.

Dad told Mum to move her head so he could search the trees.

"What are you looking for?" I asked.

"Loten's sunbirds. You can hear them if you listen carefully."

Mynah birds cawed so loudly that until they stopped their racket we couldn't hear other birdsongs.

"What does the sunbird sound like?"

My father stroked his chin while he thought about it. "The male says, *Chee, chee, chee,* where have you gone?"

"And the lady?"

"She says, *Come and find me, won't you?*"

I couldn't hear anything over the leaves shaking in the wind. Kana and I searched the branches; all we could hear and see were mynah birds.

"A sunbird roosted in the tree outside my room once," Dad said. "In the mornings, I could hear chicks in the nest."

"Which was your room?"

"See those first floor balconies? That's it, in the middle. Uncle Sohan and I jumped from there when we were about your age."

Mum said, "You're not to try it, Rohini."

I looked up at the first floor. The tallest place I'd jumped off was a wardrobe and those balconies weren't much higher than that. I knew I'd have to be careful not to break any bones, and I couldn't ask Dad to show me how to jump safely or I'd get him into trouble as well.

"I can't find a sunbird," Kana said.

I hunted through the trees with her, not noticing a man in khaki shorts and shirt come out of the house until he was near our car. I sat back in my seat. We'd come there without being invited and he was going to tell us to get off his land. Kana wasn't afraid though, she carried on looking out of the window. One of the man's sandals creaked. I moved away from the window as the squeak got louder. Dad rushed out of the car, crushing dry leaves as he went. My heart started thumping. We shouldn't have been there. I wished we weren't always caught up in a fight.

Dad hugged the man. "Dr Rajakone."

"Nathan Palar. How many years has it been?"

"Hope you don't mind us turning up like this."

"Come in, come in."

They seemed like friends but I wasn't sure. I held Kana's hand and we followed the grown-ups to the back veranda, where Dr Rajakone told his servants to bring us mango juice. "Can't beat Jaffna mangoes," he said. A maid carrying a tray, came soon afterwards and bent down to serve us. Without looking at what I was doing, I took my drink quickly so she wouldn't have to bend for long but dropped my glass, which smashed into pieces. I said sorry, it was an accident. Mum started to pick up the broken glass. I hoped she didn't cut her fingers because of me. Dr Rajakone told her not to worry and called the houseboy to come and help. He came running with a broom and dustpan and brush. We lifted our feet so he could sweep underneath and watched as he brushed the whole veranda. When I pointed at a small piece shining under Dad's chair, he brushed it into his pan then disappeared into the house. Everybody was being kind and didn't scold me for being clumsy. Kana shared her juice with me until the maid brought another glass, which I took with both hands. Without looking at her, I said thank you in my best voice.

"How long are you all here for, Nathan?" Dr Rajakone asked.

"A few nights. We're planning to go to Panchi's hotel."

"Nonsense. You must stay here."

"If it isn't too much trouble, we'd love to."

I couldn't believe we were going to stay in Appa and Amma's old house and wanted to run through all the rooms, do handstands against every wall. I asked Dr Rajakone if Kana and I could swim in the lake in the back garden. He said the water wasn't deep enough: he only used it once upon a time to keep fish. "Unfortunately they've all been eaten by birds, but those damn frogs are still there. The endless croaking drives me mad."

Dad said, "I remember. Sohan and I spent hours throwing stones at them."

"I thought you left the house when you were a baby," I said.

"We kept it for holidays until I married."

If getting a husband meant giving up places I loved, I was going to stay single like Aunty Malathi in Kandy, just having boyfriends to tell me I looked lovely when we went to parties and dinner dances.

Through an arch on the lawn, birds twittered on palm trees and I thought a sunbird might have made a nest there. As I got off my chair to get a better look, car wheels crunched on gravel in the front garden.

"That'll be my wife," Dr Rajakone said, "bringing our grandsons back from a party. The boys are with us for a week."

"How old are they?" Kana and I asked together.

"About your age."

Wow. Boys could show us how to jump off a balcony and land on the ground without breaking a leg. Kana would be frightened to do it, but if she watched me first and saw how easy it was, we could hold hands and jump together afterwards. I touched Dr Rajakone on the knee. He was like Appa.

"What shall we call you?"

"Nelson Uncle, child. You too, Nathan and Uma. None of this Dr nonsense."

Two boys in shorts and shirts and wearing bow ties ran onto the veranda shouting, "We're back." They stopped when they saw us. One was a bit taller than the other. They watched Kana and me as if we were the enemy.

"These are my two rascal grandsons," Nelson Uncle said.

The taller boy stood up straight. "I'm Ashie. This is Ruvi. If you pass a test, you can play soldiers with us."

"Girls don't play soldiers, Ashie. Is that clear?"

"Yes, *Thatha*."

"Take the girls upstairs to play. And behave yourselves with them."

I knew how to kick like boys so wouldn't have minded being in an army. I could have looked after Kana too and shown her how to fight.

We followed Ashie and Ruvi to the first floor where they showed us the room Kana and I were to sleep in. The double bed and mattress were so high that when we sat on the edge, our feet didn't touch the floor. Kana said it was like the one in The Princess and the Pea. Ashie wanted to know who the princess was so we told him the fairy story.

"I'm going to put a frog under your mattress," he said.

That night when Mum put us to bed, Kana and I looked under the mattress. We had to lift it together because it was so heavy. We didn't want to get the boys into trouble so when Mum wanted to know what we were doing we said, "Nothing." After she tucked us in and went downstairs, I thought I heard croaking in our room.

"Kana, there's one behind the door."

She snuggled up to me. "I can't hear anything."

Even though I was scared a frog might be in the room, I had good dreams in the night. Kana and I were angels playing hide and seek in clouds, flying over Appa's house. Saras and Herath lived with us, eating fried prawns every day at the dining table. God and Buddha lived together in Heaven, Buddha did the work that God was too ill to do and made sure nobody was a servant ever again. Best of all, Aunty Malathi's servant boy, Ganesh, went to school in new shoes and had a hundred shirts in his almeira.

When I woke up, I told Kana I dreamed about us in the night. She was sitting on the bed, her eyes closed. "I'm meditating," she said softly. I watched her chest going in and out and waited for her to finish so I could tell her everything. When she opened her eyes, I said, "We were in our party dresses, flying over the world." She smiled at me, didn't say anything, just held my hand. My head was quiet, like she told me to be when I tried to do Buddhism, so I thought her peace might be the same as good dreams but I didn't want to ask her about it, in case it wasn't.

Near the end of the monsoon season, the air in Yala was muggy, the grass as high as jeep doors. You never knew if you were going to hit an anthill in the undergrowth or if another danger lurked there. If not for the tracker, Sohan wouldn't have known where the pathways were. The Veddha boy was clever, no doubt about that. He could look at a pattern of leaves on the ground or a paw print in the earth and say what animal had passed by and when. Sadly, he was also conscientious and wouldn't plunder wildlife. Yet the poacher Sohan had hired ran a mile after being threatened with jail by Uncle Selva, so it was a question of relying on the Veddhas for a guide or give up on smuggling leopard skins.

"See that spoor, with claw mark?" the tracker asked. "That means sloth bear near. If leaves in print, bear here yesterday came."

"I thought you were going to say it was a leopard."

"Plenty time, plenty, Mr Sohan. Must also enjoy animals." He laughed. "Your Uncle Alagar always saying you to take it easy."

Sohan touched the scar on his thigh. It seemed redder and rougher than before. He had learned patience in Yala while they tracked spoor all day, hoping for a photo of peacocks, wild pig or even jungle fowl posing against a backdrop of forest and sunlight in clearings. Yet on that trip he was letting Uncle Alagar down by planning to shoot with a rifle, not a

Canon.

"Government gives permission to hunt three leopards a year," the tracker said. "You are lucky. This is last one. I will prepare meat in village for you to take home."

"Give the flesh to your people and you might as well take the skin off in one piece."

The Veddha boy sat upright, pulled his shoulders back. "We do not eat leopard."

"I remember now," Sohan said, embarrassed that he had forgotten. More importantly, if this was the third and last of government quota, where was he to go for the other eleven he'd set as a business plan?

The tracker told the driver to stop at a waterhole by a dense forest, where a herd of Sambhur deer had gathered. Vigilant as always, the deer lifted their heads and sniffed the air before lowering their necks to drink in spurts. Was that a leopard in the grass? Where was the kid the mother had been guarding? The boy also looked around for predators before stepping down from the jeep. Taking his bow and arrows and axe from the boot, he said, "You are safe with driver, Mr Sohan," then disappeared into the forest.

Sohan knew better than to insist he stay to track leopard. Veddhas were more proud than the money he paid for their help.

The boy hunter was soon out of sight, hidden by spreading canopies of Palu trees and the silence of his bare feet that crept across a floor of damp leaves. He must have been circling the waterhole to attack from the other side. Sohan tried to guess where he was in the forest. No doubt he was approaching the herd, choosing his target with care, never aiming at a pregnant female, the weak or the young. Madness though, to use a bow and arrow, when a gun would have done the trick more cleanly. His aim would have to be perfect. The herd would take flight after the first arrow was fired. A handful of seconds was all he had. Man against deer. Sohan tried to gauge how close the boy was to the waterhole and scanned the patch of forest ahead for signs of movement, a shadow passing through. Wasn't that what the Veddhas' ancestors had been, yaku, ghosts in the jungle? He couldn't see a thing. Not even a hint anybody was there. The young chap would be picking his way through trees and bushes, crouching to disguise his presence, on the alert for prowling leopards or a Russell's viper poised to strike if footsteps came near its resting place. Perhaps a sloth bear, unpredictable and bad-tempered, lurked nearby, sharpening its claws on the bark of a Cassia tree. When they had time, Veddhas chanted to chase away evil animal spirits before setting off on a hunt. If the boy unexpectedly came across a bear, all he could do was show no fear in the face of an attack and use his axe to defend himself. Sohan shuddered to think of what might happen. Hurry, boy. Watch where you walk. Don't step on a fallen twig. Stay downwind, so your scent doesn't carry. He thought he saw something move and squinted to see better into the light. Was that a bear climbing a tree? Hard to tell from this distance. God, a sloth could be ferocious. There'd be a roar as it ambushed its prey, clawed its face or took out an eye. Maybe there were a few bears nearby. A human would have a chance against one but being attacked by two, three, or more was a certain mauling to death. Sohan's breathing was rushed and he prayed silently for his tracker's safety.

"We should follow him," he said, as if commenting on the weather.

The driver looked him up and down, a Colombo Tamil in the jungle. "We will make much noise, spoil the hunt."

"What if he's in trouble?"

"*Tcha*, he knows what he is doing."

An arrow flew through the air into the neck of a stag, bringing it down. The soft thud as the beast fell and its dying squeals sent the herd fleeing. Even kids lagged just a pace or two behind their mothers. The boy ended the deer's life with his axe, blood gushing where the head had been chopped off. An adult male, it would feed a few families for a month or so. The driver left Sohan alone and went to help the young chap bring back the dead beast. They returned with the carcass between them, lashed to two poles that rested on their shoulders. It wasn't the first time Sohan had been close to a kill yet the musty odour of the stag, warm from life, overpowered him.

"We track leopard tomorrow night," the boy said. "Animals in fright now. No prey here."

Sohan heaved a sigh. He had twenty-four hours to get over his foolishness, to pull the trigger on *Panthera pardus kotiya*. "Don't forget the kotiya at the end," Uncle Alagar said. "That means it's Sri Lankan."

The hunting party returned to camp as the sun descended in the sky, the deer in the back of the jeep. Along the way, Sohan saw leopard tracks by the side of the road, the claw marks still visible. If he'd seen the recently-made spoor then the Veddha boy and driver must have too.


He sat for dinner with chief Aruma and his men around a fire in the quiet of the forest, disturbed only by the noise of cicadas buzzing, frogs croaking and the occasional monkey, screeching in a tree. The teardrop birthmark on the chief's right hand reminded him of Herath, brought up to be a shaman yet allowed to work as a houseboy for the Palars, sending his wages to the village to help keep alive his culture and that of his ancestors. His younger brother was allowed to go to private school, paid for by Nathan's father, because Chief Aruma was wise enough to know his people needed more than the old ways to survive.

The women served rice and *goya-tel-perume* on banana leaves. Sohan wasn't sure he could eat tail of monitor lizard, stuffed with fat from its sides. When he'd hatched his plan to poach leopards, he planned the numbers down to the last rupee, how much to spend, how much he'd earn. He hadn't expected a traditional meal. On all his previous trips, he'd been served tourist food of barbecued pork or curried beef. The chief watched him eyeing the banana leaf. "Eat," he said. Sohan took a bite of the tail, chewed it a couple of times then swallowed. A strong gamey flavour, not as bad as he'd expected. Worth the effort to win these people over. As he ate another mouthful, he noticed the chap opposite drink water from a wooden cup made from the *Gamalu* tree, the sap of which was used to treat diabetes. Given the lean diet the Veddhas followed, it was unusual to see a modern day illness in their tribe, an omen for their culture he pushed to the back of his mind.

"You remember our history?" the chief asked, stroking his beard.

"You mean how Kuveni and Prince Vijaya started your race?"

"We were here five hundred years before, in King Ravana's time. The history you learn at school is not ours. You have been here often with your uncle. You should know us well."

In all the years he'd been coming to the jungle, Sohan had never been tested on their history and couldn't understand why the questions were coming now. The chief stopped eating, picked up a twig and doodled on the ground.

"You and Kombua who went with you today are same age."

Kombua? The boy tracker? Same age? Of course they were. Years ago, they'd played at being warriors in the jungle and climbed rocks for honey. He couldn't bring himself to look the chief in the eye. After Uncle Alagar passed away, he hadn't even bothered to look at the faces of these people and had taken them for granted. He glanced across the fire at the man he'd dismissed this morning as a young tracker. Kombua smiled at him. Sohan smiled back as best he could, his eyes lingering on the other man's Veddha features, the broad nose and protruding jaw that told you here was a person of honour, fairness and kindness.

"Tomorrow you go fishing with Kombua," Chief Aruma said.

"I came here for leopard."

"First, you hunt for fish."

Sohan couldn't work out why he was being given a task to fulfil. He was sure though that he was meant to glean something from it.

The next day, breakfast had to wait while the Veddhas performed a thanksgiving dance for the deer meat. Sohan remembered from schooldays that the ritual was to secure the favour of the hunting hero, Kande Wanniya and his brother, whatever his name was. All the men went to the stream by the camp and bathed before making an offering to the spirits of rice with coconut, chillies and flesh from the head of the deer that Kombua had hunted the previous day.

The shaman squatted in front of the food, ready to repeat an invocation, *adukku denawa*, for ten minutes. He began to call the spirits. *Ayibohowa, ayibohowa. Kande haeta hat kattuwakata nayakawu Kande mulpola alut deyiannansheta Kande Wanniyata* [5]; words that sounded the same but different. *Ayibohowa, ayibohowa.* Long life, long life. Again and again, he chanted the phrase, until he was in a trance, talking to yaku.

Like the rest of the Veddhas, Sohan sat on the ground. Unlike them, he thought the shaman was a fake, the incantation nothing more than mumbo-jumbo. He scrutinised the older man's face for signs of an eye opening, a muscle twitching or a hint of a laugh. Nothing. He snorted. If there were such things as spirits in another world, they'd hardly be eating rice and curry. Yet he was in the jungle, in Veddha country, and had to abide by their rules so he played along with the ritual, loosened muscles in his body, let tension flow out, from his toes to his head. His jaw dropped until his lips were slightly parted. A wave of relaxation swept over him. He listened to the mesmerising drone of the shaman, *Ay-i-bo-ho-wa, ay-i-bo-ho-wa*, until word by word, syllable by syllable, he too was drawn into the chanting. *Ay-i-bo-ho-wa, ay-i-bo-ho-wa.* Long life, long life. His lips barely moving, he repeated the words in his mind. Long life, long life. He felt a white light shine on him; rays of warmth spread through his body, along his limbs to the tips of his fingers and feet. There was no past or tomorrow, only then. Long life, long life. Without memories, there wasn't hurt, even good times moved out of reach; everything faded, like lotus flowers in sunlight. Soon he was only aware of himself and his shallow breathing. His eyelids became heavy, drooping down to cover his eyes. Then, like a leaf dropping off a branch and floating to the ground, he descended gently to the depths of his inner being and he saw in his mind what the others were seeing: yaku hovering over the *adukku* offering.

Kana asked Ashie to show us the back garden so we could see if a Loten's sunbird was there.

"What's so special about it?" he asked.

"If we find one, it means Rohini will stay in Sri Lanka forever."

He whispered something in Ruvi's ear then called Kana and me. "Come on. Follow us. Hurry, before they fly away."

We ran behind them through an archway to a lawn that smelt of dew. I was in such a rush, I slipped on the wet grass and would have fallen over if Kana hadn't grabbed my hand. The boys took us past bushes and down paths where weeds grew everywhere. I scratched my arm on a twig as we searched every tree and branch for a nest, a purple belly or a *chee, chee* call. I didn't know what shape the nest would be, if it was going to be big or small, but I tried to find one. If there was a bird nearby, maybe Uncle would let us take it back to Colombo.

Ashie ran to a guava tree. "There's a sunbird here."

I hurried to where he was pointing and looked at every branch. "I can't see anything."

"You're too late. It flew away."

"I didn't hear it fly," Kana said.

He laughed. "Sunbirds don't come to the garden. We were just pulling your leg."

She folded her arms. "You shouldn't have lied. You're both mean. We'll ask Uncle where to find them."

He stood up straight. "You can't tell *Thatha*."

I wasn't going to tell tales on the boys but they had to be punished for playing a joke on us. I was thinking about what I could make them do when two crows that were fighting, tumbled out of a tree, flapped their wings and flew off. Suddenly I knew what I wanted.

"You have to show us how to jump off the balcony."

"It's not safe," Kana said.

"It is," Ashie told her. "If you make parachutes."

I knew when she looked down at her shoes that she thought we shouldn't do it. I didn't try to make her do what I wanted her to. She'd been Buddhist longer than me and didn't like to do dangerous things. All I could do was ask her to promise not to tell Mum and Dad what we were up to.

"I'll think about it," she said.

Even if she wasn't going to jump, she said she'd come to help us.

"You have to fold a parachute out of a pillowcase," Ashie told me. "I'll show you how."

He made one in our bedroom, using his belt to tie it to my back.

"How will it open?" I asked.

"You pull it out with your hand."

I wasn't sure he knew what he was talking about but he was older than me, so I listened to him. Also, it wasn't like I was falling out of a plane. I could jump to the ground without it. In the long mirror, I saw a big girl, ready to do a dangerous thing. I clapped my hands. At last, I was going to do something more grown-up than when Kana and I went for a walk with Shelala, and I was going to do this all by myself. I was so excited that until Kana spoke, I didn't notice she'd gone to the balcony to look at the ground.

"You'll kill yourself," she said.

Before I could stop her, she ran out of the door and down the stairs shouting, "Aunty Uma, Aunty Uma. Come quickly."

If I was going to be scolded for trying to do something I thought I might as well do it anyway. When Mum shouted, "Rohini," from the ground floor, I hurried to the balcony, put one hand on top of the stone railing and saw Dad on the lawn, winking at me. I heard footsteps rushing up the stairs so put my other hand over the railing before it was too late. Ashie and Ruvi helped me climb by pushing my bottom up. My head was over the top when Dad started laughing. He didn't think I could jump properly. I was going to show him. I pulled myself up, sat on the railing edge, then threw myself off, falling quickly and landing on him with a thump. He caught me, said, "My God," and took a step backwards. I thought he was going to drop me but he didn't. He held me tight then plonked me on the ground. Although I slipped on a damp patch of grass, I didn't fall over.

I was so proud of myself. I'd done something dangerous without praying to Buddha or Jesus and hadn't broken my neck. Mum and Dad would have to see I was grown-up enough to look after myself, and we could come back to Sri Lanka to live.

The boys and I had to stand in separate corners of the living room for most of the day. Dad said later we were only there for ten minutes but we missed afternoon shorteats, weren't allowed to talk to anybody or turn our heads to see what was going on behind us, and we had to look ahead, arms by our sides. I was there for so long I could see in the dark. In front of me were thin cracks in the wall that looked like a spider. I wasn't sure if I should let Uncle know his house was broken, or if I'd be told off for saying there was something wrong with it. I decided to keep quiet. Then I started thinking a spider might crawl out of the crack and onto me. I went stiff but was afraid to ask to come out before I'd been fully punished.

When we were freed at last, Kana gave me a kiss and said sorry for telling tales on me. The boys didn't want to be friends with her so I held her hand and told them if they were going to be nasty, I didn't want to be friends with them. Aunty saw us quarrel and made us all play Snap together. "You children shouldn't fall out with each other. And I'll be keeping an eye on you boys."

Mum told Dad she didn't know what was wrong with me that holiday. "If not for Kana, who knows what mischief Rohini would have got up to?"

"Don't worry. She's growing up and finding her way in the world."

I hoped he was joking. I didn't want to get lost one day and have to find my way home.

Sohan woke before daybreak and ventured outside his tent to lie on the ground and stare at the sky, his bare back and thin cotton sarong soaked by dew. He searched in the blackness for Polaris; other than Nathan's daughter, he'd never seen anything so flawless. Holding the North Star in his sight, he watched it as darkness started to fade. Pitch black turned to different shades of blue then gold. The sun hung in the sky, covering the forest in soft dawn light. "Perfect for photos," Uncle Alagar used to say. Sohan relished the damp, mossy smell of morning mist and the sounds of Prinia and Munia birds chirping overhead. Over their songs he thought he heard the call of a nearby leopard. Listening carefully, he peered past bushes on which migrant Brown Shrikes perched, and waited for the big cat to call again. Part of him no longer wanted to poach those animals yet the side that ignored the advice of Uncles Alagar, Roshan and Selva pressed him to get a move on.

Chief Aruma however still insisted he went fishing with tribesmen, saying there were many people to feed. Even with fish poison berries, Sohan knew they couldn't catch enough to satisfy the village. The chief was toying with him, making him earn the right to shoot a leopard. In spite of his urgency to achieve his business plan, he didn't want to risk a stand-off with the older man and knew he'd have to follow instructions.

He set off on the trip with a group of six Veddhas who wore loin cloths and carried axes over their shoulders. One fellow had a broken wrist in wooden splints and a rope sling around his neck. The *Akanda* leaf poultice under his cast had a resinous smell that blended with scents of the surrounding forest. The chap was as much help as Sohan on a fishing expedition but there they both were. Kombua's mongrel dog scampered in front, leading them to the nearest fish poison tree, an hour's walk away and near a river. Sohan watched the men laugh and joke as they picked cricket ball sized berries that they then pounded to a pulp. Drawn as he was to their untroubled ways, the ease with which they spoke to each other, he didn't think he could join in. He was an outsider, a city man used to sleeping on a bed, except when he chose to rough it in the wild.

One Veddha said, "You remember me? I am Herath's cousin, Naida. We all grew up with you. Our Colombo visitor."

"Of course."

The familiarity with which they treated him encouraged him to ask a question, yet he was unsure if he should or if he would be turned down. Sooner or later, he knew he'd have to take a chance.

"Can I help?" he asked, pointing at the berries they were pounding.

Naida gave him a club. "Take, take."

They worked together in silence, smashing berries to a pulp, careful not to let the juice seep into open wounds or cuts. Once in a while, Sohan lifted his head to glance at the others and make sure he was holding the club the same way they did, pounding berries with the same force they used. When they had enough for their task, Kombua gathered the pieces in an old piece of material and washed the toxins from the juice into the river, drawing out oxygen. Fish rose to the surface to breathe and were caught by waiting hands. Enough for a snack and a few for the chief, who ignored Sohan on their return to the village and accepted the meagre catch from his men with a nod of his head.


Dinner that night was served again in the open by Veddha women, while a deer barked in the distance, alerting the rest of the herd to a predator that skulked nearby.

After the others had gone to bed, Sohan sat outside his tent, staring into darkness. The jungle was where he felt closest to Uncle Alagar and where he missed him most. He no longer had nightmares about the old man's death yet it haunted him still, as it had done since his first year at University, when a student ran into the lecture hall shouting, "The bastards are killing Tamils in Wellawatte." The hall had emptied in seconds. Students and lecturers, Sinhalese and Tamil, men and women, all sprinted home. Even those who didn't live in the area ran to help and do what little they could. Some stayed behind at the University as if it was an ordinary day. Nobody could prove those few knew of the trouble in advance, but in the aftermath those who had gone to the rescue decided who was guilty and who was innocent.

Fires thundered through Colombo 6 that day as buildings were razed. The devil reigned supreme. So did the government who handed copies of the electoral roll to rioters for Tamil households to be targeted. Police took a day's leave or stood at street corners gossiping and ignoring the chaos. Caustic smoke stifled the air. Sohan ripped his shirt off to cover his mouth and nose with it. All around, children were screaming, screaming. He blocked out their noise, pretended he didn't know what it was.

On the way to his road, he witnessed the dregs of hatred in a side street when a crowd jammed tyres onto a man, then poured petrol on him and set him alight. An old woman prayed aloud for his soul and a quick death. A girl about Rohini's age buried her face in the woman's sari and cried, "Appa, Appa." When Sohan tried to rescue the fellow, onlookers pulled him back. "What use is there in losing your life as well?" they demanded. "Go away, before you get us all killed."

In his road, he saw smoke rise from a few houses but no fires. The mob had gone, leaving behind their destruction. Houses had been ransacked, wall mirrors and beds, even shattered sideboards were strewn in gardens and roads. People sat on front verandas, some mute from shock, others wailing. His own home hadn't been attacked. Servants had lied to rioters, told them it was a Sinhalese house, not a Tamil one. He'd hurried down the road to Uncle Alagar's place, only to hear that the old man, proud of his heritage to the end, had confronted those running amok. "This is my house," he was heard to have said. "Get off my land." Yet his defence of number thirty-five cost him his life and those of his wife and two daughters.

And when Uma returned from her school trip to Kandy, Sohan it was, who had to explain to her she'd lost her whole family. Since that day she feared the number thirty-five, never visiting anyone with that address and dreading her thirty-fifth birthday. She couldn't even bring herself to sing hymn thirty-five in church on Christmas Day.


Long before sunrise, Chief Aruma woke Sohan for the leopard hunt. "It is time," he said, popping betel into his mouth. "We have to leave."

"You're coming as well?"

"Hurry. We must find it at night, while it is in the open, hunting."

Sohan dropped his sarong, pulled on trousers and a tee-shirt. Finally, he was going to be able to kick off his plan. He loaded his gun and paused to wonder if they'd insist he use a bow and arrows instead. He was out of practice and doubted his aim would be accurate enough to bring an animal down. If he had to though, he'd try.

A flat tyre on the jeep delayed their departure from the village. The spare had worn-down thread but served its purpose. In spite of Naida's protests that he could cope, Sohan jacked up the jeep and changed the tyre while the Veddhas talked among themselves. Their language was similar to

Sinhalese and while he couldn't understand what they were saying, he could sense that something was going to happen.

Naida drove Chief Aruma, Kombua and him through scrub, down gullies and across dirt tracks. Kombua waved a torch in an arc, for the light to reflect off the eyes of night creatures, glints in the dark that turned out to be toque monkeys in trees and a pair of golden jackals on the ground, feeding on a kill. Like this they travelled, until they reached a waterhole. Sohan had his rifle by his side all the while, priming it after Naida switched off the engine. In the silence, a bull elephant trumpeted its dominance and a python slithered through trees.

"He comes here often," the chief said.

They waited in blackness, as wind blew over tree tops and monkeys shrieked in alarm at the presence of a nearby predator. Sohan wished the damn animals would shut up. They'd frighten any prey that emerged from forest, heading for waterholes in grasslands. Tiredness from the early start crept up on him, caught him unaware. His head fell forward and he dozed off until a passing cool breeze woke him up, kept him alert. Gun at the ready, he listened for a rustle in the grass.

Chief Aruma tapped him on the shoulder. "There. At three o'clock."

Sohan looked to his right and saw the white tip of a tail standing up in the bush. He picked up his rifle and aimed. Jesus Christ, his hands were trembling. He could hardly hold the gun straight.

"He's moving again," the chief said. "You will not have long. You must be ready. There he is at nine o'clock. Do it before Torn Ear runs off."

Torn Ear? Oh, for Christ's sake. They've brought me here to kill Uncle Alagar's favourite leopard, who let Uncle approach to within a few feet without snarling at him, who took cover under the jeep when it was raining. Jesus bloody Christ, they've brought me here to kill bloody Torn Ear. Sohan squeezed the trigger. His index finger seized and wouldn't go all the way. The beast must have been around fourteen years old and had done well to survive that far. The Veddhas had first spotted him when he was a cub and over the years he had posed for Uncle's photos: lapping water from a pool, strutting down a dirt track, the white tip of his tail standing tall and proud. Even while feasting on a hard-won meal, which he'd hunted and stalked for an hour, he didn't mind pictures being taken. Uncle used to say, "That leopard is like family."

Sohan couldn't do it. After all the bravado and planning of his sales and profits, he didn't have the nerve. He tried again, lifted his rifle and aimed at the big cat's head. Torn Ear stared back at him, daring him to pull the trigger, knowing he wouldn't. Sohan's chest heaved; getting rich quick had lost its appeal, his USA buyers would have to get their trophies from someone else or give up altogether. He slowly lowered the gun, made it safe and stood it by his side before wiping sweat off his forehead. Torn Ear slunk into the depths of the forest, seeking prey.

The chief spat betel juice onto the ground then patted him on the shoulder. "Your business here is finished. You are welcome to stay with us again but we cannot help you with selling leopard skins."

"You knew?"

"Herath told me."

"How did he know?"

"Your Uncle Alagar said you would need us one day. Come. It is over. My son can return to our village."

## THE WORST HAPPENS

When we came back from Jaffna, Kana and I were only allowed to play in Appa's back garden but none of the trees there had low branches we could climb onto. I missed sitting higher than my bedroom window, pretending I was an angel in the sky so sneaked to the side of the house to get to the Temple tree. I thought all the grown-ups were inside then saw Amma on the front veranda, crocheting a doily. "Get to the back of the house," she said, "before I catch hold of you."

I ran for my life.

Kana and I had to read to each other or play Veddhas at the back of the house. We'd just finished a leaf dance when Herath brought us two glasses of water and told us to stay out of the sun. We sat in the shade of the chicken coop and watched the chickens who were all asleep, apart from one who clucked because she wanted to have a chat. I talked to her for a minute then said goodnight so she could have a nap with her friends. Saras was in the kitchen making *keerai*, which sizzled as she fried it with mustard seeds. When she served the greens for dinner, I was going to pop the small black seeds with my finger.

"I wish we could play at the front," I said to Kana, "instead of always reading in the back yard."

"*Thathi's* police friend said there might be riots, and he doesn't know how to stop them."

"I'm much braver after going to Jaffna and jumping off the balcony. If the police can't stop the fights, I think we should."

"We mustn't do anything dangerous."

"We won't."

We talked about what we could do to keep our families and friends safe, and decided to practise putting out fires at Appa's house then we were going to spend the day at Uncle Theo's place to do the same there.

"Two girls aren't enough," Kana said. "We have to get more friends to help."

"I can't think of anyone."

"What about the secret club?"

I clapped my hands. "We can make it into an adventure, like in *Swallows and Amazons*."

Suddenly everything was happening at once. We were going to save our families with the club and we could help Saraswathie, Herath, Ganesh, all the poor people. I wasn't sure how we were going to do it. I only knew we had to try. I was going to pray hard to Buddha and talk to God as well, in case he was better after having his appendix taken out. All we had to do was find a way of getting Victor, the only boy, the only other person in our secret club, to come over without his sister, Leela, because she'd only spoil it for us. We sat on the ground thinking until our bottoms were numb but still didn't know how to invite him on his own. Luckily, Leela had to stay at home the next day, because she had an upset stomach after Victor gave her five cents to eat a green mango.

Kana, Victor and I went to my bedroom and shut the door to have a pow-wow in a wigwam on the bed.

Victor said, "This is man's work. I'll be in charge."

I wanted to be the one who bossed others around. He told us he wasn't going to help unless he was the leader so I gave in because we needed him to carry buckets of water.

"We need weapons," he said.

My bazooka gun that shot ping-pong balls was in London. All I had in Sri Lanka were my Baby, Sindy and Russian dolls. Even if we threw them at rioters, it wouldn't hurt enough to stop fighting.

"I don't want to use weapons," Kana said.

Victor rolled his eyes at her.

"I'm not going to fight," she said again.

The wigwam started to slip. We held it up until our arms ached then let it hang over our heads.

"Do you know what happens in riots?" Victor asked me.

"They set houses on fire."

"And they throw burning torches inside and stand outside laughing as people run away. Then they kill people like this and this and this," he said, stabbing pillows with his fist. "Then they break into Tamil shops and burn them down after stealing all the sweets, and then they take all the girls and make them into servants because boys make the best masters."

"I don't believe you," Kana said. "You're just showing off."

"You can stop the riots on your own if you're going to be like that."

"We want you to help us, Victor," I said.

"How?"

"By putting out fires."

"And fighting," he said, looking at Kana then laughing when she poked her tongue out at him.

"We can use the garden hose," I said, "and if that runs out, we can fetch water from the sea."

Appa asked me what I was doing with the hose and no, we couldn't use it to see how quickly the water comes out and why do we want to do it, anyway? He wouldn't let us go to the beach either, to practise carrying buckets of sea water to the house, to see how long that would take. And he wouldn't let Victor start a small bonfire in the back garden for us to put out. We had to make pretend fires by trees, carry water from the bathroom across the dining area, down the back veranda steps, across the back yard and throw it on the ground by the trees so nothing was wasted. The buckets were heavy and we made Victor do the carrying but he said Kana and I should also take turns to carry half buckets each. We splashed so much water on the floor by the dining table that after only two goes each, Amma came out of the kitchen and made us stop. "Enough watering the trees," she said, shooing us away. "You three are worse than monsoon weather." I was glad she stopped us because my arms were getting tired.

"Kana, do you think we had enough water to put out a house fire?"

"We can always get more from the sea if we have to."

I ran to my grandmother who was looking at puddles we'd made on the back veranda. "Amma, what happens if we run out of water?"

"That will never happen."

"But what if it does?"

"Then we have tanks. Huge lakes made by kings of Sri Lanka, thousands of years ago, with underground tunnels that let the water flow to dry areas."

"And can we make it come to Colombo if we run out of water here?"

"Why all these questions, child? There will always be enough."

She gave us cloths and made us mop up the wet floors. "It's not fair to ask Saras or Herath to clean up your mess." We had to get on our hands and knees and do it properly because she was watching us. When we finished, we went to my room and shut the door to talk about what we should do next.

"Can you come to Kana's house on Saturday?" I asked Victor. "We have to practise there as well."

"Can't. Mum's making us go to the hill country again, until it's quieter in Colombo. Dad's going to join us when he's finished his job here."

I didn't know what to do. I really thought he'd be with us if the riots happened. Even if we tried our best, Kana and I wouldn't be able to carry much water without him. He was also the only boy we could trust not to tell the grown-ups what we were up to and it was too late to find another one to help. Between the three of us we could have done something to stop the Troubles. My holiday in Sri Lanka was nearly over and if I couldn't stop the riots, I'd have to go back to England. I couldn't believe my luck had run out. We'd started our secret club to play Veddhas, wanted to use it to stop the fighting and it had finished before we could do anything.

The next morning, Kana and I were supposed to go to her house to play when Uncle Theo said she had to spend the day at her mother's instead.

"I don't want to see Jyoti," she told him.

"She's still your mother, Kana, so please call her that. And anyway, you won't be alone. Tara Aunty will also be there."

"I want Rohini to come too."

I wanted to go as well, to scold Jyoti if she was horrible to my friend and in case I needed his help, I was going to take Buddha in my dress pocket.

Uncle Theo dropped us off and said he'd pick us up before dinner. "Remember girls. Stay indoors."

Kana and I sat on a sofa opposite Tara Aunty and Jyoti, both of us holding a glass of Portello each. The sun was shining in my eyes. I looked away from the window, not wanting to ask Jyoti if I could move, in case she took it out on my friend. I was taking a sip of my drink, being careful not to spill it on the furniture when I heard shouting and firecrackers outside. The neighbours must have been having a party.

"I can smell smoke," Tara Aunty said.

If the cook had burnt something, I hoped they wouldn't get into trouble over it.

Just then, Uncle Sohan came running into the house from the back garden, his face and shirt covered in black marks. I didn't know he was going to be there as well to make sure Kana's mum behaved but was glad he'd turned up. Sometimes ladies didn't listen to each other and only took notice of being blackguarded by a man.

"What are you doing here?" Jyoti asked.

"My stepfather rang to warn me. All the police are on standby."

Oh my goodness. Everyone was making sure Kana's mother took good care of her and they'd even told the police about it. I took another sip of Portello, not worried anymore about spilling it until Uncle snatched my glass from me. I didn't know why he was being nasty. He pulled Kana and me by the hand and hurried us out of the room, stopping only to order the aunties about.

"Get some clothes from the servants' quarters. We'll be sitting targets, dressed like this. For God's sake, hurry."

He took us to a front bedroom on the ground floor where he told us to get in the almeira and stay there.

"What's happening, Uncle? Have the police come for Kana's mum?"

"What? No, no. Nothing like that."

He pulled dresses, saris and scarves from the rail on which they were hanging, and covered us with them.

"We're crushing the clothes," I said.

"It doesn't matter. Stay here and don't come out until I say so."

"What's happening?"

"Nothing. You'll be fine if you stay quiet. No talking."

He left the almeira door a little open for us to breathe then ran out of the bedroom. Kana was shivering.

"It's the riots," she said.

I didn't know where I thought I'd be if they happened but never thought I'd be stuck in a dark, stuffy almeira that was full of mothballs. A smell I liked in Amma's chest of drawers. There, it made my head hurt.

"What shall we do, Kana?"

"I don't know."

I forgot all about saving our families and friends by putting out fires and wanted instead to run to the grown-ups. I moved the clothes off my head and went to push the door open. Kana pulled me back then covered me with her mother's saris and dresses.

"We have to stay here."

"Why?"

"Because we have to."

"Why are the grown-ups pretending to be servants?"

"Rioters don't like rich people."

We shifted the clothes over our heads so we could hug each other. Kana was crying so softly she didn't make a noise. I dried her wet face with my thumbs, the way Mum and Saras did with me. I wanted my dad to fight his way through the riots and take us home but knew he wasn't going to come. He only ever wanted to fight Uncle Sohan. I wished we were in the jungle with Herath because Veddhas never started wars, and wished Uncle hadn't had to shut us in the almeira to hide us from the Troubles. Most of all, I didn't understand why God and Jesus didn't keep children safe, like the bible said they did. All we had to look after us were Buddha and the yaku, but I didn't think we should do a dance for the Veddha spirits when we were supposed to stay quiet.

"If we meditate, will that bring your peace?"

Kana shook her head.

"I'm going to try anyway."

I closed my eyes and emptied my head of thoughts, like she'd taught me. I concentrated on breathing in and out of my nose but all that did was remind me of the mothball smell in the almeira. I pushed pictures of fires out of my head, pretended I was in the jungle and Herath kept us safe with his Veddha axe and bow and arrows. As hard as I tried, I still couldn't find peace. I thought maybe it only happened in good places and you had to be happy to find it.

The shouting outside got louder until it was by the front window. Someone banged on the front door. We sat in the almeira under soft silk saris, afraid to move. When Kana carried on crying quietly, I hugged her tight and put my hand in my pocket to give Buddha a rub and pray we'd be safe.

"If anyone finds us," I said. "I'll show them Buddha. They won't hurt us when they know we love the Sinhalese."

"I'm going to wet myself."

I didn't hear her doing *choo*, then I felt my bottom getting wet through my dress. As my dress got wetter, I heard shouting outside the room. Someone kicked open the bedroom door. If Kana was still wetting herself, they might have seen it come out of the almeira.

"There's nobody here," a man said in Sinhalese.

"Try the almeira."

The door opened then someone moved the dresses and saris apart. The clothes slipped off our heads and onto the floor. The smell of *choo* and mothballs made me feel sick but I stopped myself from vomiting. Kana opened her mouth to say something then she opened it wider. I thought she was going to scream. A man holding a rifle stood in front of us. Some of his teeth were missing and his shirt was torn and covered in dirt and red stains. His sweat was the strongest I'd ever smelt. He stared at Kana. She started shaking again and moved closer to me. He gave her a funny look then lifted his gun. I thought he was going to kill her with a bang. I had to do something to stop him. I put my hand in my pocket but couldn't find Buddha and he was all I had to save us. If I didn't find him soon, it would be my fault if Kana died. I searched the floor of the almeira with both hands. The man was in the way of the light and I couldn't see what I was doing. I didn't remember dropping Buddha but wasn't sure of anything anymore. Even though I searched and searched, I still couldn't find my statue. The man gave me a funny look and pointed his rifle at me. I moved closer to Kana. She stared at him while she leaned across and fished in my pocket. I thought she was looking for a hanky to wipe her nose and gave it to her but she kept searching my pocket. She took Buddha out and showed it to the man. I watched him to see what he was going to do, if he was going to shoot. He screwed up his eyes and stared at us before he walked out, slamming the bedroom door shut.

"What have you found?" someone shouted from the hallway.

"Nobody here," he said.

After he left, the room went quiet again and we waited for something to happen. When it didn't, I whispered, "I think it's safe to go out now."

"Uncle told us to stay here."

People shouted on the front veranda then Uncle yelled back in Sinhalese. "Go away. *Mahathya* isn't here, only servants. This is Sinhalese house, no Tamils. Get out of here."

I didn't want him to get into trouble for hiding us, especially after he saved me when I fell in the sea, but wasn't sure if I should disobey him and leave the room. Then I remembered I was Dad's brave daughter who jumped from a first floor balcony in Jaffna and I looked after Kana like her mum should have. I was also a Veddha like Herath. I remembered the shouting in Appa's house after Dad and Uncle Sohan fell out with each other, and how grown-ups stopped fighting when children were in the room. I gave my statue a rub and pushed open the almeira door.

Kana grabbed my dress. "Where are you going?"

"I have to save Uncle. Buddha will look after me."

I climbed out of the almeira and went to close the door so she'd be safe inside.

"I want to come," she said, following me out. "But Mum will be cross when she sees I've wet myself."

"You can change first."

She took off her wet *jungies* and dress, put on one of her mum's tee-shirts from the chest of drawers, and gave me one to wear too. I changed, then we stood by the bedroom door for a few seconds. As I pulled the handle and was about to go outside, she said, "We should stay here."

"I can look after you," I told her, wishing I had my bow and arrows as well as Buddha to keep us safe.

We held hands and walked out of the bedroom to the hallway where the grown-ups and rioters were arguing. Uncle Sohan's eyes opened wide as soon as he saw us. He covered his mouth with his hand and was surprised how brave we were, coming out of the almeira to help him. Everybody looked at us. One rioter couldn't stop watching Kana and smiled at her, showing his yellow teeth. He laughed then used the long stick he was carrying to lift her tee-shirt. She pulled it down again and cried. He grabbed her hand and tried to pull her from me to make her his servant, like Victor said the rioters would, but I wouldn't let go of her. Kana's mum came over and was about to say something to the man when I showed him Buddha. He didn't take any notice of me and pulled Kana free. Her mum grabbed her back. "You're not taking my daughter." Uncle Sohan took my hand and kept me by him.

The rioters started shouting at each other. The man who found us in the almeira, pointed at Kana and called her to stand with him. He'd been kind before and not told anyone about our hiding place, so I didn't understand why he had to show off when he was with his friends, and try to make her go with them. He moved forward to take her. Her mum stood between them and wouldn't budge. She told the man she'd go with him instead.

"No, Jyoti," Uncle said. He talked to the men in Sinhalese but they wouldn't listen. When one man looked towards the front door, Uncle grabbed him by the throat, snatched his gun and pointed it at the rioters. I ran behind Kana's mum.

The man who found us, aimed his rifle at Kana and said to Uncle, "Don't be a fool."

"Give them the gun, Sohan," Aunty Jyoti said.

"I'll die first."

She touched his cheek and stroked it gently. "For the children's sake. Please."

Uncle swore then threw his gun on the floor and kicked it to the man he'd taken it from.

Aunty Jyoti bent down to kiss Kana on the head and said in a gentle voice, "I have always loved you and always will." She walked outside with the rioters, taking tiny steps until the man with the long stick told her to get a move on.

I was afraid without a grown-up to hide behind, grabbed my friend's hand and took her to stand by Uncle. He put his arm around us then called out, "Kana will be fine, Jyoti. I'll see to it."

She stopped walking, looked back at Kana and nodded her head.

## ON GALLE FACE GREEN

Although the shouting in the road had stopped, I could still smell smoke and Uncle made us stay indoors until long after lunch. The phones weren't working so we couldn't ring Appa's house or Kana's dad to say we were all right. After checking the road a few times, Uncle said it was safe to drive us home.

"What about emergency curfew?" Tara Aunty asked.

"What curfew? The only people on the streets are rioters and they've got the government and police helping them."

"If they've got help, my mum can leave them soon," Kana said, smiling.

Uncle and Aunty looked at each other. I'd never seen my friend that happy before, not even after meditation. She must have really loved her mum after all.

Tara Aunty said that even when the mess on the streets was cleared up, people still wouldn't forget for a long while what had happened in Colombo. I was going to do my best to think only of good things and even if I did remember hiding in the almeira, the riots had finished without anybody getting hurt. Everything the grown-ups had been afraid of had happened and we were all safe. Kana and I could play again in Appa's front garden and we could climb the Temple tree. We wouldn't have to be scared that there might be more riots because Buddha would make sure those were the last ones.

Kana didn't want us to change out of our tee-shirts, even though the servants gave us clean clothes to wear. She put on one of her mum's gold necklaces and when Uncle called us to get into the car, she ran into the bedroom and took a bottle of perfume. "Blue Grass is my Mum's favourite," she said. "I'm going to keep it under my pillow and give it to her when she comes back."

I wanted Aunty Jyoti to come back soon so she could be a proper mother to Kana. I was proud of Buddha that day: as well as keeping us safe in the almeira, he made Aunty love her daughter then sent her with the rioters to stop the fights against the Tamils. I was disappointed in God and Jesus. I didn't know what they were thinking about, letting the Troubles happen in the first place. Buddha would have to make them stand in a corner so they didn't do it again.

Uncle Sohan told Tara Aunty to get in the car too but she wanted to stay at the house. "I'm not ready to leave Jyoti's house yet. You understand? I'll be fine with the servants."

He kissed her on the mouth. "I'll come straight back after dropping off these two. I won't be long."

The roads were empty apart from people sweeping rubbish, leaves and flowers. I'd never seen so many Temple flowers on the ground. The rioters shouldn't have knocked them off the trees. They were holy. A few houses were black from smoke and there were smashed tables and rattan chairs in gardens and on the roads. On one front veranda, an old lady sat on a rocking chair, crying and rocking while her husband held her hand. Most of the shops were boarded up or closed, like it was a Sunday. Those that weren't shut had broken windows and were smoking. I thought the fires had only happened in Aunty Jyoti's road.

"Uncle, do you think the riots were at Appa's as well?"

". . . No."

He didn't say it like he was sure. I sat forward in my seat, worried I hadn't been with my family when they needed my help.

"What about my dad?" Kana asked.

"He's fine too."

He dropped me off first then was going to take Kana home. I wanted her to stay with me so I could look after her until her mum returned but he said she needed to be with her family.

The Temple tree in Appa's side garden was the same as that morning. There weren't many petals or leaves on the ground so the riots couldn't have happened there. I couldn't smell the shoeflowers though, only smoke from other roads. Everyone hugged me as soon as I got out of the car. Their eyes were red, like Mum's were when she thought I was lost. Dad came down the steps to talk to Uncle through the car window. Uncle looked at him and nodded before driving off. He was telling my father he'd taken good care of me.

Once I was back with my family and knew they were safe, I didn't want to be with Tamils or Sinhalese anymore. I only wanted to be with Veddhas who never start fights.

"Where's Herath?"

Dad held me close. "Never mind the servants. You're safe. That's all I care about."

"He's at the back with Saraswathie," Amma said. "Go to him. He's been asking the yaku to keep evil spirits away from you."

I ran to the servants' quarters, calling, "Herath, Herath."

Saras saw me first and held me tight. "Come, kunju. He's been waiting for you."

He was at the kitchen table, a bowl of coconut milk and his arrow in front of him. Saying something in his Veddha language I didn't understand, he sat me on his lap.

"Did you do Kiri Koraha for me?" I asked, dipping my finger in the milk.

"Yes, naga. It's the ceremony I know best as a shaman."

That night, Mum and Dad told me to sleep in their room but I didn't want them with me, only Herath, so he was allowed to put his mattress next to my bed. After Mum tucked me in he checked to make sure I was alright and said he'd come to sleep later. I asked him to keep the bedroom door open so I could hear the grown-ups talking in the sitting area.

"Do you think there's something going on with Herath?" Dad said. "Can we trust him?"

"Don't be ridiculous," Amma said. "I trust him with my life."

"Then why does Rohini want him to keep her safe and not her own father?"

"Ask yourself that question, Nathan."

In the morning, I followed Saras and Herath around while they cooked or swept the outside corridors. Amma let me have my breakfast with them in the kitchen and didn't even once tell me not to get in their way. Saras sat next to me at the table and stroked my hair while I ate purple yam mashed with milk and sugar. Mum popped in to see if I was all right then left me alone. The sun shone on the outside corridor, like it had when I first knew Saras was an angel. A hairy caterpillar crawled along the wall in sunbeams, but it didn't look holy like my ayah had.

Herath let me play with the chatty he used for Kiri Koraha. I pretended I was a shaman in his village, far away from Colombo, calling Veddha spirits. I didn't feel like doing a dance so I put coconut milk in the chatty and took it to the veranda steps by the kitchen, to listen to the chickens clucking as they told each other about the riots and how happy they were that we were all safe. I stirred the milk with my finger and said a thank you prayer to the yaku for saving Kana and me in the almeira. I didn't want to talk to anybody. Although Appa, Amma and Mum didn't bother me, Dad stood in the dining area and watched me across the courtyard. I thought he might try to find out if I still loved him, even though it was Uncle Sohan who saved me from the rioters, not him. I knew he wanted to cuddle me but I didn't want to touch anyone. He went inside again when Amma called him. "It's been a shock for her," she said. "She needs to handle it in her own way." He stayed away after that and only looked at me every now and then. Although I didn't want to get close to him, I liked to know he was keeping an eye on me.

Saras, Mum and my grandmother cooked all day for the people whose houses and shops had burned down. First there was a smell of cut ginger, garlic, onions and chillies in the kitchen then a curry smell while the food cooked.

I stood next to Amma and leaned against her. "Are you going to make yellow rice as well to cheer them up?"

"There isn't enough time, girl."

While the ladies cooked, Dad and Appa drove cardboard boxes of food to anyone who was hungry or whose shops and homes had burned down. I also helped by sitting quietly on the back veranda steps with my chatty. When I couldn't feel my bottom anymore, I went to the kitchen. I knew I'd be in the way but nobody minded me being at the table and they cut up vegetables around me.

Mum cried once when Amma asked if she was all right after her family ran away in the last riots. I wanted to say sorry to her for losing her family but couldn't.

Herath took me for a walk so I could see there weren't any fires burning in our road or in Colombo. Before we went outside the garden, I made him stop by the front gate to look left and right. I couldn't see any smoke but held his hand tight while we went to see Uncle Selva and make sure Shelala was safe. Uncle had gone to work to put rioters in prison and his maid let us in. I cuddled Shelala, pulled out twigs and leaves from her fur then played with her for a few minutes before saying goodbye. She followed us all the way to the garden gate.

"You can't come with us today," I said. "You have to stay here and guard the house. I'll see you soon."

Herath and I walked down Perth Avenue past the field where the cobra lived. I wasn't afraid of it anymore and knew it wouldn't bite me if I didn't frighten it by getting close. At the beach, the waves were still in the sea and nobody had thrown furniture onto the sand. Tiny crabs were in their pools and there was driftwood all over the place.

"Do you want to collect shells?" Herath asked.

I picked up two and put them in my pocket.

We stayed out for a little while, walking along the sand, until we had to go back for dinner. Dad was waiting for us on the front veranda. His chess book was open in his hands but he wasn't reading. I gave him a cuddle then took him to the dining table. Uncle Theo dropped in while we were eating and Amma called Saras to bring an extra plate for him. I put down the ball of rice and curry I was making with my fingers.

"Uncle, where's Kana?"

"She's staying with her grandmother in Matara. You'll see her soon."

"Is Aunty Jyoti with her?"

He looked at Dad then said, "She's gone to India for a holiday."

"With the rioters?"

"She escaped from them."

Now that she loved Kana, I knew she'd come back soon from India to look after my friend. I picked up my food again with my fingertips and made another ball of rice and curry. For once, without even trying, the palm of my hand wasn't covered in food. It made me feel more grown-up than learning the two rude words, beginning with F and C, that Uncle Sohan called the rioters who took Aunty Jyoti.

"Look," I told Mum and Dad. "There's no food on my palm."

"Well done," they said and carried on eating.

"Good girl," Appa and Amma said.

Uncle Theo smiled at me but it wasn't a happy smile.

I looked at my clean palm. I didn't like being older and wished I hadn't seen the riots. If I listened to Mum and Dad and always obeyed them, I thought I could be a small girl again but I still wouldn't forget the burning and shouting and broken furniture thrown into gardens.

"I'm thinking about going to live in Australia," Uncle said. "They've eased the White Australia rules and besides, everybody needs engineers."

"But if the Troubles have happened and are finished," I said, "like Buddha and the yaku promised, why do you have to leave? And we can come back to live in Sri Lanka now they're over, can't we, Dad?"


Under a blue-grey sky that absorbed the last cloud of the day, Sohan arrived at Perth Avenue for a farewell dinner with Nathan and his family. A smell of roasted coriander drifted through the house and lingered on the veranda, to disappear into salt air that hung around the neighbourhood. In the falling darkness, a male Loten's sunbird flew through the garden, calling to the female, *Chee, chee, chee,* where have you gone? Over the sounds of dogs barking in the distance, came the female's reply, *Come and find me won't you?*

"Fancy a stroll on the beach, *machan?*" Sohan asked Nathan.

"Why not?"

They left the others and walked down the steps, both barefoot, neither returning for their sandals. Rohini jumped down from the Temple tree.

"Can I come too, Daddy?"

"Tomorrow, girl."

At the beach, the men perched on boulders by the shoreline, to listen to waves heave and crash while white froth dragged seaweed and debris onto the shore. They stared ahead at the horizon, as if the answers to their friendship were hidden beyond it.

"What happened, Sohan?"

"Jyoti stepped outside with those *thadiyans*. They wanted blood, didn't care whose. She knew that."

Nathan stepped down from his perch and rubbed his neck as he gazed into the sea. "Then what happened?"

"She gave her daughter a goodbye kiss and said she loved her. A mother for seven years and she waits until then to show affection. She was always more concerned about her French polished nails and furniture." Stony pebbles dug into his soles as he jumped onto the sand and walked towards Nathan, whipping him round so they were face to face. "If I could have stopped it, you know I would have. Don't you?"

They locked eyes and stood still, breathing to the rhythm and roll of ocean waves. A red-backed sea eagle circled the boulders then darted into the water, its white head plunging onto a fish. Without warning, Nathan also pounced. He grabbed Sohan by the throat and pushed his thumbs in, a pressure more uncomfortable than painful. Sohan let his friend's hands linger for a second before levering them off with his own.

"There was nothing I could do. You have to believe me."

"What if they tried to take Rohini?"

"You think I would have let them take one of the children? You believe that?"

"Tell me everything."

Sohan said that as the lines were dead, he couldn't ring his stepfather for help after Jyoti left with the rioters. And he couldn't have offered the *thadiyans* money because he'd passed himself off as a servant.

"Those were no ordinary rioters. They had the devil in them. When I saw Jyoti again, it was to identify her blood-covered body."

"Gun shots?"

"Beatings and rape."

Both men stood silent, to pay homage to the woman who in death was more to her husband and child than she'd been while alive.

"What if something had happened to you, Sohan?"

"If it had, would you give a damn?"

Nathan stepped back and spoke softly, his words muffled by the cries of the eagle. "I always have."

Hushed by the memory of their shared youth, they stayed side by side to remember how they had changed from happy-go-lucky children playing *carom*, to teenagers who captained cricket teams, to young men going from one party to the next.

A strolling couple walked by, hand in hand, laughing at a private joke. Sohan waited for them to pass then said, "*Machan*. That day. All I wanted to do was give you a hug, wish you the best for your wedding."

"I know."

"And you turned to kiss me."

Nathan stared right through him and beyond the animosity that had gnawed at the later years of their friendship. "Yes."

"And I let everybody think it was me, to spare your feelings, to let you have the marriage you wanted."

"I loved Uma then. I still do."

Sohan watched him. He had never doubted his friend's feelings for his wife. "So, buddy, what happens now?"

"We go on as normal."

"Bloody hell, Nathan. I hope you don't mean the fighting."

"Not that."

"Then what?"

"I don't know."

Part of Sohan wanted to punish his friend for letting him take the blame for an innocent hug that had turned into a kiss. And why should he let him off the hook? Nobody had stood by him all these years, after Uncle Alagar passed away. Uncle who understood his rebellious years, who led him to Chief Aruma, who showed him the power of forgiving those he wanted to keep in his life.

"Father Woodgate told me something on Christmas Day," he said.

"You went to church?"

"He said love shows itself in different ways. You understand what I'm saying? You and me, we're like brothers. It's okay."

Nathan gazed at him. "It was pre-wedding nerves. That's all. I should never have let you take the blame for it. I was afraid of losing Uma."

"I know, and there's no need to explain to the others. I have broad shoulders."

"I have to be honest with Uma."

"We should go back. They'll be wondering if we're killing each other."

"There's something else. This poaching game you planned. You think I was going to let you get away with putting my name on the export licence, passing off the skins as tea?" He grabbed Sohan's shirt collar, squeezed it then let go. "You bloody fool. You risked my reputation. Did you think I wouldn't find out?"

"*Machan*, that's the second time you've tried to strangle me tonight. Go easy, will you?" He massaged his Adam's apple. "I assume you found out through Uncle Selva."

"How did you know?"

"Sometimes, *machan*, we want to be discovered. I used his neighbour to organise export licences and joked how did he know I wasn't trying to sell leopard skins? I guessed you'd eventually find out about it. It doesn't matter anyway. Chief Aruma understands me better than I do. He knew I couldn't go through with it."


The day before we flew home, Appa took us to Galle Face Green for Sunday tea and to fly kites. Uncle Theo had promised to bring Kana from Matara so we could see each other one more time.

"Can Saras and Herath come too?" I asked my grandmother.

"Today is for family and friends. You can say goodbye to them tomorrow."

"You said Saras is like family and Herath is your cousin."

"Enough, Rohini," she said in a gentle voice.

I started crying. She put me on her lap and stroked my head until I stopped. I didn't feel any better afterwards, like I usually did after a cuddle. "I don't want to wait until next Christmas to see you all again. Why can't we live here now the riots are finished?"

Even though it wasn't bedtime, she sang me a lullaby in Tamil. "Your mum knows it too. Ask her to sing it to you when you miss us."

"It isn't the same. And I saw a Loten's sunbird last night when Uncle Sohan was here so we have to stay in Colombo. You promised."

"We will always be together, darling girl, because love keeps us close. Now hurry. We have to leave soon for tea. Ask Saras to plait your hair."

I was the last one to get ready because I kept pretending to Saras that the plaits were too tight, so she had to keep doing and undoing them. As she brushed my hair, I sat on my bed, looking at the bedside table I'd kept Buddha on, remembering how Kana and I had played with my dolls in that room. Saras took so long over my hair that in the end Mum came in and told me I looked lovely, not to waste any more time.

I wanted to give Kana a present so she wouldn't forget me but all the shops were shut. I decided to give her the Russian dolls she played with every time she visited and my *Swallows and Amazons* book. I wrote on the inside: *To my best friend in the whole world, with all my love, Rohini.*

"Rohini, will you get a move on?" Mum said from the front veranda.

"I'm just saying goodbye to Herath," I shouted as I ran to the outside corridors where he was sweeping.

"What's the real word for Veddha?" I asked him.

"Wanniya-laeto."

"Wan-ya-lto?"

"Wann-i-ya-laeto,"

"Wann-i-ya-laeto." I was so proud of myself for remembering my promise to say it properly before we went back to London.

Appa said he was going to drive us to the hotel. Amma didn't put up a fight or say she wanted Mum to drive. After I said I'd stay away from the door handle, I was allowed the special treat of sitting by the door. I waved to the *kadillai* man, who was walking to the beach, and asked Amma to buy from him every day, so he'd have enough money to buy new clothes for his daughter. Dad said later that my grandmother bought dresses for the girl afterwards and paid for her to go to a good school. We turned left into the main road and towards Galle Face Green. I prayed to Buddha to look after the beggars sitting on the dirty street, especially those with bleeding hands and fingers falling off.

"Why don't they wear bandages?"

"Lepers get more money looking like that," Amma said. "It's not as if they can't get free medical treatment."

I asked Buddha to take special care of them because he wasn't like God, only helping those who help themselves. Sometimes people are so sad they don't know what to do and nobody will listen to them.

We passed a group of schoolgirls in white dresses and red ribbons in their hair. "Mum, why are they wearing uniform on a Sunday?"

"Must be a school outing."

When I went back to England, I was always going to wear my hair in plaits, with blue ribbons for school to match my uniform and red ribbons at weekends. I tried to remember as much of the shops, temples and people as I could, even old women carrying umbrellas to keep the sun off their head, and stray dogs searching for food on pavements. The only thing I looked away from was the thick, black smoke from buses and tuk-tuks.

Galle Face Green was full of families flying kites, sitting on benches to watch the sea, or eating *kotthu* roti or *kadillai* they bought from stalls at the edge of the grass. Uncle Theo and Kana were already on the green and called us to join them. They weren't far away from the stalls but after we got to them, I couldn't get the spicy smell of fried chick peas anymore. When my friend smiled at me, I remembered how she was always happy, except when her mother hadn't loved her and that had changed. I wanted to run along the grass with her, holding hands, best friends forever, never falling out like my father had with Uncle Sohan.

Uncle Theo bought two kites, a yellow cobra with a tail for Kana and a diamond-shaped one with a long tassel for me. I hadn't flown a kite before so Dad showed me how to run with it, then let the wind carry it into the sky until it flew with all the others. Kana and I watched our cobra and diamond fly in and out of clouds.

Appa stared at the sky. "Only a few more minutes until tea, girls. And it looks like it's going to be one hell of a sunset."

My grandmother looked the other way and acted like she hadn't heard him swear.

The sky turned gold then orange then made the whole sea orange too. Sea spray blew in the air, making my lips taste of salt. Kana flew her kite and I gave mine to Dad so I could watch it fly without worrying that the wind might blow it away. It went up and down, up and down then stayed up for a long while, flapping in the sky. When another kite got caught up with it, Dad untangled them, keeping mine safe.

I looked up and saw angels and yaku flying in and out of clouds, watching over us. Herath must have done Kiri Koraha for my last evening in Sri Lanka. I didn't know if I'd ever live with Appa, Amma, Saras and Herath for more than just Christmas holidays, or if my best friend would move to Australia and we'd never see each other again. I really wanted to help servants, especially children like Ganesh in Kandy, but was too small to save them on my own. I hadn't even been to see Herath's family in Nilgala.

Then Buddha whispered in my ear, telling me not to worry anymore. Everything was going to be all right; he and the yaku were going to look after all living things and Jesus was going to do God's work. I went empty inside and looked over to where Kana flew her kite. She smiled at me, same as she'd done all holiday. I couldn't smile back because my head was quiet, like she said it would be. Two ships left the harbour, sailing away from Colombo. I picked up a white feather a seagull dropped on the grass as it flew over us. I felt all alone but wasn't afraid because at last I had peace. It was different to what I thought it would be like. I wasn't happy, just calm inside. After all the times I tried to find it on my own at Appa's house, or with Kana at her place, it came to me on Galle Face Green when the sky was orange. Buddha said from inside the clouds that he only let me have it then because I didn't need it before the riots. He also wanted me to remember that wherever I was, the people I loved would always love me.

Dad and Appa had their hands in their pockets while they chatted to Uncle Theo. Mum stood between the wind and my grandmother to stop Amma's sari flapping and my best friend flew her cobra kite. Suddenly I didn't mind so much about going back to England or that I'd grown up and I waved to Kana.

## Our Father (Saras' dream)

At the end of my existence,
a fish eagle hunts
in sapphire-blue skies,
over the Lake of Faith;
silver carp dart around lily pads
in the shadow of weeping figs.
On the shore of holy waters,
I embrace friends and relations,
their bloodied wounds healed.
All mourning comes to an end.
My betrothed waits by a raft,
holding orchids of love,
nurtured since he last saw me.
We sail in endless time
to where prayers are not needed.
Quietness is all that I feel.
When a voice calls my name,
I lift my eyes to see
a congregation of sunbirds,
dancing in a triangle of sunlight.
The Lord opens His arms.

# REFERENCES

1 Charles G. and Brenda Z. Seligmann. "Songs." 2010. The Veddas. Cambridge University Press 1911. 368. Print.
2 Charles G. and Brenda Z. Seligmann "Songs." 369
3 Charles G, and Brenda Z. Seligmann. "Ceremonial Dances." 252
4 Charles G., and Brenda Z. Seligmann. "Songs." 367
5 Charles G. and Brenda Z. Seligmann. "Invocations." 285

# ABOUT THE AUTHOR

When she's not working as a bean counter in England, Renuka David writes novels and screenplays and goes on safari. She also dabbles in writing poetry. Her first novel is buried in a lead box, which is the best place for it and her next one is on the much-travelled road of being rewritten.

**Words from the author**
I first wrote this novel to highlight the plight of the Veddhas, the aboriginal race of Sri Lanka. However, nostalgia took over and the story adopted its own form. All the same, I hope I have managed to raise awareness of their endangered culture, even if it seems that in ten years they will all be absorbed into mainstream Sri Lankan society.

# CONNECT WITH ME ONLINE

Twitter: http://twitter.com/Renuka_David
Email: info@renukadavid.com
Website: www.renukadavid.com

www.ingramcontent.com/pod-product-compliance
Lightning Source LLC
Chambersburg PA
CBHW022112040426
42450CB00006B/675